PERGAMON INSTITUTE OF ENGLISH (OXFORD)

Language Teaching Methodology Series

EPISODES IN ESP

Other titles of interest:

ALTMAN, Howard B. and C. Vaughan James
Foreign Language Teaching: meeting individual needs

BRUMFIT, Christopher J.
Problems and Principles in English Teaching
English for International Communication

CARROLL, Brendan J.
Testing Communicative Performance: an interim study

FISIAK, Jacek (ed.)
Contrastive Linguistics and the Language Teacher

FREUDENSTEIN, BENEKE, PONISH (eds)
Language Incorporated: teaching foreign languages in industry

FREUDENSTEIN, Reinhold
Teaching Foreign Languages to the Very Young

JOHNSON, Keith
Communicative Syllabus Design and Methodology

JUNG, Udo
Reading: a symposium

KELLERMAN, Marcelle
The Forgotten Third Skill: reading a foreign language

KRASHEN, Stephen
Second Language Acquisition and Second Language Learning
Principles and Practice in Second Language Acquisition

KRASHEN, Stephen and Tracy Terrell
The Natural Approach

LEONTIEV, Alexei
Psychology and the Language Learning Process

LOVEDAY, Leo
The Sociolinguistics of Learning and Using a Non-native Language

ROBINSON, Pauline C.
ESP (English for Specific Purposes)

SHARP, Derrick W. H.
English at School: the wood and the trees

STREVENS, Peter
Teaching English as an International Language

TOSI, Arturo
Immigration and Bilingual Education

YALDEN, Janice
Evolution, Design and Implementation

See also SYSTEM *the international journal of Educational Technology and Language Learning Systems* (sample copy available on request).

ESP Journal, an international journal of English for Specific Purposes

EPISODES IN ESP

A source and reference book on the development of English for Science and Technology

JOHN SWALES

University of Michigan

PERGAMON INSTITUTE OF ENGLISH

a member of the Pergamon Group

Oxford · New York · Toronto · Sydney · Frankfurt

U.K.	Pergamon Press Ltd., Headington Hill Hall, Oxford OX3 0BW, England
U.S.A.	Pergamon Press Inc., Maxwell House, Fairview Park, Elmsford, New York 10523, U.S.A.
CANADA	Pergamon Press Canada Ltd., Suite 104, 150 Consumers Rd., Willowdale, Ontario M2J 1P9, Canada
AUSTRALIA	Pergamon Press (Aust.) Pty. Ltd., P.O. Box 544, Potts Point, N.S.W. 2011, Australia
FEDERAL REPUBLIC OF GERMANY	Pergamon Press GmbH, Hammerweg 6, D-6242 Kronberg-Taunus, Federal Republic of Germany

First edition 1985

Library of Congress Cataloging in Publication Data

Main entry under title:
Episodes in ESP.
(Language teaching methodology series)
Includes bibliographical references.
1. English language—Study and teaching—Foreign speakers—Addresses, essays, lectures. 2. English language—Scientific English—Study and teaching—Addresses, essays, lectures. I. Swales, John. II. Title: Episodes in E.S.P. III. Series.
PE1128.A2E64 1984 428'.007 83-25011

British Library Cataloguing in Publication Data

Episodes in ESP.—(Language teaching methodology series)
1. English language—Textbooks for foreigners
2. English language—Technical English
I. Swales, John II. Series
428.2'4'0245 PE1128

ISBN 0-08-029428-6

Printed in Great Britain by A. Wheaton & Co. Ltd., Exeter

That was the real lesson to learn; never to make an end of the means, never to be so immersed in the medium, the formulae, the techniques, as to forget the end to which they were but subsidiary.

A. L. Rowse
Discoveries and Reviews
(Macmillan, 1975, p. 2)

— ACKNOWLEDGEMENTS —

I am grateful to the following for giving permission to reproduce material used as the core of each Episode:—

Dr Charles Barber and Gothenburg University Library for 'Some Measurable Characteristics of Modern Scientific Prose', originally published in *Contributions to English Syntax and Philology* (Gothenburg Studies in English, 14), 1962.

The Longman Group Limited for extracts from *The Structure of Technical English* by A. J. Herbert and *Nucleus General Science* Student's Book by Martin Bates and Tony Dudley-Evans.

The Oxford University Press and The British Council for the articles 'Hard Facts (Notes on Teaching English to Science Students)' by John J. Higgins and 'Further Notes on Developing an English Programme for Students of Science and Technology' by J. R. Ewer and E. Hughes-Davies, from *The English Language Teaching Journal*, and an extract from *Reading and Thinking in English*, Book Four by John Moore, © The British Council 1980.

Thomas Nelson & Sons Limited for an extract from *Writing Scientific English* by John Swales.

Julius-Groos-Verlag, Heidelberg, Germany, for permission to reprint the article by J. P. B. Allen and H. G. Widdowson: 'Teaching the Communicative Use of English', first published in *IRAL* XII, 1, 1974, pp. 1–20.

Tom Hutchinson and Alan Waters of the Institute for English Language Education, University of Lancaster, for 'ESP at the Crossroads' from *The ESP Newsletter*, 26, 1980.

The article 'Teaching and Learning Materials' by Karl Drobnic, James B. Herbolich, Paul Fanning and Phil Skeldon was first published in *ESPMENA Bulletin* No. 10.

'How to Arm your Students: A Consideration of Two Approaches to Providing Materials for ESP'. *ELT Documents* 101, 1978, pp. 23–35. Reproduced by permission of the British Council.

'An Experiment in Team-teaching of Overseas Postgraduate Students of Transportation and Plant Biology'. *ELT Documents* 106, 1980, pp. 6–23. Reproduced by permission of the British Council.

Every attempt has been made to trace and acknowledge ownership of copyright. The publisher will be glad to make suitable arrangements with any copyright holders whom it has not been possible to contact.

I would like to thank all those colleagues and students from many parts of the world who offered comments on a preliminary version of this book and made valued suggestions for its improvement. I am also very grateful to Fiona Waterhouse for her rapid and accurate typing of the manuscript; and last but not least, I am indebted to Claire, Harvey and Kirby, without whose equanimity this book would not have been possible.

CONTENTS

— INTRODUCTION —

With one exception, the currently available books on English for Specific Purposes are all collections of articles, either with or without some editorial commentary. Better known examples of these collections are *English for Specific Purposes* edited by Mackay and Mountford (Longman 1978) and *English for Academic and Technical Purposes* edited by Selinker, Tarone and Hanzeli (Newbury House 1981). Such volumes certainly contain much material of lasting interest, but the articles are usually written by specialists for specialists and the volumes as a whole tend to offer the shared views of like-minded contributors as to 'the state of the ESP art' in, say, 1975, 1978 or 1981. As a result, the articles they contain are not easy to evaluate by those relatively unfamiliar with this branch of English language teaching; in particular it can be difficult to see why and how the arguments presented are reactions *against* previous approaches and reactions *to* current developments in linguistic and educational thinking. Therefore, one of my main purposes in *Episodes* is to offer a volume that does attempt to explain and illustrate the major lines of development in what David Wilkins has described as 'the sometimes bewildering world of English for Specific Purposes'.

The exception I referred to at the beginning of the previous paragraph is Pauline Robinson's *ESP (English for Specific Purposes)* (Pergamon 1980). Robinson provides a succinct and coherent overview of ESP work produced up to about 1979; she discusses various definitions of ESP, surveys a number of influential theoretical positions, analyses the available ESP teaching materials and concludes with a justly-admired 500-item bibliography. It is not my intention that *Episodes* should compete with or update Robinson's book in any way; rather, I see *Episodes* as complementary—as a companion volume. The scope of the present volume is in some ways broader and in others narrower than in Robinson's survey.

The scope is broader in a historical sense, for I have selected and arranged in chronological order fifteen actual items from the ESP literature. These fifteen Episodes are made up of eleven articles and four extracts from textbooks. Although this volume is in no sense a history of ESP, I have deliberately set out to try and establish a historical perspective. One reason for this I have already mentioned: that is, a wish to try and show something of the causes and effects that link the Episodes together. Another is my wish to demonstrate the value of pioneering contributions. My own experience of the ESP profession over a period of fifteen years or more is that the profession as a whole, and with all too few exceptions, operates within the 'here and now' of their actual teaching situation. The profession itself is composed of ESP *practitioners*—the term I prefer because it nicely illustrates the range of teaching, materials production, course design, and research activities that make up many ESP job-specifications. ESP practitioners tend not to look *across* to other ESP situations and to other ESP endeavours, whether similar or dissimilar to their own, to see what lessons might be learnt, what insights might be gained, or what useful short-cuts can be made. Nor do they often look *back* to previous work in their own departments or in others. My feeling is that such 'isolationist' attitudes can lead to reduplication of effort and inefficient use of time, and my hope is that this volume will do something to persuade the profession that contributions from other places and other times are at least potentially relevant to the 'here and now'. A third reason for a historical approach relates to the fact that ESP—like many other recently developed areas of social and educational science—has been subject to marked and perhaps exaggerated changes in fashion. A source book like *Episodes*, with its emphasis on the emergence of longer-term trends, can perhaps show that beneath the clash and controversy of debate, there is more agreement about the appropriate principles and practices for carrying out ESP work than appears on the surface.

ESP is a relatively recent development in the major worldwide industry of Teaching English as a Second or Foreign Language; indeed, nobody has yet retired from spending a professional lifetime working within it. Moreover, it has no clear and indisputable beginning; the fixing of the moment when the prehistory of ESP became the beginning of its history must be a personal and somewhat arbitrary choice. Peter Strevens has observed that phrase-books for foreign tourists have been in existence for four hundred years and Kurt Opitz has shown that mariners have been making use of highly-specialized bilingual maritime dictionaries for more than half of that long period. But for me the real history of ESP is shorter than that by an order of magnitude, and I have set the beginning of the story in 1962 with the publication of Barber's article 'Some Measurable Characteristics of Modern Scientific Prose'. And at least the choice of 1962 allows me, when writing the final section of this volume in 1983, to consider the question of whether English for Specific Purposes has yet come of age.

If the choice of Barber for Episode One was not altogether an easy one to make, the choice of each succeeding Episode became increasingly harder. The ESP literature has expanded enormously over the twenty-year period covered by this volume. I believe I can illustrate this most easily by showing the increase in the number of items held in the ESP Reference Collection built up by my colleagues and myself, originally at the University of Khartoum and now at the University of Aston in Birmingham:

Items held in a working ESP Reference Collection

Date	Number of Items (approximately)
1972	30
1975	60
1978	150
1981	400
1984 (estimate)	1300

Therefore selecting as few as fifteen items illustrating the development of ESP has been an invidious task and many sacrifices of really excellent work have had to be made. Further, I have fairly rigorously applied two criteria:—

(1) I have tended to choose items that actually exemplify teaching material or deal fairly closely with either an actual teaching situation or with the language of science and technology. In view of my aim to put together a volume that may be of use to English teachers venturing into ESP for the first time or to those undergoing teacher-education courses in ELT and Applied Linguistics, I have restricted the entries to those directly concerned with the ESP classroom or with an understanding of the specialized language that will be taught (by one route or another) in that classroom. I have therefore decided to exclude papers dealing entirely with higher-order matters such as course and syllabus design, needs analysis, the management of ESP projects, and ESP evaluation and testing.

(2) In order to create a reasonable basis for chronological comparison over a twenty-year period, I have further restricted the selection to English for Science and Technology, or EST. EST is the senior branch of ESP—senior in age, larger in volume of publications and greater in number of practitioners employed. It therefore seemed to me that because of the predominant position of EST, the major developments of ESP as a whole could best be told through it. With one or two exceptions, particularly in such areas as games and simulations, English for Science and Technology has always set and continues to set the trend in theoretical discussion, in ways of analysing language, and in the variety of actual teaching materials. Further, I have tended to concentrate on Episodes which deal with the mainstream areas of reading and writing scientific and technological English at tertiary level. However, in order to see the implications of all these restrictions, it is first necessary to review some of the divisions typically accepted—and occasionally rejected—in English for Specific Purposes.

One way of subcategorizing EST (and other ESP activities) is into educational level, and here the normal and self-evidently sensible procedure is to subcategorize according to institutional setting. Thus we have courses differently designed for:—

A *Schools* (especially technical secondary and trade schools)
B *Technical Colleges*
C *Polytechnics and Universities*—undergraduate level
D *Polytechnics and Universities*—postgraduate level
E *Polytechnics and Universities*—research and academic staff
F *Specialized Institutions* (technical translation, patents, research administration etc.)

Category C has attracted the lion's share of attention; and indeed nine of the fifteen Episodes are firmly targeted on providing improved service English courses for first- and second-year students on BSc programmes. Reasons for this concentration are not hard to find. Those in charge of tertiary administration see the early years as being the most obvious place for service courses of various kinds; the medium of instruction may change from the first language to English on entry to the University or Polytechnic; and most entering students will find that they are required to use a large library for the first time in their lives, and will also find a considerable part of that library stock will be written in English, whatever the medium of instruction used in lectures and classes. Although there continue to be doubts about the wisdom of putting all the EST eggs in the basket of the first two or three semesters, there is little doubt that in practice the amount of materials preparation and the amount of teaching is greater on this level than on any of the others.

A second way of subcategorizing English for Science and Technology is in terms of subject-matter. Again the common practice has been to follow institutional boundaries:

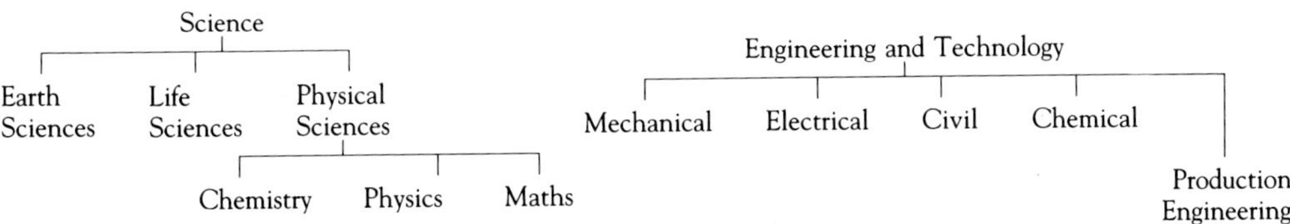

And again the central areas of the above diagram (particularly the physical sciences) have produced more research and pedagogical work than those on the sides. The emphasis on physics, chemistry, mechanical and electrical engineering is particularly apparent in the earlier Episodes, but in the later ones I have been able to choose extracts that illustrate work on a wider or on a more general range of subject-matter. I do not want at this stage to face up to the question of whether such a subject-matter subcategorization is well motivated as far as ESP programmes are concerned, nor do I wish to consider at this point what sort of evidence would establish (or disestablish) the need for, say, a specific course for geologists. Questions such as these occur and recur throughout this volume and are best discussed against fairly specific historical and educational backgrounds.

A third way of dividing up the broad area of EST is to establish a set of activity-types that our students of sciences and engineering are required to engage in. Such a set might include:—

A Reading and making notes on textbooks
B Reading scientific articles
C Following and taking notes on lectures
D Carrying out and writing up experiments
E Writing technical reports
F Answering examination questions
G Taking part in seminars and tutorials
H Using technical manuals and other instructional literature

Once more, the literature in general, and this book in particular, reflects clear priorities. The major area of interest has been in developing a capacity to process information in textbooks; quite a lot of attention has been given to developing writing, especially at a fairly straightforward descriptive level; the listening and speaking skills have received rather less. In fact, none of the Episodes in this volume deals principally with the matters relating to spoken scientific English, although several make some reference to it.

I have in the previous paragraphs given three separate ways of looking at EST, but of course they are all interrelated. However, how they are interrelated remains at the moment rather obscure. Which is the really important *variable*? Is it *educational level*, or *subject-matter*, or is it *activity-type*? Or is it none of these, but something else like *communicative purpose*? And a further set of questions about the relationship between science and its linguistic expression also arises. Does science have a general methodology, or do its component disciplines have distinct methodologies and cognitive styles? Or is it the case that a particular educational institution exerts a powerful influence on what takes place within it? We have at present no definitive answers to such fundamental questions, but at various places throughout this volume partial answers are proposed and discussed.

We can now see that EST is central to ESP in another way. ESP itself is often, if somewhat uncomfortably, divided into a set of operating categories that further specify the *specific*:—

English for Academic Purposes
English for Occupational or Vocational Purposes
English for Professional Purposes

Courses in other areas such as business and commerce are largely concerned with the second and third of those categories, whereas, as we have seen, EST is more likely to fall within the first. Although at a training level teaching English for Science and Technology may be seen to be EOP or EVP, and at a level where graduating students are being prepared to be effective communicators within industry and government various professional elements may become important, it remains true that the great majority of EST programmes are designed to help their customers survive and succeed in an academic environment. This is particularly the case in the 'classic' context of courses for first-year students aimed principally at improving their comprehension of textbooks in the physical and engineering sciences.

Because of the criteria I have applied to the selection of Episodes my scope is considerably narrower than Pauline Robinson's. I have attempted to elucidate the development of one central area of ESP interest rather than (like her) to offer a survey of the scene as a whole. The restrictions of both level of discussion and content have also meant that actual examples of the writings of certain key figures in ESP are missing. There is no Episode containing an article by Peter Strevens because his articles have offered clarifications of ESP as a whole rather than dealt with classroom practice. For rather similar reasons, I have not been able to find a place for even one of the many papers written by Ron Mackay. Henry Widdowson is only represented by the well-known 1974 article of which he was joint author. Yet Widdowson's influence on EST over the last fifteen years has been greater than that of anybody else; for establishing subtle distinctions, for level of argument, for confident evaluation of the relevance of the work of linguists and for elegance of expression he is unrivalled. However, Widdowson's own intellectual development is well chronicled in the volume entitled *Explorations in Applied Linguistics*, and indeed his thinking is detectable at numerous places in this anthology. The names of Christopher Candlin and John Sinclair do not feature on the contents page at all, again largely as a result of the criteria I have used. Nevertheless, their work is represented here by their associates; the paper by Hutchinson and Waters has been chosen to illustrate Lancaster radicalism and the work of Sinclair's Department at Birmingham can be seen in Episode Twelve.

I equally regret the fact that all the principal authors of the Episodes are native speakers of English. As it happens, EST is one area where up until now the impact of non-native speakers on development has been relatively minor. In other branches of ESP the situation is rather different; elsewhere we find major contributors who do not speak English as their first language, such as Angele Tadros in English for students of Economics and Vijay Bhatia in English for Academic Legal Purposes. That said, I venture to think that the selection I have made does have certain merits. First, the contributors represent a wide cross-section of professional activity; one or two are academics, one is now a full-time textbook-writer, many are practitioners in the sense that I have defined that term, a few would consider themselves as pre-eminently classroom teachers. Secondly, the provenance of the work reported is equally wide; certainly Britain and the United States are well represented, but there is also work that originated in such diverse countries as Chile, Colombia, Iran, Kuwait, Libya, Sudan and Thailand. In this way I have hoped to show that ESP excellence is neither the preserve of developed countries nor the preserve of those who hold important positions in the ELT hierarchy.

Each *Episode* has five sections. Each opens with a *Setting* wherein I try to place the textbook extract or article that follows against its background, to assess its relationship to other work, to highlight its novel and original elements and to signal its limitations—in short, to offer the reader a framework through which he or she can approach the original with some idea of its movitations and repercussions. The second section is the Episode itself accompanied by a number of commentary notes. Some of the notes pick out topics and themes that recur in other Episodes, some explain or exemplify observations and technical terms that I felt some readers would have difficulty in understanding, some comment on the uses other practitioners have made of ideas and suggestions contained within the Episode itself, and others are essentially questioning or critical. I have set some store by the last in that I hope it will show readers new or relatively new to this type of literature ways of developing a critical awareness of what precisely is being described or claimed or concluded.

The third section is entitled *Activities* and offers a small number of exercises based on the particular Episode. In teacher-training situations one or more of these may be set as individual, pair or group work. (I have not provided a key because many are rather open-ended, but if anybody would like possible outline solutions I should be able to provide them.) Section IV is entitled *Evaluation* and asks the reader to review what he or she has just read and to come to various sorts of judgment about that reading. If this book is used with students or student-teachers a number of these *Evaluations* could be set as written assignments. The Episodes close with a short annotated list of *Related Readings* that are designed to steer the user of this book towards comparable work if he or she should be so inclined. In fact, my original intention was to round off *Episodes* with a comprehensive update of Robinson's ESP bibliography, but the number of items to be included is now approaching fifteen hundred and an entry of this size would make this volume both excessively long and seriously unbalanced. I am therefore hoping that the Bibliography will appear as a separate volume.

At the end of the day, *Episodes in English for Science and Technology* is a selection of items that I personally have found and still find imaginative, significant and exciting. I suspect that in making the difficult decisions of choosing so few from so many I have, as ever, been influenced by my essentially pragmatic approach to ESP—by my distrust of theories that do not quite work out in the litmus-paper realities of the classroom. Colleagues who have also spent years charting the coastlines of the mysterious and fascinating world of ESP might have made a different selection, and might well want to make different assessments of the Episodes that I have chosen. Only time—and comments both favourable and unfavourable—will tell whether I have persuaded the ESP profession that their judgments might accord with mine.

References

K. Opitz, **'Linguistics between Artificiality and Art: Walking the Tightrope of LSP Research'**, *CILA Bulletin 37*, Neuchâtel, 1983.

P. Strevens, **'Special-purpose Language learning: a perspective'**, *Language Teaching and Linguistics Abstracts*, 10, 3, 1977.

EPISODE ONE 1962

C. L. Barber, 'Some Measurable Characteristics of Modern Scientific Prose' in *Contributions to English Syntax and Phonology*, Almquist & Wiksell, Stockholm, 1962.

I

SETTING

For those few people involved in ESP in the mid-sixties this article had a special importance. First, it was a clear demonstration that the descriptive techniques of Modern Linguistics, as most influentially represented in *The Linguistic Sciences and Language Teaching* by Halliday, MacIntosh and Strevens (Longman, 1964), could be successfully applied to the language of science and technology. Secondly, the useful statistical information it contained provided ammunition for those EST teachers trying to convince their colleagues and superiors in Departments of English that 'Scientific English' was different from 'General English' or 'Literary English' in ways other than its use of technical or specialized vocabulary. After all, we need to remember that in the early sixties syllabuses were essentially structural, and, for example, all the tenses of English were taught simply because they were *there*—as part of the language system. Barber's results could be—and were—used as an argument for *not* teaching the progressive tenses in 'Scientific English' classes. The article additionally served as a model for further work on frequency analysis. With one difference, however: Barber chose to express his findings in terms of traditional grammar, whilst other workers chose some version of Halliday's category and scale grammar.

Copies of this article have always been difficult to obtain, and I believe a certain belated justice is being done by giving 'Some Measurable Characteristics' pride of place in this collection. There was in fact a certain amount of similar research taking place in England and elsewhere at this time and in the years immediately following, usually by students on postgraduate courses, but the resulting projects and dissertations have long been buried in departmental and university libraries and are now almost completely forgotten.

Although I have just suggested that the type of frequency analysis as represented by Barber has found little favour in British (and American) ESP work in recent years, it has by no means been abandoned in all quarters of the globe. On the continent of Europe—and perhaps especially in the Eastern bloc—a tradition of 'lexicostatistics' continues. Indeed it may well be undergoing something of a revival as a result of the fact that frequency analysis is ideally suited to computerization.

Twenty years on, Barber's study of scientific syntax and vocabulary still seems, within the limited scope he has set himself, thoroughly professional. The suggestions for the teacher of scientific English are cautious and sensitive, and the honesty with which he relates problems and difficulties sets a standard of intellectual responsibility that has not always been maintained. This is not to say that Barber's study does not have serious limitations, even within its own narrow objectives. A further reason, therefore, for selecting Barber as the opening Episode is that it offers an excellent opportunity for developing a capacity to read ESP papers critically. In particular, a close reading should raise questions about the selection of a corpus (or body of texts) for analysis, about the consequences of choosing a particular scheme of analysis, and about the interpretation of statistical findings. The point of such questioning is not, of course, to arrive at a position whereby we dismiss Barber's article simply because it is not in tune with contemporary thinking; rather we should be looking for ways of incorporating the more useful of his findings within our knowledge of scientific English for our specific teaching purposes. To this end, I have written rather longer commentary notes for the first Episode than for most of the subsequent ones.

Barber's original 1962 article is quite long, and for this volume I have included only the first two-thirds which deals with syntax; the final section on vocabulary is omitted.

II
TEXT AND COMMENTARY

Some Measurable Characteristics of Modern Scientific Prose

by C. L. Barber *University of Leeds*

During recent years, English has increasingly become a medium for the teaching and learning of other subjects. This use of English as an auxiliary language is especially important in those countries where a great deal of university-teaching is carried out in English (e.g. India); but it is also important in many other countries, which rely to a great extent on textbooks written in English, especially at the university level. This dependence on textbooks in English seems to be particularly marked in scientific and technical subjects, and there must be many thousands of students of these subjects who rely wholly or largely on books published in Britain or the United States. It is therefore of interest to teachers of English abroad, and especially of course to those who teach English to scientists and technologists, to examine the characteristics of modern scientific English; and some of these characteristics, as exemplified in small samples of recent scientific writing, will be examined in this article. Since the bias is towards the needs of the teacher, I shall use traditional terminology (e.g. in the discussion of verb-tenses and of subordinate clauses); but I hope that the material will also have some general stylistic and linguistic interest.

The investigation reported in this article must be considered merely as a preliminary one; it is only a small-scale study, confined to a limited body of material, and this must be borne in mind when the results are considered: they are obtained from a small sample. As material for analysis, I have chosen three different texts: Text A is an excerpt from a textbook of university standard on the engineering applications of electronics;[1] Text B is more concerned with basic research, (*a*) and is in *the field of biochemistry*;[2] Text C is from an elementary university textbook on astronomy, and consists of a chapter on astronomical instruments.[3] The approximate lengths of the three passages are 7,500 words, 6,300 words, and 9,600 words respectively. All three passages are from American books; this is partly an accident; but in any case it is desirable, given so small a body of material, to confine oneself either to British or to American English; and it is clear that the United States is now the main source of technical and scientific writing in English, and will continue to be so. On the surface, there is not much difference between British and American scientific English;[4] though a statistical comparison would no doubt reveal differences.

[1] D. G. Fink, *Engineering Electronics* (New York 1938), pp. 3–13, 306–21.
[2] L. Michaelis, 'The nature of the interaction of nucleic acids and nuclei with basic dyestuffs', in *Cold Spring Harbor Symposia on Quantitative Biology* XII (1947), pp. 131–40.
[3] H. N. Russell, R. S. Dugan, and J. Q. Stewart, *Astronomy* (rev. ed. Boston 1945), pp. 37–73.
[4] See T. H. Savory, *The Language of Science* (London 1953), pp. 28–30.

(*a*) Barber's choice of texts calls for some comment. Huddlestone (1971) categorized his science texts into three 'levels of brow':—

(1) 'High-brow', e.g. scholarly journal articles;
(2) 'Mid-brow', e.g. undergraduate textbooks;
(3) 'Low-brow', e.g. popular science for the general reader.

However, it could be argued that 'level of brow' is not as important as the expected relationship between the

(*a*) *continued overleaf*

The texts that I have chosen, besides coming from totally different scientific fields, also (b) straddle two fields each (electronics and engineering, biology and chemistry, astronomy and instrumental optics). In this way I hope, even with so little material, to get some idea of the things that are *generally* useful to the foreign reader or teacher, by seeing what things are common to all these fields; this is especially important in the study of the vocabulary.

Occasionally, I shall compare my findings with those of two colleagues, who have done similar work as part of their postgraduate studies at the University of Leeds, and whose unpublished findings I quote with their permission. Mr W. Rumszewicz, of Olsztyn in Poland, has examined the language used in four recent English textbooks in the sphere of agricultural studies (crop husbandry, animal husbandry, agricultural chemistry, agricultural botany); for the purposes of comparison, he has also examined four passages of recent prose drama. He thus has eight texts in all; they are very short (1,000 words each), but he has analysed them in great detail. Mr M. Siddiqui, of Karachi, West Pakistan, has done a study of the vocabulary of scientific textbooks, on the same lines as my own (to be described later in this article), but using more material: he has five texts from five different fields (civil engineering, organic chemistry, physics of matter, plant botany, meteor astronomy), each running to about 15,000 words.

My own analysis falls into two main parts: (1) a study of sentence-structure and verb-forms, and (2) a study of vocabulary. Ideally, one would like a complete analysis of structures used, but in this preliminary investigation I have had to content myself with a small part of this: I have examined sentence-length, clause-types, verb-tenses, and the uses of non-finite verbs. The figures for sentence-length and clause-types refer to Text C only; the remaining statistics refer to the whole material.

(c) Text C, consisting of 9,648 words (tokens), contains 350 sentences; for the purposes of (d) analysis, a sentence has been considered to begin with a capital letter and to end with a full-stop.[5] Of these 350 sentences, 2 are commands; 3 are statements with commands in parenthesis; and 345 are statements; there are no questions or requests. Rumszewicz has similar results from his material: in his scientific texts, all sentences are statements; but in his dramatic texts, only two-thirds are statements, the remainder being questions or requests.

---

[5] In two exceptional cases, I have reckoned a sentence as ending at a colon, when no alternative analysis seemed realistic. My figures for numbers of words and sentences do not include captions to figures, or section-headings.

---

author and reader. In (1) the researcher is reporting results to his fellow-researchers; in (2) the relationship is that of teacher and student; and in (3) a journalist/scientist is attempting to interest a section of the general public. Thus, we can see that 'high-brow' and 'low-brow' texts are essentially informational, whereas 'mid-brow' textbooks are essentially instructional. Barber's Texts A and C are textbooks, but his text B is a high-brow research article. Putting the two sorts of text together may have been unwise. We can, however, get some idea of why Barber did this by reconsidering the opening paragraph. He begins by correctly identifying the textbook as representing the type of text of greatest importance to teachers of Scientific English, but he closes with the hope that his findings 'will also have some general stylistic and linguistic interest'. Presumably it is this hope that led him to include a basic research text written to provide information for colleagues.

(b) Certainly today not many people would consider Electronic Engineering, Biochemistry and Astronomical Instrumentation to be *interdisciplinary* fields.

(c) *Tokens and types. Tokens* are the actual occurrences of any words. *Types* are the occurrences of different words. Thus, in the two short sentences I have just written, we have the following numbers of tokens and types.

Tokens (i.e. total number of words) = 15.
Types (i.e. number of different words) = 10.
(tokens/are/the/actual/Occurrences/of/any/words/types/different)

This is then expressed as a type–token ratio, i.e. 10/15 = 1/1.5.

The ratio thus gives some measure of *lexical density*; in other words, the number of times words recur. The *lower* the type–token ratio, the *fewer* the number of repeated words. For example, if the fifteen words in my two sentences had been all different the type–token ratio would have been 1/1, and if they had been all the same—

In my material, the average sentence-length is 27.6 words. The distribution of sentence-(e) lengths is shown in Table 1. The modal length is 16–20 words, which seems surprisingly short for expositional prose; there may possibly be another peak, however, at 26–30 words. In Rumszewicz's scientific texts, the average sentence-length is slightly less, 23.6 words, and most numerous are sentences in the group 20–29 words; in his dramatic texts, on the other hand, the average sentence-length is only 7.0 words, and most numerous are sentences in the group 1–9 words.

TABLE 1. *Text C: Number of Sentences of Different Lengths*

Length in words	1 to 5	6 to 10	11 to 15	16 to 20	21 to 25	26 to 30	31 to 35	36 to 40	41 to 45	46 to 50	51 to 55	56 to 60	61 to 65	66 to 70	71 to 75	76 to 80	81 to 85
Number	5	24	51	64	38	46	30	25	20	15	12	6	6	4	2	1	1

I have also analysed the sentences of Text C according to the number of main and subordinate clauses that each contains. The results are given in Table 2; one sentence, containing 7 main and 2 subordinate clauses, has been omitted from the table, for simplicity of presentation. In the Table, the figures in the matrix show the number of sentences having the clause-structure indicated; thus there are 8 sentences in Text C that have 2 main clauses and 3 subordinate clauses. The striking thing about this table is the degree of simplicity it reveals in the typical clause-structure of the passage, which is shown by the density of the figures in the top left-hand corner of the table. Out of 350 sentences (one of which, it will be remembered, is omitted from the table), no less than 250 (71%) have only one main clause; only 12 sentences (3.4%) have more than two main clauses. No less than 190 sentences (54%) have no subordinate clauses at all; only 24 sentences (6.9%) have more than two subordinate clauses. Only 17 sentences (5.2%) have a total clause-number exceeding 4. By far the commonest type of sentence (144, 41%) is that with one main clause and no subordinate clauses, i.e. what is traditionally known as the 'simple sentence'. Not all such sentences, indeed, are simple in the

TABLE 2. *Number of Clauses per Sentence* (*Text C*)

Subordinate Clauses		0	1	2	3	4	5	Total
Main Clauses	1	144	57	36	9	4	0	250
	2	41	23	14	8	1	1	88
	3	5	4	0	0	0	0	9
	4	0	2	0	0	0	0	2
Total		190	86	50	17	5	1	349

as might happen in a computer print-out—it would have been 1/15. As might be expected, type–token ratios tend to be much lower in the life sciences than they are in mathematics. A final but important point about type–token ratios is that only texts of the same number of words can be compared. This is because as longer samples of text are taken, so the higher the type–token ratio will tend to be.

(d) In the previous paragraph Barber has announced his intention to examine sentence-length. He now needs a criterion to judge the end of sentences and he (entirely reasonably) relies on the traditional *full stop* or *period*. Unfortunately, this criterion becomes very much less useful if the text contains equations, chemical formulae and so on. It is by no means clear how such symbolic material is best handled by a sentence-grammar; for an interesting if difficult discussion, see Peter Roe, *Scientific Text*.

(e) *Modal* here means 'most common'; notice that it does not mean 'average'. *Expositional* is an unusual term; the more usual one is *expository*. Other researchers have found that scientific sentences have an average length of 20–30 words. The highest figures for sentence-length so far reported are those for legislative texts, which have a sentence-length of approximately double that of science.

(f) ordinary sense: some are quite long, and can have involved structures, often using non-finite verbs, as will be seen later.

In Text C, there are 118 junctions of main clauses within sentences. At 32 of these junctions, there is no conjunction, but only a mark of punctuation (in most cases a semi-colon). In the other 86 cases, conjunctions are used, in most cases *and* (62 times) or *but* (20 times).

Of the 264 subordinate clauses, 102 are adjective clauses (52 defining, 50 non-defining). The commonest relative pronoun to open these adjective clauses is *which* (22 defining, 40 non-defining); in 13 of these cases, the *which* is governed by a preposition. The next commonest is *that*, with 15 clauses (14 defining, 1 non-defining). Six of the clauses begin with *when*, one with *who*, and one with *whose*. The remaining 17 have no explicit subordinating word.

Only fifteen of the subordinate clauses are noun clauses, most of them beginning with *that*. Twelve of the subordinate clauses are adverb clauses of degree, introduced by *than*, *so . . . that*, or *as . . . as*. These two groups, then, are relatively small.

The remaining subordinate clauses are what would traditionally be called adverb clauses (g) modifying a verb (though a number of them would better be considered as sentence-modifiers). The largest sub-group is formed by clauses of time (53), most of them introduced by *when* (30); the next commonest subordinators in these clauses are *until* (7) and *while* (7); most of the clauses with *while* are really continuative rather than temporal, but formally they are clauses of time. The only other large sub-group is formed by clauses of condition (32); most of these (26) are introduced by *if*. A medium-sized sub-group is formed by the clauses of result (18), nearly all introduced by *so that*. Other types of adverb-clause (place, manner, reason, concession, purpose, explanation) are infrequent.

On the whole, adjective clauses are the largest single type; adverb clauses of time and condition are also frequent. Moderately frequent are noun clauses, adverb clauses of result, and adverb clauses of degree. Nothing else gets into double figures.

Of the words used to introduce subordinate clauses, by far the commonest is *which*, with 62 examples (all adjective clauses). Also very common are *that*, *when*, and *if*. *That* occurs by itself 33 times, mainly in noun clauses (12) and defining adjective clauses (14); it occurs a further 22 times in conjunction with *so*, mainly in adverb clauses of result, but also in clauses of degree, manner, and purpose. *When* occurs 36 times (30 in adverb clauses of time, 6 in defining adjective clauses). *If* occurs 26 times, all in adverb clauses of condition. Subordinators that occur with moderate frequency are *as* (11), *where* (7), *until* (7), *while* (7), and *since* (7). Other subordinators are infrequent.

(f) It is now time to review this paragraph, principally because it is a particularly good illustration of an important characteristic of all types of linguistic investigation; that is, the results and conclusions are at least partly determined by the type of analysis adopted. As Barber states, Table 2 suggests that scientific sentences have a simple sentence structure: 'by far the commonest type of sentence (144, 41%) is that with one main clause and no subordinate clauses, i.e. what is traditionally known as the "simple sentence"'. It is only when we read the last sentence in the paragraph that we realize that for Barber subordinate clauses must have a *finite* verb. Structures using non-finite verbs are not clauses, and so do not enter into Barber's measure of sentence complexity. Thus Barber's scheme of analysis requires him to analyse the following sentence (quoted by him later from Text A) as *simple* because, on his criteria, it contains one main clause and no subordinate clauses:—

(1) To explain this remarkable behaviour, each electron is considered to possess an electric charge, the charge being a numerical measure of the force of repulsion experienced between two electrons.

However, if the sentence had been:—

(1a) To explain this remarkable behaviour, each electron is considered to possess an electric charge, which is a numerical measure of the force of repulsion that is experienced between two electrons—

It would have been placed as amongst the 25% most complex sentences. Doubtless the reader can appreciate the effect of a scheme of analysis on the conclusions that are reached.

(g) As its name suggests, a *sentence-modifier* modifies the whole sentence:

She laughed unhappily (Adverb of manner—'in an unhappy way').
She laughed, unhappily (Sentence-modifier—'it was unfortunate that she laughed').

The majority of the subordinate clauses are directly dependent on a main clause or some word within it, and are not contained within some other subordinate clause. In fact the number of sentences that contain sub-dependent clauses is only 25, the number of sub-dependent clauses involved being 30. There is only one example of a sub-sub-dependent clause (an adverb clause of reason contained within an adjective clause which is itself contained within an adverb clause of degree); there is one sentence where three sub-dependent clauses are contained within the same subordinate clause (a noun clause, direct object of the main verb); there are two sentences where two sub-dependent clauses are contained within the same subordinate clause (in both cases a noun clause), and in the remaining 21 cases there is simply one sub-dependent clause within a subordinate clause. Of the 30 sub-dependent clauses, 15 are adjective clauses (9 defining, 6 non-defining), and 8 are adverb clauses of time. The subordinate clauses containing the sub-dependent clauses are more miscellaneous; 7 of the sub-dependent clauses are dependent on noun clauses, 6 on adjective clauses (1 defining, 5 non-defining), 4 on adverb
(h) clauses of time, 3 on adverb clauses of condition, and 3 on adverb clauses of result.

The figures given so far have been for Text C only, but the remaining figures are for all three texts. First there is an analysis of the verb-forms used; in this matter, there is no great variation between the three texts, and I shall give total figures.

The total number of verb-forms in the three texts (counting compound verbs as only one form) is 2,903, i.e. about one for every 8.1 words of running text. Of these, 61% are finite verbs, and 39% non-finites (infinitives, past participles, *-ing*-forms).[6] Obviously, the non-finites are of some importance, and I shall come back to them later.

There are 1,763 finite verbs, about one for every 13.3 words of running text; the differences between the three texts are negligible. These finite verbs can be divided into those that include
(i) a modal auxiliary, and those that do not. For this purpose, I have adopted the traditional breakdown into tenses, and have not counted *shall* and *will* as modal auxiliaries (although formally they behave like them), but as parts of traditional compound tenses, like auxiliary *be*, *have*, and *do*. When they are divided in this way, 84% of the finite verbs fall into the traditional tenses, while 16% employ modal auxiliaries. However, even 16% means 288 examples, which is quite a sizeable number in such a relatively small body of material.

Let us first take the 1,475 finite verbs without modal auxiliaries. Of these, 28% are passive, and 72% non-passive (and the three texts agree to within 1%). This confirms the common view that the passive is relatively frequent in this kind of writing. Rumszewicz's material gives very similar figures—26% passive, 74% non-passive; whereas his dramatic texts have a much smaller number of passives—only 3%, against 97% non-passives.

Perhaps the most interesting thing about these finite verbs is their breakdown into tenses. The simple form of the verb in English can be modified by any combination of four tense-markings—the past, the perfect, the progressive, and the passive; this gives a possible sixteen tenses. In my analysis, we have to add to these the future forms (*shall*/*will*); these can be modified by any combination of the perfect, progressive, and passive markings, which gives us another 8 tenses. To these 24 tenses we can add the Imperative, making 25; formally, of course, the imperative is simply the unmarked form of the verb, identical with the form used in the Present Simple; but for our purposes it is convenient to distinguish it. Many of these 25 tenses,

[6] The figure for non-finites, however, includes about 80 *-ing*-forms which are really pure nouns.

(h) The preceding paragraphs on subordinate clauses have probably been rather hard going. The conclusions that we need to keep in mind are that relative clauses are by far the most frequent (nearly 40%) and that relatives are followed by time clauses (20%) and conditionals (12%). Other types of clauses are relatively infrequent.

(i) Barber's decision to accept the traditional grammatical belief in the existence of a *future tense* in English is unfortunate in the sense that other researchers, including Huddlestone, have (correctly) included *will* and *shall* with other modals. We will need, as a result, to re-arrange Barber's figures if we want a direct comparison between his results and those of others.

of course, are rare; we seldom feel any need to use the Past Perfect Progressive Passive, or the Future Perfect Progressive Passive (to take extreme cases); but they are at any rate possible.

Now in my material no less than twelve of these 25 tenses are completely unrepresented. These are: the Past Progressive Active; the Perfect Progressive Active; the Past Perfect Progressive Active; the Past Progressive Passive; the Perfect Progressive Passive; the Past Perfect Progressive Passive; the Future Perfect Active; the Future Progressive Active; the Future Perfect Progressive Active; the Future Perfect Passive; the Future Progressive Passive; and the Future Perfect Progressive Passive. Three other tenses are represented in my material only *once* each: these are the Past Perfect Active, the Past Perfect Passive, and the Present Progressive Passive. So in my material no less than 15 of the 25 tenses are of quite negligible importance. As a matter of fact, the great bulk of the forms fall into two tenses only: the Present Simple Active (64%) and the Present Simple Passive (25%), leaving only 11% divided among the other eight tenses. The dominance of the Present Simple Active is not really surprising, since this is the completely unmarked, and so most general, form of the English verb.[7]

The complete ranking-order of the ten tenses in my material is as follows:

1. Present Simple Active (64%). 2. Present Simple Passive (25%). 3. Future Simple Active (3.7%). 4. Present Perfect Passive (1.7%). 5. Present Perfect Active (1.4%). 6. Past Simple Active (1.2%). 7. Past Simple Passive (1.2%). 8. Future Simple Passive (0.7%). 9. Present Progressive Active (0.6%). 10. Imperative (0.3%).

It will be noticed that the *progressive* forms are of very small importance: only one progressive tense is represented at all (the Present Progressive Active), and this comes bottom-but-one on the list, with only 0.6% (9 examples). Rumszewicz's scientific texts give a very similar pattern, with the Present Simple Active and the Present Simple Passive as the dominant tenses, and with hardly any progressive forms.

This does not mean, of course, that the less frequent tenses can be completely neglected by the teacher dealing with this kind of English; even a figure of only 1% means 14 examples of the tense in the material studied. But the figures do give some ideas about what should be the *priorities* of such a teacher in the matter of tenses: it is obviously undesirable, for example, to spend a great deal of time on the progressive tenses, and to neglect the Present Simple Passive. At the same time, my ranking-order cannot be taken as definitive, because of the smallness of the material. For example, if *prescriptive* works had been included as well as descriptives ones (if, for example, the material had included maintenance instructions for technical equipment, (j) or instructions for carrying out experiments), then the Imperative might well have come higher on the list.

There are two interesting points about the Present Simple Active, the predominant tense. First, no less than 45% of the examples are parts of the verb *to be* (nearly all *is* and *are*); no other (k) tense is dominated in this way by one verb; and no other verb, not even *have*, is outstandingly frequent. Second, hardly any of the examples of the Present Simple Active are forms with auxiliary *do*, either periphrastic or emphatic; in fact of the 949 examples of the Present Simple Active, only 18 are *do*-forms (1.9%). Of course, the 429 examples of the verb *to be* in the Present Simple Active cannot have the auxiliary *do* in any case; but even if we leave these 429 examples out of account, we still find that only 3.5% are *do*-forms. The same trend can be seen in the past tense: there are 18 examples of the Past Simple Active, and not one of them has auxiliary *did*. It is possible, therefore, that auxiliary *do* plays a relatively small part in this kind of writing; in my material it occurs much less frequently than some of the modal auxiliaries.

[7] I am, of course, disregarding the *-s* singular marking of the verb, since this is not really a *tense* marking. It is misleading to use the words 'present' and 'active' in the description of English tenses; but, as explained earlier, I am using traditional tense names with an eye to the needs of the teacher, who is often tied to such terminology.

(j) This paragraph shows Barber at his best. On the one hand, he makes a number of pedagogical suggestions, whilst, on the other, he exposes the fragile nature of the evidence from which those suggestions derive.

We can now turn to the finite verbs with a modal auxiliary. There are 288 of these, representing 16% of all finite verbs. Two auxiliaries are especially frequent: *can* (110 examples) and *may* (101 examples). Some of the examples of *may* look a little odd to the eye of an Englishman, and it is possible that a British scientist would have written *can* in several places where the Americans have written *may*; if this is so, *can* is perhaps even more predominant over *may* as the main modal auxiliary in British scientific writing; and in fact in Rumszewicz's scientific texts (all British) *can* is twice as frequent as *may*. A third very frequent auxiliary in my material is *must* (46 examples). The complete list of modal auxiliaries found is as follows:

1. can (110, 38%). 2. may (101, 35%). 3. must (46, 16%). 4. should (13, 4.5%). 5. would (10, 3.5%). 6. could (5, 1.7%). 7. might (2, 0.7%). 8. let (1, 0.4%).

Once again, the size of the material means that caution must be used in interpreting these results; for example, if a geometry textbook had been included, the auxiliary *let* might well have been more frequent.

Of the verbs following the modal auxiliaries, 58% are passive and 42% non-passive. The vast majority are present forms, only 3 examples (1%) being perfect.

If we now combine the results from finite verbs with and without modal auxiliaries, we get the following overall ranking-order:

1. Present Simple Active (949, 54%).
2. Present Simple Passive (364, 21%).
3. *can*-forms (110, 6.2%).
4. *may*-forms (101, 5.7%).
5. Future Simple Active (54, 3.1%).
6. *must*-forms (46, 2.6%).
7. Present Perfect Passive (25, 1.4%).
8. Present Perfect Active (21, 1.3%).
9. Past Simple Active (18, 1.0%).
10. Past Simple Passive (17, 1.0%).
11. *should*-forms (13, 0.75%).
12. Future Simple Passive (10, 0.57%).
    would-forms (10, 0.57%).
14. Present Progressive Active (9, 0.51%).
15. Imperative (5, 0.28%).
    could-forms (5, 0.28%).
17. *might*-forms (2, 0.11%).
18. Present Progressive Active (1, 0.06%).
    Past Perfect Active (1, 0.06%).
    Past Perfect Passive (1, 0.06%).
    let-forms (1, 0.06%).

Certain methodological objections can be made to this table: it could be argued, for example, that the forms with modal auxiliaries ought to be divided into active and passive, like the traditional tenses; and that *shall* and *will* ought to be shown separately (like *should* and *would*), instead of being combined in the future tenses. Such changes would, in fact, make very little difference in the overall pattern given by the table, which will suffice for our requirements.

It will be seen that the Present Simple Active is still the overwhelmingly predominant form, followed by the Present Simple Passive. Among the remaining forms, the verbs with modal auxiliaries are clearly the most important: they occupy three of the next four places on the

(*k*) A simple statement of the frequencies of Active and Passive can often be misleading, especially if the percentage of passives is taken as an indication of the degree of impersonality. This is because the degree of 'deverbalization' is a key further factor. Consider these three sentences:—

A We can divide 9 by 3 without a remainder.
B 9 can be divided by 3 without a remainder.
C 9 is divisible by 3 without a remainder.

We can see that although A and C share the active voice, it is really B and C that have more in common. A case can therefore be made for a threefold classification:—

A Active.
B Passive.
C Equative *be* as the main verb (see Wingard for an implementation of this).

The real question is what the textbook writer does when he has a *choice* of either active or passive, and why he chooses one or the other (a question taken up in Episode 15).

(l) table, and account for 64% of the forms (the Present Simple Active and Passive being left out of account). It will be remembered that in the Present Simple Active the forms with auxiliary *do* numbered 18, which is the same frequency as the Past Simple Active (ninth in the table), and a much lower frequency than *can*, *may*, and *must*. It is interesting to notice that the Future Simple Active comes high in the table, and that Present Perfect forms are rather more frequent than Past Simple ones.

Rumszewicz's material yields a very similar pattern. The Present Simple Active is the predominant form (51%), followed by the Present Simple Passive (10%), but third on his list comes the Present Perfect Passive (8%), followed by *can*-forms (6%), Past Simple Active (6%), Present Perfect Active (4%), Future Simple Active (4%), *may*-forms (3%), *would*-forms (2%), and Past Simple Passive (2%); other forms are infrequent. In view of the smallness of his material, the correspondence with my own findings is really very close. From his dramatic texts, however, Rumszewicz gets a rather different pattern: the Present Simple Active is still the predominant tense, with 47%, but is followed by the Past Simple Active (10%), the Imperative (9%), the Future Simple Active (7%), and the Present Perfect Active (6%); the progressive tenses are more important than in the scientific texts, the Present Progressive Active coming sixth with 5% and the Past Progressive Active thirteenth with 1%, but they are still not really outstandingly frequent; the passive forms, on the other hand, are much less frequent in the dramatic texts, accounting for only 3% of the forms (against 26% in the scientific texts).

We can now return to the *non-finite* verbs. There are 1,140 of these in my material, representing 39% of all verb-forms. Rumszewicz also finds a high proportion of non-finites among the verb-forms of his scientific texts (35%), whereas in his dramatic texts the figure is only 17%. Of the non-finites in my material, 532 are *-ing*-forms (47%), 350 past participles (34%), and 221 infinitives (19%). All three types, therefore, are of some importance, and in fact all play a considerable part in sentence structure. It will be remembered that, in clause structure, there is a strong tendency in my material towards simplicity (Table 2); but sentences with simple clause-structure are nevertheless sometimes quite long and complicated, and the non-finites play a large part in providing the complications. For example, the following are all 'simple sentences' in traditional terminology (i.e. they have only one main clause and no subordinate clauses), but they are all moderately complex in structure; I italicize the non-
(m) finites, and it will be seen that many of them play key-parts in the phrase-structure:

(i) *To explain* this remarkable behaviour, each electron is considered *to possess* an electric charge, the charge *being* a numerical measure of the force of repulsion *experienced* between two electrons.

(Text A, p. 9)

(l) As the section on finite verb forms draws to an end, we can now attempt some evaluation of Barber's approach. First, we would do well to remember his title, 'Some Measurable Characteristics of Modern Scientific Prose', and recognize how limited an objective he has set himself. He presents us with surface statistics, such as tense frequencies, of a variety of English. This approach has been severely criticized in recent years; here is Widdowson:

> The fact that scientific text exhibits a relatively high proportion of certain syntactic features and a relatively low proportion of others may be useful for identifying scientific English texts should we ever wish to do such a thing. In fact this approach has proved useful for establishing authorship; it can reveal, with the help of a computer, who wrote what. But it cannot reveal the communicative character of what was written. It cannot of its nature deal with discourse.

Although this criticism is well founded, it identifies sins of omission rather than of commission. It is true that Barber merely *describes* and does not *explain*, but it is not his intention to offer explanations. He merely points out that the passive is relatively frequent, as is the Present Simple, as are relative clauses, and leaves it to others (including ESP practitioners) to explain *why* such things should be the case. Frequency analyses are not discovery procedures. But they can often indicate *which* features do call for some sort of explanation. Further, they also provide evidence for generalizations about a variety, type or style of the language. It is one of the ironies of ESP research that those who are most critical of frequency work are those most given to making claims that such-and-such a feature is *important*, *frequent* or *interesting* without any evidence to support these claims.

(m) The author uses 'phrase-structure' because, as we have seen, he has defined *clause* as requiring a finite-verb. This use of 'phrase-structure' is entirely different from its use in transformational grammar.

(ii) Resistance *welding* is performed by *passing* a very heavy current through the pieces of metal *to be joined.*

(Text A, p. 317)

(iii) First of all we consider the dye solution at *varied* concentrations, but always *keeping* within the range of very dilute dye solutions, the solvent *being* a highly *concentrated* solution of nucleic acid (1 to 3%).

(Text B, p. 137)

(iv) These effects combine *to make* the brighter stars visible with the telescope in the daytime, the star image *being* far brighter and the background of the sky *seeming* fainter.

(Text C, p. 40)

(v) In this way, exposures *extending* even over several successive clear nights can be made, the plate-holder *being shielded* from the daylight and the instrument *set* again, with the aid of the *guiding* star, upon exactly the same point of the heavens as before.

(Text C, p. 55)

(vi) The final test of all the adjustments, and of the accurate *going* of the clock, is obtained by *observing* a number of Almanac stars of widely different declination, *reversing* the instrument in its pivots midway in the process.

(Text C, p. 62)

(vii) Often a réseau, *consisting* of a network of lines *ruled* with the utmost attainable precision and *forming* squares five millimetres on a side, is printed photographically on the plate before development, thus *affording* a system of coordinates permanently *attached* to the plate (Fig. 155).

(Text C, p. 68)

The three texts vary somewhat in the extent to which they use non-finites. Text B is the most sparing, with about one non-finite to every 30 words of running text, whereas Text C has one to every 20 words, and Text A one to every 17 words. There are no great differences, however, in the uses made of the non-finites in the three texts.

The largest group of non-finites is the *-ing*-forms (532). However, no less than 82 of these (15%) are in effect pure nouns, like *welding* in passage ii above, and of little interest from the point of view of sentence structure. Another 24 are verbal nouns like *going* in *the accurate going of the clock* (passage vi), where the *-ing*-form is the head-word of a noun-phrase.[8] Apart from this type, there are not many examples of *-ing*-forms as the head-words of nominal expressions, except in expressions governed by prepositions, like *by passing a very heavy current* . . . (passage ii) and *by observing a number of Almanac stars* . . . (passage vi). Such phrases governed by prepositions are in fact very common—there are 132 of them, representing 25% of the *-ing*-forms. The most popular preposition is *by*, which occurs in 57 of the examples; next comes *in* with 18, and then come *for* and *of* with 17 each. There is some variation between the texts in this respect: Text B contributes only 3 of the examples of *by*, and none of the examples of *in*, but has 11 examples of *on*, which is not found in the other two texts.

Almost as large as this group of nominal uses is the group of *-ing*-forms used adjectivally: there are 206 of these, representing 39% of all *-ing*-forms. However, no less than two-thirds of

[8] Constructions of this type are potentially equivocal. In the phrase *the mounting of the telescope* (which occurs several times in Text C), *mounting* can be read either as a concrete noun or as the name of a process. I have not distinguished between these two types in my figures.

these are examples of the simple attributive use, like *guiding* in passage v, which are not of interest for sentence-structure.[9] In most of the remainder (64 examples), the *-ing*-form is the head-word of an attributive phrase, which can be defining, like *extending even over several successive clear nights* (passage v), or non-defining, like *consisting of a network . . . a side* (passage
(n) vii). This, then, is a fairly important structural device in my material.

There are various other uses where the *-ing*-form is the head-word of a phrase dependent on some nominal expression (which provides the subject of the *-ing*-form), but where the use can hardly be classified as adjectival. Examples of this are the phrases *but always keeping . . . dye solutions* (passage iii) and *thus affording a system . . . the plate* (passage vii). These uses shade off into ones where the phrase is only very loosely or uncertainly attached to a nominal expression, or becomes absolute, so that we get what is sometimes called a 'detached participle', as in the following examples:

(viii) The most recent instruments are provided only with coarsely graduated circles, sufficient for finding the desired object (thus *saving* much expense).

(Text C, p. 50)

(ix) *Restricting* ourselves to the dyestuffs of the thiazine class, the following statement may be made.

(Text B, p. 133)

These various uses are fairly common, accounting for 50 examples.

Less common is the type where the *-ing*-form has a separate subject of its own, thus forming an absolute phrase, as in *the charge being a numerical measure . . . two electrons* (passage i); there are also examples in passage iii (*being*), in passage iv (*being*), and in passage v (*being shielded*). There are 29 examples of this construction in my material.

(o) The second-largest group of non-finites is formed by the past participles, with 387 examples. Of these, 123 are used as simple attributive adjectives, and are not of much interest for

[9] In fact more than one type is involved here: *magnifying glass* exhibits a different type from *magnifying power*; but I have not distinguished between these in my figures.

(n) It is now becoming clear that Barber has done something rather strange. He has included *all* occurrences of words ending in the *-ing*-morpheme in his data—presumably to make his counting procedure more automatic. He has therefore counted *-ing*-forms that are better regarded as nouns or adjectives, as well as those more properly taken as non-finite verb forms. Let us now see what happens if we try and separate out the two major types of *-ing*-forms:—

	Barber's groups	*No. of non-finite verbs*
	82 Nouns (resistance *welding*)	0
	24 Verbal nouns (the *mounting* of the telescope)	0
	132 non-finite verbs following prepositions (by *passing* the current)	132
206 {	*-ing*-forms as premodifiers (the *guiding* star)	0
	64 non-finite verbs in reduced relatives (exposures *extending* over)	64
	50 non-finite verbs in 'detached' clauses (thus *affording*)	50
	29 non-finite verbs in 'absolute' clauses (the *plate*-holder *being* shielded)	29
Total	523	Total 277

We have now identified 277 *-ing*-forms as constituents of non-finite clauses and 246 as constituents of noun-phrases. Even though we are now reduced to 277 *-ing*-clauses, we can see that they still make an important contribution to the organization of sentences in Barber's scientific texts. Remember that Barber found 250 finite subordinate clauses in Text C and that Text C represented about 40% of his corpus. We might therefore expect to find some 600 finite subordinate clauses in his three texts and we already have 277 non-finite clauses containing an *-ing*-verb form.

We can also notice that Barber classifies his clauses into formal, grammatical types; he says nothing about the *function* of *-ing*-clauses. The relevance of *function* and of *use* are matters that will be taken up in later Episodes.

(o) Barber's use of the term 'past participle' is traditional. Casual observation will show that the majority of the participles are in fact *passive* rather than *past*.

sentence-structure; the vast majority are placed in front of the noun, as in *varied concentrations* (passage iii) and *the desired object* (passage viii), but a few are placed after. In even more cases, no less than 196, the past participle is the head-word of an attributive phrase; in 43 of the examples, the phrase comes before the noun, as in *a highly concentrated solution* (passage iii); in the remaining 153 examples the phrase comes after the noun, as in *experienced between two electrons* (passage i), *ruled with . . . precision* (passage vii), and *permanently attached to the plate* (passage vii). This, plainly, is an important structural device in my material.

Predicative uses of the past participle are much less common, but occur occasionally, as in the following passage:

> (x) With this arrangement the image remains *fixed* in the focal plane.
> (Text C, p. 53)

There are 37 predicative examples; in 13 of them the past participle is used like a simple predicative adjective; in the other 24 it is the headword of a predicative phrase (as in passage x). With these predicative uses can be grouped the 27 cases where the past participle is the head-word of an expression introduced by *as*, *when*, *unless*, *if*, or *though*.

The third group of non-finites is formed by the infinitives, of which there are 221 (of which only 10% are passive infinitives). The infinitives thus form by far the smallest group in the non-finites, but on the other hand a very high proportion of them are important in the phrase-structure (whereas a considerable number of the *-ing*-forms and past participles operate as simple adjectives or nouns). The infinitives are difficult to classify briefly, but some of the main uses in my material can be picked out. No less than 64 of the examples (29%) are used to introduce phrases of aim, intention, or purpose, like *To explain this remarkable behaviour* (passage i). Of these 64 examples, 9 are introduced by *so as to*, and 7 by *in order to*; the remainder have simply *to*. On the other hand, phrases of result, like *to make . . . the daytime* (passage iv), are not common.

Another common use of infinitives is after adjectives. There are 10 examples of the following type:

> (xi) The band in the ultraviolet . . . is difficult *to observe*.
> (Text B, p. 132)

Commoner is the type where *it* is used as a substitute subject, and the infinitive forms the head-word of the real subject, as in the following example:

> (xii) It is not possible . . . *to secure* a perfect correction of the color.
> (Text C, p. 43)

There are 33 examples of this type; the adjectives most commonly used are *possible*, *necessary*, *easy*, and *difficult*.

Another group, of 20 examples, consists of cases where the infinitive is dependent on a nominal expression, as is *to be joined* in passage ii; particularly frequent in this group are infinitives depending on nouns like *tendency* and *ability*. In a smaller group, of a dozen examples, infinitives are used in expressions of degree with adjectives, as in the phrase *too numerous to examine* (Text A, p. 4).

Most of the other examples of the infinitive occur in various constructions after finite verbs. There are a few examples like the following, where the infinitive has its own subject:

> (xiii) If we cause the current . . . to pass between the electrodes . . .
> (Text A, p. 10)

Commoner, however, is the same construction turned round into the passive, as in *each electron is considered to possess an electric charge* (passage i); there are 20 examples of this. There are 25 examples of the infinitive as the head-word of a noun-phrase which forms the complement, usually after the verb *to be*; many of these infinitives are passives, but active infinitives also occur, as in the following example:

(xiv) the function of the tube is *to modify* the electron flow in some predetermined manner.

(Text A, pp. 9–10)

Many of the remaining examples of the infinitive occur after the verbs *have* and *seem*, after the passive *is said* (*are said*), and after verbs of desiring.

All the examples given, it will be noticed, are of infinitives with *to*. The name 'infinitive' is also often given to the base-form of the verb without *to*, when used for example as in the following sentence:

(xv) Tightening the clip and using the vernier screw, he makes the lower edge, or limb, of the sun just *graze* the horizon.

(Text C, p. 71)

In my material, however, such uses of the infinitive without *to* are quite negligible in number.

III
—ACTIVITIES—

(1) (*a*) Work out the average sentence-length of the first two paragraphs of Barber's article. Although this looks easy—especially as there are exactly ten sentences in the corpus—certain procedural problems remain. What are you going to do about the following?

(i) hyphenated forms, i.e. *University-teaching*
(ii) abbreviations, i.e. *e.g.*
(iii) letters, i.e. Text A
(iv) numbers, i.e. 6,300

Obviously there are no *correct* solutions; can you arrive at a clear and consistent policy?

(*b*) You will find that the average sentence-length is surprisingly high, although the sentences do not *seem* particularly long or complex. Scan the paragraphs for uses of the semi-colon (;) and colon (:). Are you still prepared to accept that a written sentence only ends with a full stop? Define your position.

(2) Re-read note (*n*). Carry out a similar separation for Barber's discussion of *past participles*.

IV
—EVALUATION—

(1) 'Barber's study is thus of interest not so much for the information which it provides or the light it sheds on a scientific English style, as for its attempt at a statistical approach, and its illustration of what should and what should not be done in such an investigation'. (Don Porter, 'Scientific English: An Oversight in Stylistics', *Studia Anglica Posnaniensa*, 8, 1976.)
After your careful reading of Barber, how far do you agree with Porter? If you disagree, justify your point of view by pointing to findings that throw some light on Scientific English style.

(2) Barber's title is 'Some Measurable Characteristics of Modern Scientific Prose'. What other kinds of characteristics (if any) could be usefully measured?

V

RELATED READINGS

H. G. Widdowson's *Explorations in Applied Linguistics* (OUP, 1979) is a key volume. Widdowson's influence on ESP and EST over the last decade has been pre-eminent, and this selection of his papers is indispensable for anybody with a serious professional interest in these areas. The paper entitled 'The Description of Scientific Language' is one of the most straightforward and the one most easily related to Episode One.

Peter Wingard, 'Some Verb Forms and Functions in Six Medical Texts' in *English for Academic and Technical Purposes* (edited by Selinker, Tarone and Hanzeli), Newbury House, 1981. Wingard's paper is an accessible *late* example of a Barber-type frequency analysis; the volume as a whole is one of the more important collections of ESP articles.

Rodney D. Huddlestone, *The Sentence in Written English*, CUP, 1971. This scholarly volume is subtitled 'A Syntactic Study based on an analysis of Scientific Texts', and derives from a large corpus of some 135,000 words of written Scientific English. The theoretical framework is mainly that of transformational grammar and restricted to a consideration of the syntax of single sentences. Reviewers and commentators have not found it of major or direct help in preparing EST courses, but it is a valuable source of reference, being rich in data and subtle grammatical distinctions. At the time of writing, out of print.

Peter Roe, *Scientific Text* (Discourse Analysis Monograph, English Language Research, University of Birmingham, UK), 1977. As note *(d)* implies, Roe's abridged doctoral thesis is rather difficult reading, but it does propose an interesting way of coping with equations and formulae in English grammar.

EPISODE TWO 1965

A. J. Herbert, *The Structure of Technical English*, Longman, London, 1965.

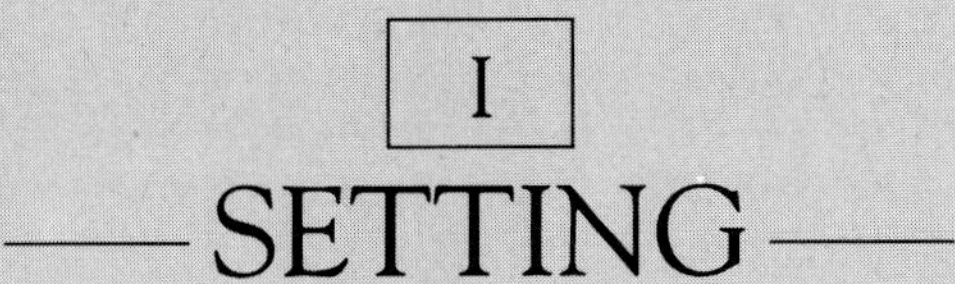

I SETTING

The Structure of Technical English (hereafter STE) was the first 'real' ESP textbook. The only other possible claimant for this pioneering position would be Pittman's *Preparatory Technical English*, which was published in 1960. However, Pittman's book, although very interesting in parts, exhibits marked idiosyncracies in course design and methodology. It was, therefore, very much a personal statement, and it was not until the appearance of STE five years later that we had an EST textbook based on a serious and detached investigation into the characteristics of the language found in science and engineering written texts.

STE has a clear and restricted aim. As the Preface states, 'this practice book is intended for foreign engineers or students of engineering who have already mastered the elements of English, and who now want to use their knowledge of the language to read books on their own subjects'. Herbert therefore is interested in making engineering literature in English more accessible. In order to achieve this specialized reading objective, he selects 'special structures and linguistic conventions of the English used in technical and scientific writing'. This in turn requires that a certain background knowledge is assumed of the readership—'I have taken for granted a knowledge of the terms of elementary mechanics and physics of the kind that would be studied in High Schools'.

Not only then does STE have a precise aim, it also has a precise title. It does indeed concentrate on *displaying* the structure of Technical English as this is expressed through a series of technical statements. Like Barber, Herbert believes that by placing emphasis on the typical forms of language found in written engineering texts, by highlighting the typical sentence patterns and by isolating certain aspects of vocabulary, the foreign student of engineering will be substantially aided in his specialist English-language reading. Immediately, we can see that this approach is consistently single-minded. First, Herbert understands by 'the structure of Technical English' *not* the structure of engineering passages *but* the structure of sentences. Second, there is no attention given to the development of reading strategies or reading skills as such. The problems are seen as lying within the grammar and vocabulary of the sentences.

The Preface to STE is particularly interesting for what it has to say on vocabulary. However, in order to appreciate Herbert's contribution in this area, we need first to see what Barber has to say (in the final section of his paper, which was omitted from Episode One). Like practically everybody else involved in English for Science and Technology, Barber holds the view that teaching specialized technical terms falls neither within the responsibility nor the competence of the English teacher. He continues:—

> 'What the English teacher can usually hope to do is to teach a vocabulary which is *generally* useful to students of science and technology—words that occur frequently in scientific and technical literature of different types. Some of these words will be technical ones, but many will not. I have therefore made the basic point in my vocabulary analysis the *number of texts* that a word occurs in; secondly, total number of occurrences is also taken into account.'

We may, I think, conclude from this that Barber's emphasis on the *range* or distribution of vocabulary items will indeed produce a list of general (and by implication non-specialized) words. However, he is clearly uninterested in *categorizing* the words that will thus emerge. Let us now compare Barber's position with that of Herbert. Herbert likewise begins by making clear that highly technical words are not his concern, and then goes on to say:—

> 'Much more difficult are the semi-scientific or semi-technical words, which have a whole range of meanings and are frequently used idiomatically. One of the aims of this practice book is to present as many of these words as possible, and as often as possible; words such as *work* and *plant* and *load* and *feed* and *force.* Words like these look harmless, but they can cause a lot of trouble to the student. And there is another kind of word which is important; the verbs, adjectives and adverbs that are not specifically scientific, but which belong to the phraseology of science. These are usually formal, dignified and foreign-sounding words, like *extends* and *propagate* and *obviate* and *negligible*, which are partly responsible for the slightly fossilized appearance of the typical scientific statement. A wide selection of these words will be found in this book.'

This concept of *semi-technical* (or *sub-technical*) vocabulary has become an important one in EST; and equally important has been the appreciation of the role of formal, 'elevated' equivalents of such ordinary-language words and phrases as phrasal verbs.

STE contains 28 sections (or Units) which follow a highly standardized format. Each section opens with a reading passage, accompanied by a line drawing, of about 500 words. The passages have been specially written by Herbert (in consultation with engineering colleagues) 'to illustrate features of technical style, and for no other purpose'. There are no comprehension questions on the passages. The middle part of each section is made up of *Word Study*, which contextualizes and comments on semi-technical vocabulary relatable to the passage. The third element in a section is entitled *Patterns.* There are three Patterns to each section, usually dealing with a particular aspect of technical statements and usually followed by a single sentence-completion exercise. The bases of the patterns vary. Here, for example, is Section 12:—

Patterns (1) Explanations of Cause (1)
(2) Contracted Relative: Passive
(3) Problems, Difficulties and Solutions

We can see that Pattern (1) is functional or communicative, Pattern (2) is structural and Pattern (3) is conceptual.

The Structure of Technical English is still in print and is still being used today, especially for its *Word Study* and *Patterns* elements. This is because STE shows a highly professional concern with the language of EST; a quality that is not totally obscured by an unexciting methodology. I have chosen Section 8 for Episode Two, which is given complete apart from the third Pattern.

Commentaries for (a) and (b) on opposite page

(a) The opening sentence is somewhat abrupt, but this is explained by the fact that Section 6 has dealt with *Steam Boilers* and Section 7 with *Steam Locomotives.* Nevertheless, Herbert's selection of topics is questionable, ranging as it does from steam locomotives, impulse turbines, jet engines, aerofoils, chain reactions and so on. These Engineering applications are usually studied in the final years of Engineering courses, whereas STE is typically used with first- or second-year undergraduates.

(b) The italicized parts of the text represent by-phrases which signify *means*; *means* is taken up by Herbert in Pattern 1. 'In order that/so that' are in bold type because they form the basis of Pattern 2.

II

TEXT AND COMMENTARY

The Structure of Technical English

by A.J. Herbert

Section 8

Reading: Condensation and Condensers

(a) Steam which is admitted to a cold engine cylinder is liable to be partially condensed by contact with the cylinder walls. That part of the steam nearest to the walls is cooled and condenses as a film of water. The volume of steam in
(b) the cylinder is *thereby* considerably reduced, and more steam must be admitted **in order that** the pressure is sufficiently high to drive the piston along the cylinder. Condensation in a cylinder therefore raises the steam consumption of the engine and *thereby* lowers its efficiency. It is therefore necessary to devise means of getting rid of this condensation as far as possible, and in modern reciprocating steam engines, condensation problems have been practically eliminated.

This is effected *by superheating* the steam in the boiler and also *by fitting* steam jackets round the cylinder. These are fitted into the annular space between the cylinder and the cylinder liner, and are connected to the steam supply. *By raising* the temperature of the cylinder walls in this way, the outward flow of heat is greatly reduced.

Steam which is exhausted from the cylinder still has a considerable heat content, and **in order that** this heat energy should not be wasted, the steam is condensed and passed back to the boiler as hot feed water. Rapid condensation is accomplished *by means of a condenser*. In this condenser, a liquid coolant is circulated through banks of metal tubes. *By flowing* over these tubes, the steam is caused to transmit some of its heat to the liquid, and a rapid drop in temperature occurs. The steam condenses, and is collected at the bottom of the condenser as condensate. *By ensuring* that there is no contact between the condensate and the coolant, a pure distilled water can be produced which is ideal for boiler feed water. This type of condenser is commonly used where pure water is not plentiful. The condensate is usually re-heated, **so that** it may be circulated back to the boiler at an adequate temperature.

In other types of condensers, which are known as jet condensers, the steam is cooled *by allowing* it to mix intimately with jets of cold water which are injected into the condenser. *By this means*, rapid condensation takes place, and the mixture of condensate and coolant is withdrawn *by means of an extraction pump*. The water which is normally used as a coolant cannot usually be utilised in the boiler, and cannot therefore be re-circulated. It is either pumped up to a cooling tower or it gravitates into a cooling pond, and is stored for later use in the condenser.

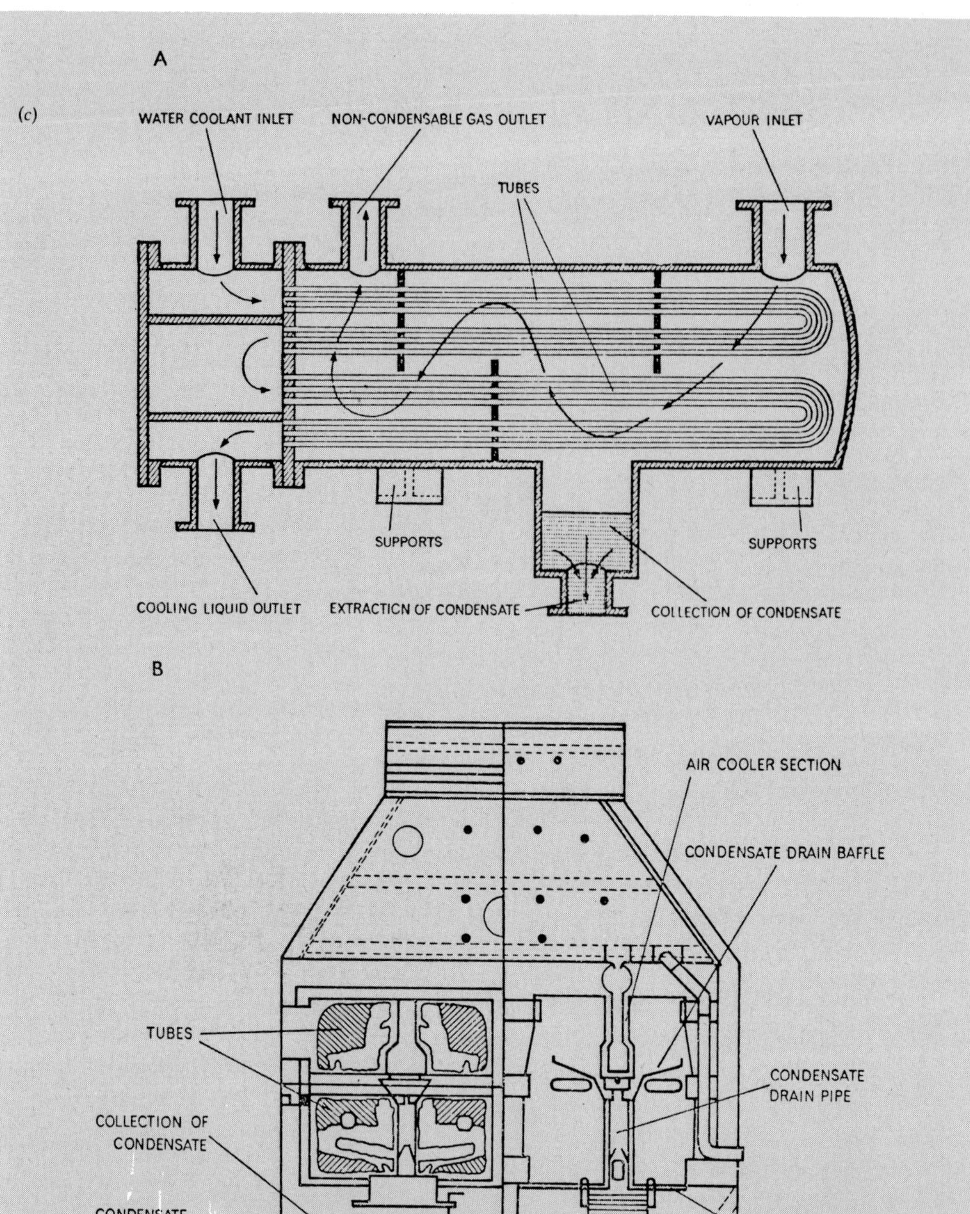

Cross-sections of (A) horizontal-process condenser
(B) steam surface condenser

(c) One of the peculiarities of STE is the lack of connection between texts and diagrams. It would seem that diagram A refers to the second half of the third paragraph of the text, and that in line 4, 'this condenser' refers to a condenser of a horizontal-process type. However, the relationship between text and diagram is not very explicit, to put it at its mildest. Indeed, whether diagram B illustrates a 'jet condenser' remains obscure, at least as far as the textual evidence is concerned. Clearly, Herbert has missed a valuable opportunity here, especially as the overt linking of text and diagram is precisely one of the most characteristic features of Engineering texts. The diagrams are neither integrated with the reading passage nor exploited for student activity.

(d) **WORD STUDY**

Produce, Product, Production

1. *a.* The company	*produces*	1000 cars a day. (= makes)
b. The boiler		high-pressure steam. (= generates)
c. Combustion		very hot gases.
2. *a.* Most of our industrial	*products*	are sold abroad.
b. These hot gases are the		of combustion.
c. Petrol and kerosene are		of crude petroleum.
3. *a* Motor-car	*production*	is increasing rapidly.
b. Recent		figures show an improvement on last year.
c. A new		line will be set up in the factory.

Consume, Consumption

1. *a.* The boiler *consumes* 3 tons of fuel per hour.
   b. The reactor *consumes* less material than it produces.

2. *a.* Engine efficiency may be measured by steam *consumption.*
   b. Family cars are designed for low fuel *consumption.*

Achieve, Obtain, Effect, Accomplish (= bring about)

1. A reduction in condensation is	*achieved* / *effected* / *accomplished*	by the use of steam-jackets.
2. Control of the power output is		by varying the fuel supply.
3. Rapid closing of the valve is		by fitting a heavy spring.
4. Removal of excess heat is		by means of a radiator.

Withdraw, Extract, Abstract (= take out or draw out)

1. The condensate is	*withdrawn* / *extracted* / *abstracted*	from the condenser by a pump.
2. The molten metal is		from the furnace, ready for casting.
3. Some of the steam is		for heating and other purposes.
4. The exhaust gases are		from the cylinder.
5. The fuel-rods are		from the reactor core mechanically.

(d) As the reader can see, the items chosen for *Word Study* are only semi-motivated by the text. *Produce*, for instance, occurs only once in the text, and *product* or *production* not at all. Nevertheless, these 'sentences with common features' as Herbert calls them are usually well done. Of course, it is easy to criticize; we might, for example, want to point out that *produce* in its geometrical sense of 'extend' is not included, nor are related words like *productive* or *productivity*. The key difference between *product* and *production* is there but, as so often with Herbert, an imaginative and alert teacher is needed to bring the difference fully into the open.

(e) *Inject* (= squirt through jet or nozzle)

1. The fuel is 2. The oil is 3. Pulverised fuel is	*injected*	into the cylinder by compressed air. directly into the combustion chamber. into the furnace.

Eliminate, Get Rid of

1. The use of oil in hydraulic systems largely *eliminates* / *gets rid of* corrosion.
2. In the interview, all except one applicant was *eliminated* for one reason or another, and this one man got the job.

(e) The gloss for *inject* is somewhat unfortunate in that it could be argued that the explanation ('squirt through jet or nozzle') is more advanced linguistically than the term being explained. The problem of glosses in EST textbooks is a major one, and few materials writers consistently escape the trap that Herbert has fallen into here.

(f) So far the commentary on STE has been largely negative. However, on reaching *Pattern 1*, the quality of Herbert's descriptive work should become apparent. In order to recognize the innovative character of this page, we need to remember that in the sixties the approach to the passive was to see it as a simple transformation of the active:—

The driver started the car.
The car was started by the driver.

In Sections 5 and 6 Herbert has already implied that his study of engineering texts suggests that *human agents* are rare, and the appropriate passive version of 'the driver started the car' should be:—

The car was started.

He has also maintained that where the agent is not a person it may be necessary to add it:—

Large quantities of steel are required by modern industry.

Section 8 contains his third and final *Pattern* on this subject. He opens with the observation that *by* is particularly important to indicate *means* or *method* (to which we might now want to add *process*). This has been an influential observation and has had a wholly beneficial effect on EST teaching and materials writing. However, Herbert now runs into one of the major theoretical problems in the grammar of Scientific English: the differentiation of agentive and non-agentive uses of *by*. He side-steps this issue—understandably enough—by remarking that 'it can occur in both active and passive statements', continues with a very useful summary of *by means of*, *with*, etc., and concludes his explanatory section with the celebrated pair of sentences about the bulldozer.

The substitution table is exceptionally well thought out, but it does carry forward the unresolved issue that I

(*f*) **PATTERNS**

1. Means (by + *noun* or -ing)

In Section 6, we noted that **by** + *an agent* sometimes follows the verb in a *passive* statement

Large quantities of steam are required by modern industry

A second and more important use of **by** is to indicate the *means* or *method* of doing something or achieving some result.
It can occur in both *active* and *passive* statements.
It often occurs with the phrase **by means of.**
Sometimes it is possible to use **with** instead of **by** before a *noun*.
With really means **with the help of,** and there is a slight difference in meaning; it is not advisable to use *with* unless the meaning is truly instrumental.

The road was cleared **by (means of)** *a bulldozer.*
The road was cleared **with (the help of)** *a bulldozer.*

Heat losses can be reduced We can reduce heat losses	*by*	firebricks. the use of firebricks. *lining* the furnace with firebricks.

This can be	done effected achieved accomplished	*by means of*	firebricks.

By	lining the furnace with firebricks,	heat losses can be reduced.

N.B. You will notice in the last example that a clause or participial phrase may come *before* the main part of the statement.
The word **thereby** means **by means of this.**

By means of cannot be used before a participle; only **by** is possible in such a case.

referred to in the previous paragraph. We might want to claim, for instance, that the table could just as well have been like this:—

Firebricks The use of firebricks Lining the furnace with firebricks	can reduce heat losses

This question of interpretation is too complex to be discussed here, except to point out that since some work in transformational grammar in the sixties we have come to recognize a relationship between the verb *to use* and the instrumentality of *means*:—

This can be done by means of firebricks.
Firebricks can be used to do this.

(g) EXERCISE ONE

Complete these statements in the same way, using the verb in brackets.

1. We reduce the ore to pig-iron ...... it in a blast furnace. (*smelt*)
2. Production will be greatly increased ...... the new machinery. (*introduce*)
3. A hot steel bar can be hardened ...... it in water. (*quench*)
4. Bars of steel can be made ...... them through rollers. (*pass*)
5. The heat-resistant properties of steel are improved ...... more chromium and nickel. (*add*)
6. ...... roller bearings, the friction is reduced still further. (*use*)
7. ...... the bearing in an oil-bath, adequate lubrication is ensured. (*dip*)
8. ...... a flux to the metal, we can prevent oxidation. (*apply*)
9. ...... forced circulation in the boiler, better results are obtained. (*employ*)
10. ...... a gas rapidly in a cylinder, we raise its temperature. (*compress*)
11. ...... steam over the hot coke, producer gas is formed. (*blow*)
12. A casting is produced ...... molten metal into a mould. (*pour*)
13. Improved heat-transfer rates were achieved ...... fins to the outside of the cylinder. (*fit*)

EXERCISE TWO

Complete these statements with *by*, *by means of* or *with*, whichever you think most suitable.

1. Production can be greatly increased ...... the introduction of new machinery.
2. We can prevent oxidation of the metal ...... a flux.
3. Rapid heating in the boiler is achieved ...... forced circulation.
4. The work is firmly held in the lathe ...... the centres.
5. Better combustion is obtained ...... a hemispherical combustion chamber.
6. The heat-resistant properties of the steel can be improved ...... the addition of chromium and nickel.
7. Frequent measurements of the bar were made ...... a micrometer.
8. Lubricant is forced into the bearing ...... pressure of the grease gun against the nipple.
9. A soldered joint may be made ...... a soldering iron made of copper.
10. The temperature of the liquid is raised ...... the application of heat.
11. Greater speeds can now be attained by modern aircraft ...... the new metals which are now being developed.
12. More rapid burning is made possible ...... the use of pulverised fuels.

(g) Unusually Herbert has two exercises on this pattern, presumably because he needs a way to cover both the structure of participial completions and the choice of *by*, *by means of* or *with*. We can note that the Exercise One is entirely mechanical and does not require the student to understand the sentences he is completing. We may also observe that the instruction 'Complete these statements in the same way' might be improved.

2. Purpose (Clauses)

(h) See also Section 7.

Here is a further structure which is used to indicate purpose.

The steam is superheated	*so that* *in order that*	it	is may be can be should be	fairly dry.

EXERCISE

Complete these statements in the same way.

1. Phosphorus is added to the metal ...... better castings ...... produced.
2. ...... the iron ...... demagnetised, it is necessary to apply a negative magnetising force.
3. ...... the metal ...... properly soldered, the metal and the solder should both be made clean.
4. The steam velocity across the tubes is kept high, ... any stationary air ...... swept away.
5. The storage tank is elevated, ... its contents ...... withdrawn by gravity.
6. The condenser water is cooled ...... it ...... re-used in the condenser.
7. The coal gas is sometimes compressed ...... condensation in the gas mains ...... avoided.
8. A by-pass road is being constructed ...... the traffic ...... (not) need to go through the city centre.
9. ...... deposits ...... not form on the tubes, only pure feed water should be used.
10. Water is sprayed into the cylinder ...... immediate condensation of the steam ...... occur.
11. ...... the amount of expansion ...... calculated, the coefficient of expansion of the metal must be known.
12. The diameter of the bar should be measured frequently ...... too much metal ...... (not) taken off.

(h) Section 7 deals with:—

The purpose of __________ is to __________.
aim
object

and the use of non-finite verbs following *in order to, for the purpose of*, etc.

III

ACTIVITIES

(1) (a) The Reading Passage contains the following examples of *this/these.* Complete the table showing what the demonstratives refer to:—

	line	item	reference
(i)	8	this condensation	
(ii)	11	This	
(iii)	12	These	
(iv)	14	this way	
(v)	17	this heat energy	
(vi)	19	this condenser	
(vii)	20	these tubes	
(viii)	25	This type of condenser	
(ix)	30	this means	

(b) Which three uses of this/these do you consider to be likely to be most difficult for non-native speakers of English? And why?

(c) In the passage, there are nine examples of the demonstrative in about 430 words. Do you think this frequency will be greater, lower or the same as authentic science or engineering texts? Check it out against any texts of interest to you.

(2) Sketch out a way of making Exercise One less mechanical.

(3) A group of your students worked together to produce the following answers for Exercise Two:—

1.	by	7.	by
2.	with	8.	by means of
3.	by	9.	with
4.	by means of	10.	by
5.	with	11.	with
6.	by	12.	by

How many of these answers do you accept? Where you disagree, what explanation would you give to your group of students? (In the Key to the Exercises at the end of STE, Herbert does not agree with these answers to 2, 4, 7 and 8; make of this what you will.)

IV

EVALUATION

(1) Numerous ESP practitioners have observed that STE is a difficult book to teach. One reason frequently given is that there is no teacher's book. On the basis of the extract given, what other reasons might be put forward?

(2) In this Episode, I have argued that STE still has value for its presentation of the patterns of the technical statement. Have I made a reasonable case?

V

RELATED READINGS

(1) I know of no review of STE in an easily accessible journal; there is a review by André Cyr in *Review and analysis of thirteen ESP Textbooks* (1977) edited by Ron Mackay (available from the English Language Institute, Oregon State University, Corvallis, Oregon 97331—see also Episode Eleven).

(2) A relevant MA dissertation is 'An Outline of a suggested taped accompaniment to A. J. Herbert's *The Structure of Technical English*' (Ray Williams, the University of Lancaster 1973).

EPISODE THREE 1967

John J. Higgins, 'Hard Facts (Notes on Teaching English to Science Students)', *English Language Teaching*, 21, 1, 1967.

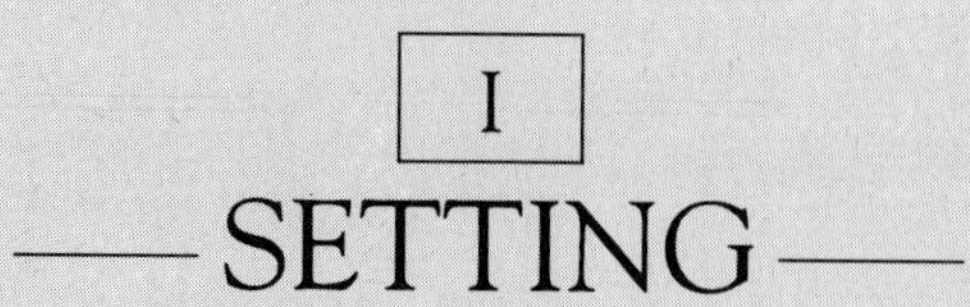

I SETTING

This is the first Episode in which we find discussion of an actual teaching situation. In this respect, therefore, it differs from both Barber's research orientation and from Herbert's offering of actual teaching materials. *Hard Facts* also differs in another way, and in a way that reflects the fact that ESP has developed in a rather different manner from that of say, general linguistics or language learning theory. In ESP significant innovations have taken place in a wide range of countries and a wide range of institutions, and indeed, very often in countries and institutions that have lesser reputations for research output or for educational quality. Thus it is that the most successful ESP textbook so far, *Nucleus General Science* (Episode Eight) was developed in the isolated and mountainous province of Azerbaijan in North-West Iran. And thus it is that Higgins here relates developments at the University of Chiengmai in Northern Thailand, that the next Episode illustrates materials developed at the University of Libya and that in Episode Five Jack Ewer reports on his experiences at the University of Chile. These next three Episodes, therefore, move away from the European perspectives of Barber and Herbert and in turn illustrate developments in three of the major growth areas in ESP: South-East Asia, the Arab World and the Pacific States of Latin America.

It is not hard to see why the ESP scene has been more active—at least until comparatively recently—in these regions rather than in Anglophone Africa, the Indian subcontinent or Northern Europe. By and large, the standards of School English in the latter group have been higher and so the need for Service English as a support for a wholly or partly English-medium higher education sector has been less apparent. Conversely, in situations where English is only one of many subjects in the school curriculum but, for various reasons, is used as the 'reading language' or the 'teaching language' at University, then ESP as a bridge-building exercise attempting to span the gap between secondary and tertiary education has received greater attention and support. Nor is it surprising that of the countries in South-East Asia falling within the Anglo-American rather than French sphere of influence, it was Thailand that first developed ESP programmes. In other countries of the region, such as Malaysia, the process of establishing a national language as the medium of instruction in secondary schools was delayed by social and political considerations.

Hard Facts opens with a rejection of a 'liberal studies' approach to English for Science students at Chiengmai and other Universities in similar circumstances. Higgins claims that the aims of English courses for such students should be functional and of immediate and tangible benefit to the students in their difficult 'switch-of-medium situation'. 'Cultural inspiration' is a luxury. He then follows this with three problems, or 'hard facts':—

(1) The students are demotivated towards English because of past failure;
(2) The standards of English in the relatively large classes are very variable;
(3) There is a lack of time for English on the timetable.

Higgins then describes how he and his colleagues reacted to this situation, firstly in terms of syllabus, secondly in terms of methodology. Like Barber he undertook a linguistic analysis of a textbook in order to establish principles, and he observes that 'we gave prominence to the structures that I had noted in the textbook'. And like both the previous authors in this volume, he asserts that 'it is not the job of the English teacher to teach technical vocabulary'.

However, it is for the closing paragraphs on Methods that *Hard Facts* is chiefly memorable. Re-reading these paragraphs some fifteen years after they were originally published, one is struck by their contemporary appeal, and by their preserved qualities of imagination and educational involvement. Indeed, for many Service English Departments around the world, the ideas that John Higgins had in Thailand in the mid-sixties represent a combination of methodological practicality and inventiveness that has rarely been attained and even more rarely maintained.

I know from both conversation and correspondence that quite a number of ESP practitioners were much influenced and encouraged by Higgins' report on his own and his colleagues' work in Thailand, and among those practitioners are the authors of the two Episodes that follow this one.

II

TEXT AND COMMENTARY

Hard Facts
Notes on Teaching English to Science Students

by John J. Higgins *Chlengmal University, Thailand*

There seems to be a belief current in some English language teaching and publishing circles that 'English for Scientists' means brief biographies of Marie Curie and Thomas Edison, or else accounts of the development of flying or modern medicine, full of lavish praise of intrepid airmen and dedicated doctors. The teacher or the glossary can define *intrepid*, *dedicated*, *microbe*, and *glider*; after that we can move on to culture again, confident that our duty to the science student has been done.

There is plenty of 'the romance of discovery' in such an approach, plenty of uplift but lamentably little hard scientific fact or description of processes. Reading such passages may well encourage the impressionable student to be a doctor or an engineer, but once he has decided to study for one of these careers he should have something more than encouragement. In this article I want first to show that there is a need for a more specialized approach to the teaching of English to scientists and then to make some suggestions for the inclusion of certain items in an English course. I shall refer my remarks to the background I know best, teaching in a university in south-east Asia. I feel I can safely generalize from my experience, since the school system in
(a) the country where I work provides a good illustration of the shortcomings of a literary approach to English teaching when applied to science students, and I know from discussions with colleagues and visitors that the problems may be encountered anywhere in the area.

Thailand does not have the kind of internal language problem that some African states have, since the Thai language, in its written form at least, is standard through most of the country. At the school level English is a subject and not a medium, and books used for science subjects are available in the vernacular. Consequently the science teacher and the English teacher occupy different worlds. When the student reaches our university, he discovers that three of the science lecturers are British and that most of the books which he has to read, including basic course books, are in English. A little translating has been done, but translation as a large-
(b) scale policy is not feasible because of the cost and the fact that many texts would be out of date before the translation could be made available. The English department of the university
(c) therefore gives four hours' instruction a week to all students in all faculties. This teaching is

(a) The 'literature' tradition in secondary school ELT programmes is a strong one. Although these days there tend to be many more pupils in Science rather than Arts courses, a reasonable emphasis on 'factual English' and on functional study skills has been slow to emerge.

(b) For many smaller countries with a national language little used outside their borders, the problems of translating technical and academic works remain as acute today as they did in 1967.

(c) Notice we do not know whether the English instruction extends to all *years* as well; also notice that there is as yet no indication of a 'Service English Department' or 'Scientific English Section' being established independently of the main degree-giving English Department. However, at about this time, the strong pressures for separation were just beginning to be felt in other places.

carried out by four Thais with American or Commonwealth degrees, two locally recruited Americans and four British lecturers recruited by the British Council. Our job in the science faculty is to make English books and the English scientists' lectures intelligible, and so our priorities are comprehension before production and writing before speaking. Most of the students have had anything up to eight years of English before reaching university, but the standards of teaching at the lower levels are mixed, and the whole system consists of a series of false starts. Children start to learn English at the age of eleven and have two years in primary school. On going to high school at thirteen, they start again at the beginning to repair the faults of the previous instruction. When they enter the pre-university classes at sixteen, they once again start at the beginning of a course, learning 'This is a book'. When they come to university the first thing we give them is a one-term grammar revision course. Our first
(d) problem, then, is that we have students who are heartily sick of learning English and apparently never getting anywhere.

Our second problem is the variety of standards. The best Bangkok schools produce students
(e) who are fluent, while country schools, which cannot attract well-qualified staff, send us boys and girls who are almost inarticulate in English. Educational policy and practice in Thailand are opposed to any kind of streaming. The students choose their instructor rather than vice versa. With classes of nearly fifty of widely mixed ability, one does not know what standard to teach to.

The third problem is lack of time. Four hours a week may sound like a generous allocation, as indeed it is in the wider context of the curriculum. However, one never has enough time in a remedial course. Our task with the science students is very specific, but it is still an enormous one, and so we were forced to recognize that any work on literature or 'the beauties of language' must be ruthlessly trimmed from the syllabus, and the work on which we should concentrate, structure drills and comprehension practice, must be very closely matched to the students' needs. At first the course did not seem to be producing enough improvement, and, since we could not ask for more time, we had to think of ways of using the time more efficiently.

As a first step I analysed a sample of scientific English from a course book on chemistry and observed structures with verbs. Passive forms were slightly commoner than active forms of lexically full verbs, and the impersonal passive structure with *it* occurred frequently, 'It was observed that . . .', 'It should be noted that . . .', etc. Great use was made of the defining past participle following a noun, 'The results obtained were checked . . .', 'All the compounds provided are listed in this manual . . .', etc. The commonest modal verbs were *may* and *should*. *Should* occurred very often with the passive in instructions, 'The solution should be tested . . .' The simple present and present perfect tenses were the most used, and very little use was made
(f) of any progressive tense. (Only two were recorded in a sample of five hundred forms.) *If* clauses with the present tense and present or future in the main clause were found, but the conditional *would* or *could* did not occur. At the same time I analysed a 'scientific' chapter in the English reading anthology which we had begun to use. There was a marked dissimilarity; for example, passive structures comprised only an eighth of all finite verbs, and past tenses predominated. The subject matter and the historical approach used determined the tenses, but it seemed to me

(d) This problem is treated in more detail in Section 1 of Episode Seven.

(e) Although there can be no doubt that students living in the capital of a Third World country will have certain advantages, it is not always the case that 'country schools' come out badly. This is particularly not the case in isolated boarding schools where the absence of entertainments and distractions may well create an appreciation of the value of reading for pleasure. Within the major towns too, significantly different patterns of permitted behaviour may exist for boys and for girls. In the Arab world today, the number of girls achieving outstanding results in secondary school leaving examinations is climbing fast, at least partly because they are more housebound. As a result, girls are increasingly occupying the prized places in Faculties of Medicine—places traditionally reserved for those who have done best at school.

(f) See Episode One for similar results.

(g) that the author had deliberately eschewed passives in order to keep his style simple, and in doing so had done the science student a disservice. However much the literary specialist may deplore the style of scientific language, it is still the style which the student needs to learn for comprehension and, since the science teachers demand it, for his own writing of reports.

It is not the job of the English teacher to teach technical vocabulary; it consumes too much time, and he will probably not do it well. The most he can do is to encourage the student to use a dictionary. However, we made, with the help of the science staff, a list of 'frame' words which
(h) were causing difficulty, words which, although not technical terms, are frequently used in technical writings. The scientist cannot teach these words properly, since they need to be demonstrated in contexts and then drilled, rather than merely defined, and the scientist does not have the time or the training for this. The list is not, of course, comprehensive; the words are mainly those which cause persistent errors here. Some of them would give little trouble to speakers of a western European language, and one or two items (the distinction between 'boil' and 'heat' for instance) are included because of specific differences between Thai and English which lead our students to misuse them. However, I offer the list for what it is worth.

contain	increase (n. & v.)	separate
include, including	decrease (n. & v.)	combine
consist of	obtain	boil/heat
record (n. & v.)	determine	fill
consume	react	assemble
materials	chemicals	proportion
quality	figures	theory
average	exceptional	theoretical
similar	identical	pure
accurate	inaccurate	impure
exact	approximate	

For the students who would transfer to the medical school, we added some of the 'frame words' of medicine.

symptom	relapse	cure
diagnose, diagnosis	heal	treat, treatment

This work gave us some idea of specific items to put into a course. Although there were still large gaps, we could be reasonably sure that these items at least would not be irrelevant. On our grammar syllabus we gave prominence to the structures I had noted in the textbook: passive forms; impersonal passive with *it*; *if* clauses; *should* and *may*; *must* and *need not*; simple present and present perfect tenses. Realizing that students have to write reports as well as read instructions, we included some further structures which we hoped would be useful: simple past
(i) tense; past perfect in clauses with *when* and *after*; comparisons. We did not teach these items to

(g) *eschewed* = avoided

(h) It is not entirely clear what Higgins precisely means by 'frame' words; clearly some are semi-technical words of wide *range*; and others known to be problematic in the local situation.

(i) The Past Perfect in Report-Writing is rather tricky. Consider:—

(i) When the liquid boiled,
(ii) After the liquid boiled,
(iii) When the liquid had boiled,
(iv) After the liquid had boiled,
(v) When the liquid boiled for 30 seconds,
(vi) After the liquid boiled for 30 seconds,
(vii) When the liquid had boiled for 30 seconds,
(viii) After the liquid had boiled for 30 seconds,

} the test-tube was removed from the heat.

Nos. (iii), (iv)(?), (v) and (vi) seem unacceptable. What is your judgment? Do you have a rule that *works*?

the exclusion of all else, but we did decide to concentrate on these items and on any further ones that we might uncover with more experience.

In method we made two innovations intended to close the gap between the English lesson and the science lesson. Firstly, we included the fortnightly sheets of laboratory instructions put out by the science departments as texts for comprehension, using them alongside the reading book. This was applauded by the science teachers, and it seemed to bring more co-operation from the hard core of students in each class who had hitherto regarded English as a tedious imposition. As a second step we began to give the students practice in writing reports based on tabular data, for example rainfall statistics, comparative alcohol consumption figures for various countries, sporting records, and cost of living calculations. One useful model for this kind of writing is the consumer research report, and so we used as data performance figures for several imaginary makes of car. We then carried out in class a comparative test of all available local brands of matches (which the teacher could afford to buy in large quantities) and worked out a fairly elaborate report based on the results. Other subjects which we have proposed for similar treatment are ballpoint pens and locally made sweetmeats.

Aural comprehension has always been a part of our regular work, but we have become rather more selective about the kind of passage we use for this. We divide them into two main kinds. The first are ones we write ourselves, describing simple processes, how a bicycle is propelled, how to perform a simple conjuring trick, how a match ignites, how to make the perfect Chinese meal, and so on. We include several examples of a grammar structure and make the passage a springboard for grammar drills, and the final aim of each lesson is to get the student to reproduce, either written or orally in response to questions, the content of the passage or to
(j) describe an associated process.

We also use another type of aural comprehension in which we test only retention of facts. For this we have used popularizations of scientific material or newspaper reports containing a good deal of information expressed numerically. Students are told to take notes, and we endeavour to duplicate the conditions of their science lectures, giving only one reading but dwelling on and repeating important points. Since we are only interested in the absorption of facts and not in expression, we generally give true/false tests or ask questions demanding a one-word factual answer. We do, however, try to avoid a parrot-like repetition of the facts, which is what the students are inclined to give in their examinations if allowed to. If, for instance, the passage quotes sets of figures in support of a theory, then we would test this by means of true/false statements using *more than* and *less than*, to see whether students had grasped the meaning
(k) of the figures and the relationships between them. This work is complementary to the report-writing exercises described above.

The 'new' programme has not yet been under way long enough for us to tell how well it is working, but we have begun to notice that there is slightly more interest in English and slightly less resentment of it as a compulsory subject. Written classwork still contains a number of howlers, but it does seem to be less spoiled than before by the confusion of thought which arises when both the language and the subject-matter being studied are strange. We now try to make sure that the students write only about what they know, so that they only have one level of difficulty to deal with at one time. Then, when we are dealing with a familiar framework of expression (e.g. the laboratory instructions) and a familiar set of language items, but introducing new subject-matter, we sometimes uncover evidence of muddled thinking and can point it out and correct it. A recent article in the *Saturday Review* deplored the tendency of teachers to think that when a student produces a confused report or essay, this is 'bad science' or 'bad geography', but when a student writes using incorrect grammar or spelling, then and only then is he guilty of 'bad English'. The English teacher, the article maintained, has the

(j) 'Describe an associated process' is presumably a reference to a writing task that is 'parallel' or to be done on similar lines to the one illustrated.

(k) 'Complementary' work could either be as *preparation* for report-writing, or could be to 'consolidate' it; in either case it is seen as 'means to an end'.

equipment and the responsibility for helping his students to think straight. The writer was thinking of English as a native rather than a foreign language, but our experience here has shown that the language teacher can help the science student to think more clearly about his chosen subjects, and that the science teacher, both Thai and foreign, can play a vital part in improving the students' command of English by noting persistent errors and by providing the English teacher with suitable comprehension material. I only wish that publishers of language
(l) teaching material would go to the science teachers for advice.

(l) In conclusion, we can now see that Higgins's title *Hard Facts* is a play upon words: on the one hand it refers to the harsh realities of his Service English situation; on the other, it refers to the need to teach real Scientific English, 'hard facts' and all.

III

ACTIVITIES

(1) At the end of the first paragraph dealing with *method*, Higgins writes:—

'We then carried out in class a comparative test of all available local brands of matches (which the teacher could afford to buy in large quantities) and worked out a fairly elaborate report based on the results'.

(a) Specify four different tests to be carried out in order to compare two brands of matches. Carry out the tests and write up a simple report.

(b) Identify where and why a group of students might have difficulty in writing a report like yours.

(2) In the next paragraph, Higgins describes the use of scripted monologues for listening comprehension. Complete the following table by putting ticks in the appropriate boxes.

	Agree strongly	Neither agree nor disagree	Disagree strongly	It depends
1. Listening passages should be recorded not scripted because speech is quite differently organized to writing.				
2. Recorded listening passages tend to be unnaturally word-perfect, and so not like real speech.				
3. In scripted sentences the information is usually too densely packed to be followed by the ear alone.				
4. A written reproduction of an oral process description involves complex changes of style and structure and thus is not suitable for the sort of student referred to in this *Episode*.				

IV
EVALUATION

(1) At the close of the article, Higgins refers to the English teacher as helping the Science students to think more clearly about their chosen subjects. How far do you think this is a confusion between thinking itself and the organized expression of that thinking in English?

(2) Looking at *Hard Facts* from the vantage point of more than sixteen years later, how far do you think Higgins succeeded in closing 'the gap between the English lesson and the Science lesson'? And what more might he have done?

V
RELATED READINGS

Given the amount of ESP work that has gone on in Thailand over the last fifteen years, published reports are surprisingly rare. There are, however, a number of unpublished descriptions held in the British Council ELD Archives in London (for details see Robinson's entries 35–37).

Chulalongkorn University Language Institute publishes a Journal called PASAA, which usually contains an ESP article; for example Volume X, Number 1 (1980) contains:—

Stephen Edmonds, 'The CULI English for Academic Purposes Writing Course'.

After this Episode, to my mind the most impressive paper emanating from Thailand is David Cobb, 'Aural Comprehension Materials for Tertiary Level Science/Technical Students' in *The RELC Journal* 3, 1972 (Singapore). This remains the classic description of what to do with a language laboratory on an EST course. Highly recommended.

EPISODE FOUR 1971

John Swales, *Writing Scientific English*
Thomas Nelson, London 1971.

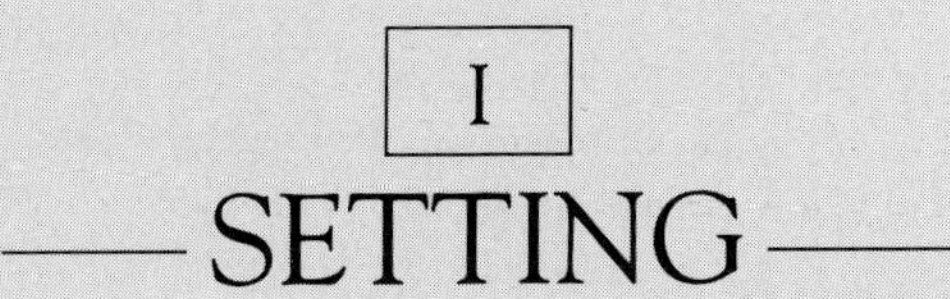

SETTING

Writing Scientific English was the first of a continuing line of EST textbooks to be based on Middle East teaching experience. The book contains twelve Units and the extract that follows is from Unit 8, which has the general title *Experimental and Explanatory Descriptions*. The first half of *WSE* is predominantly grammatical and owes something to Herbert in the way features of scientific English are displayed and explained. The second half is more functional. In general, the book is 'heavy' on grammatical and functional explanations, this being a reflection of the fact that *WSE* is determinedly 'cognitive'. Such a 'cognitive' approach was, on the one hand, a reaction against the *pattern–practice* methodologies so common in the sixties and, on the other, a recognition that the clientele were intelligent undergraduates.

The reasons for including an extract from *WSE* are essentially two. First, it offered a wider variety of exercise types than had been hitherto, several of which were to be further developed as the seventies progressed. One of these exercise types was 'the matching table', of which the following is a part illustration:

Join one sentence from the left-hand column and one from the right-hand column.

Tungsten is a metal.	It contains acetic acid.
Water is a liquid.	It contains a large proportion of copper.
Vinegar is a liquid.	It retains hardness at red heat.
Brass is an alloy.	It consists of two parts of hydrogen and one part of water.

It seemed to me that 'matching tables' were an important variant of the 'substitution table' as used by Herbert, principally because the students cannot do them without making an attempt to understand the *meaning* of the language being used to consolidate a grammatical structure. Admittedly, they are very artificial and also rather uneconomical in terms of words written per minute. However, the students found 'matching tables' challenging and interesting, and they are simply excellent for pair-work.

If I am right in thinking that *WSE* was innovative in terms of the range and variety of student activity required, I do not think this can be ascribed to the author having a particular flair; rather, it was the result of extensive trialling over a three-year period and of a decision not to provide a set arrangement for each Unit. Apart from the fact that the Units were kept to roughly the same length, in almost every other way each Unit was allowed to develop in the direction that seemed to best suit its main teaching points. Hence variety was not discouraged by a stereotyped Unit format.

Secondly, *WSE* was bold enough to offer 'models' of what today we might call the information structure of scientific paragraphs. My colleagues and I had the feeling that teaching the form of isolated functional statements was not enough. We felt that our Arab students had been brought up in a different rhetorical tradition and that some explicit work on how scientific writing in English was organized would be beneficial.

WSE was essentially the end-product of four years' preparing and teaching English courses at the Faculty of Engineering, the University of Libya, Tripoli (now known as Al-Fatah University). It is a writing course. As I claimed in the Preface, 'I have excluded comprehension work because I have found that the way in which a comprehension passage is best handled depends principally on how much the students know of the scientific subject-matter. For this reason I believe that the selection and presentation of comprehension passages should be carried out within an actual teaching situation.' Moreover, our courses at the University of Libya had concentrated on the productive skills (writing in the classroom and speaking in the language laboratory) even though the students' needs in terms of the traditional language skills could be ranked in decreasing order of importance as Reading, Listening, Writing and Speaking. It has, of course, usually been assumed that such skill priorities will be translated into appropriate time allocations in a properly-run ESP programme. However, this is at least arguable; because reading (say) has been identified as being the greatest need, it does not necessarily follow that reading should be assigned the lion's share of English class time. The final decision will also depend on what we consider the language teacher can most usefully do in the limited time available to him. In other words, as I have said elsewhere, 'decisions about course priorities should be partly based on an assessment of the circumstances under which teacher intervention in the learning process is essential, where it is useful, and where it is of marginal advantage.' And, of course, our students attended many lectures and intensively studied a few set mathematics and engineering textbooks. We decided, therefore, that we could best help them by concentrating on the productive skills; by teaching, discussing and correcting writing we could improve an aspect of our students' performance that they found particularly difficult to do for themselves.

Writing Scientific English is still used today, but largely in an ancillary role. It still functions as a remedial grammar, particularly for individual students thought to have problems with the typical basic structures of Scientific English. Additionally, numerous comments over the years suggest that it has served as a partial reference grammar for teachers of Scientific English—a role for which it was, of course, never intended. Three common complaints are justified: there are too many single-sentence exercises; the scientific content is both arbitrarily selected and often tending towards that found in information handbooks rather than textbooks; and there is no key to the exercises nor any teacher's notes. As far as the last is concerned, I can at least say that a Key *was* prepared, but it was never published because the publishers decided that sales of the textbook would never justify it—a prediction that was not entirely right.

II
TEXT AND COMMENTARY

Writing Scientific English
by John Swales

(a) **Descriptions of how things work**

This type of description usually requires a diagram. A diagram makes the explanation easier to follow. A diagram can also be used to avoid the problem of vocabulary. Sometimes you will not know the name for a part of a machine or a piece of apparatus. Never mind! Draw a diagram and label the parts you do not know *A*, *B*, *C*, etc.

Read this explanatory description carefully:

A water tap is a device for turning on and off a flow of water. Its most important parts are a rod with a handle on the top and a washer which is fixed to the bottom of the rod. The metal parts of a water tap are usually made of brass because brass resists corrosion. The washer is made of a flexible material such as rubber or plastic.

A Water Tap

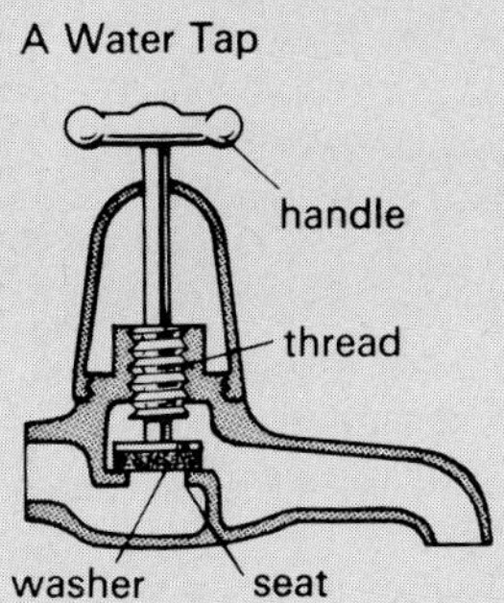

When the handle is turned the rod either rises or descends because of the spiral thread. The column descends until the washer fits firmly in its 'seat'. (This position is shown in the diagram.) The tap is now closed and no water can flow out of the pipe.

(a) *Descriptions of How Things Work* is the second section in Unit 8. It follows a section on writing up experiments and, additionally, builds upon Unit 6 which dealt with Definitions and Expanded Definitions.

(b) (c) ○ **Exercise 8(a)** Cross out the wrong alternatives. (*S* = sentence)

1 This description consists of 1/2/8 paragraphs.
2 The first paragraph describes a tap/explains how it works.
3 The second paragraph describes a tap/explains how it works.
4 Each paragraph contains 1/3/4/6 sentences.
5 The first sentence (*S*1) is/is not a definition.
6 *S*2 describes the main moving parts of a tap/the main fixed parts.
7 *S*3 explains why brass resists corrosion/why brass is used.
8 *S*4 explains/does not explain why rubber is often used for a washer.
9 *S*5 begins with a subordinate clause/a main clause.
10 *S*6 explains/does not explain why the column goes down.
11 *S*7/*S*8 links the description to the diagram.
12 *S*7 must come before *S*8/it doesn't matter which sentence comes first.

(d) ○ **Exercise 8(b)** Write a description of how a water tap works, choosing only five of the eight sentences given in the original passage. In other words, decide which are the five most important sentences and write them out.

(e) ○ **Exercise 9** Write a continuous description of how a bicycle pump works choosing one of the given alternatives each time. Your description should therefore contain nine sentences arranged as a passage of continuous English.

(b) Each exercise was prefaced by one of three symbols (○, △ or □) which were supposed to indicate to the teacher or the self-study student the following information:—

○ — exercises are simple and should give little difficulty if the explanations and examples have been studied carefully

△ — exercises usually require students to produce a certain amount of their own work. However, quite a lot of help is given in terms of example sentences and in the organization of the written material

□ — exercises are rather more advanced and nearly always require students to produce passages of continuous scientific or technical English.

(c) Exercise 8(a) nicely illustrates the cognitive, analytic aspect of *WSE*. As far as I know, there is little research evidence that directly bears on the question as to whether such exercises are valuable or valueless.

(d) Such selection exercises are easy enough to construct and often indeed concentrate the student's mind, but they can leave the EST teacher exposed in front of his class with unconvincing explanations of *why* some selections are better than others.

(e) This exercise has been abundantly 'borrowed' and I have seen it in local textbooks in at least three (nameless) countries. Controversially, some of the selections need to be based on linguistic form and others on meaning, and there is no indication of which criterion is to be applied in any particular case.

A Bicycle Pump

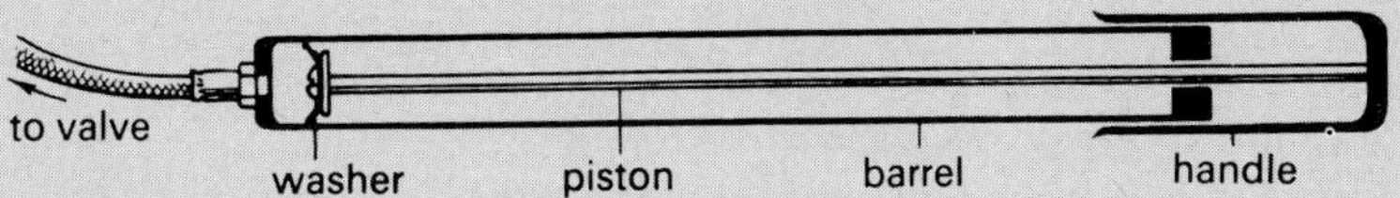

1 A bicycle pump is a device
- for forcing water through a narrow tube.
- for extracting air from tyres.
- for moving air against a pressure difference.

2 It
- can
- cannot
- might

work without the valve in the bicycle tyre.

3
- Essentially,
- Firstly,
- Importantly,

it consists of a hollow barrel, a piston with a handle, and a leather washer at the end of the piston.

4 If the piston is left at the bottom of the barrel the pressure is approximately equal
- that of the atmosphere.
- to that of the atmosphere.
- to that of the atmospheric.

5 When the piston is drawn sharply upwards the air below the piston rises, thus causing the pressure
- to fall
- to rise
- to remain constant.

6 Atmospheric pressure then pushes the sides of the leather washer
- away from
- against
- through

the barrel, allowing air from outside to enter.

7 When the handle is pushed down the air pressure below the piston
- is rising.
- rose.
- rises.

8 This pressure forces the sides of the soft leather washer against the sides of the barrel,
- stopping air from entering.
- stopping air from escaping.
- allowing air to escape.

9 The air is then pumped
- through the tyre-valve into the tyre.
- through the tyre into the tyre-valve.
- by the tyre-valve into the tyre.

H

(f) Notice that three of the nine sentences end with an *-ing* clause:

5 .... *the piston rises, thus causing* .....
6 .... *pushes* .... *the barrel, allowing air from outside to enter.*
8 .... *forces* .... *the barrel, stopping air* .....

Finally, here is an example from the last section:

The phosphorous burns, producing dense white fumes of phosphorous pentoxide.

These are *-ing* clauses of result:

x happens, causing y to happen.

Such *-ing* clauses are particularly useful in descriptions of how things work, because with them we can avoid describing a series of events
(g) using a series of 'ands':

x happens, and y happens, and then z happens.

A typical sentence structure is subordinate clause + main clause + *-ing* clause. (5) is an example of this:

(a) (subordinate clause)	*When the piston is drawn sharply upwards,*
(b) (main clause)	*the air below the piston rises,*
(c) (*-ing* clause)	*thus causing the pressure to fall.*

(h) ○ **Exercise 10** Here are the mixed-up parts of ten (a) + (b) + (c) sentences of this type. Join them together correctly. The first one has been done.

(a)
When the piston is drawn sharply upwards,
When the oven rises in temperature,
As the oven cools,
When the mixture is ignited,
If a bubble of air is introduced into a barometer,
If one end of a metal bridge is fixed to the ground,
When water is heated from 0° C,
If there is a good head of water,
As a rivet cools,
When plates of copper and zinc are placed in dilute sulphuric acid,

(f) The following section illustrates the rather 'heavy' explanatory material referred to in the Setting.

(g) Arabic prose has a tendency to be loosely structured and relies heavily on 'and'.

(h) In retrospect, this seems a competent exercise and provides quite an interesting way of generating a useful sentence type.

(b)

the zinc reacts with the acid,
it pushes the mercury down,
the invar rod is pulled back,
the gas is re-admitted,
the air below the piston rises,
it contracts,
the combustion forces down the cylinder,
the turbine will rotate at high speed,
the other usually rests on a roller,
it contracts,

(c)

thus producing energy.
making the instrument inaccurate.
reaching its maximum density at 4° C.
so cutting off the gas.
drawing the two plates together.
causing the crankshaft to turn.
thus generating large quantities of electricity.
raising the temperature.
thus allowing the bridge to alter its length.
thus causing the pressure to fall.

As some of these (c) clauses show, the 'result' nature of the *-ing* clause can be emphasized by putting *so, thus* or *thereby* at the beginning.

(i) △ **Exercise 11** Complete as many of these sentences as you can, by writing main clauses of your own.

1 ...., causing the water to condense.
2 ...., thus causing the bell to ring.
3 ...., producing a spark.
4 ...., thereby showing that the solution is acidic.
5 ...., causing the vehicle to lose speed.
6 ...., thus controlling the speed of the engine.
7 ...., indicating that a chemical change has taken place.
8 ...., so breaking the current.
9 ...., thereby forcing the rocket into the air.
10 ...., showing that the water molecules pass across the membrane into the sugar solution.

△ **Exercise 12** Write a simple explanatory description of one of the following (diagrams may be used):

1 a bunsen burner
2 a burette
3 a bus
4 an electric switch
5 a fountain pen
6 a thermometer

(i) It is not so easy to be complimentary about Exercise 11, and perhaps the problems are already recognized in the rubric 'Complete as many of these sentences as you can'. The difficulty for the writer is that he is asked to do something very unnatural—start a sentence he has completed!

III ACTIVITIES

(1) You are teaching writing and want your students to produce passages like that on the *Water Tap*. Produce an alternative to Exercise 8(a) which you think might be more useful (gap-filling, scrambled sentences, missing subjects, or whatever). Compare your exercise with 8(a) and 8(b).

(2) Produce three more sentences of (a) + (b) + (c) Exercise 10-type.

(3) Neither Swales nor Herbert (unlike the authors of many later courses) provided a teacher's book. What should teacher's notes for this extract contain?

IV EVALUATION

(1) The section has the clear intention of taking the student from analysis in 8(a) to a free composition on 'How Something Works' in Exercise 12. How successful are the transitions from one part to another and what improvements can you suggest?

(2) *WSE* attempts to teach writing largely independently of reading. Is writing a separable skill in this way? What problems of subject-matter does an independent writing course have to face? And what solutions are possible?

(3) Would you prefer to 'teach' the extract from Herbert or that from Swales—and why?

V RELATED READINGS

(1) The background to *WSE* is discussed in fuller detail in John Swales, 'Writing Scientific English', in *English for Specific Purposes* edited by Ronald Mackay and Alan Mountford (Longman 1978).

(2) Although there were a number of shorter notices of *WSE* soon after it first appeared, the only longer review I know of is by Raymonde Johnson in the review collection referred to in the *Related Readings* for Episode Two.

EPISODE FIVE 1971–2

J. R. Ewer and E. Hughes-Davies, 'Further Notes on Developing an English Programme for Students of Science and Technology', *English Language Teaching*, 26, 1 & 3, 1971–72.

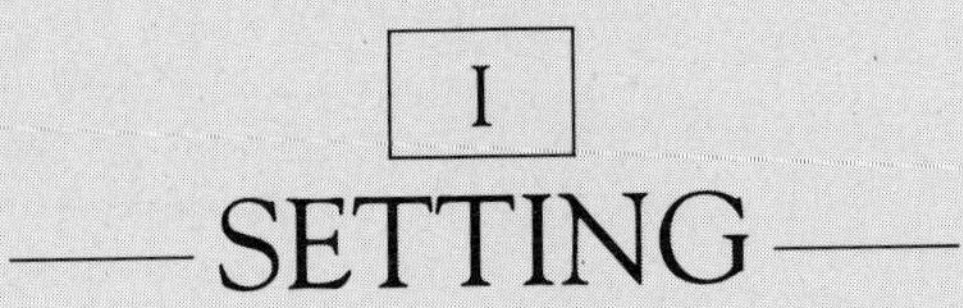

I SETTING

Further Notes was originally a two-part article, but the parts have been combined for the purposes of this volume. *Further Notes* comprises the second and third articles on ESP that Ewer wrote. He went on to write about twenty more before his untimely death in a climbing accident in February 1982. Jack Ewer was one of the great pioneers in ESP, and over the twenty years of his life that he devoted to English for Science and Technology he gained an increasing international reputation, despite the fact that his activities were almost entirely restricted to Chile. As far as I am aware, only twice did he leave Latin America on 'official ESP business', the second time to attend a conference in Singapore in 1975. But perhaps it is wrong to suggest that his reputation was achieved *despite* his physical isolation in the southernmost country of Latin America. The fact that Jack Ewer remained so many years at the University of Chile in Santiago became a source of unusual strength. He was protected from the rapid changes of fashion and the desperate searches for innovation that characterize English language teaching in the USA and Britain. He came to know his own teaching situation—and its attendant possibilities and limitations—better than most ESP specialists know theirs as they move from post to post and country to country every few years or so. Jack Ewer was able to evaluate and revise methodologies and teaching materials in the light of the experience gained with several generations of apprentice teachers of English and technical translators. He was able to plan and execute a number of major and long-term projects into the characteristics of scientific and technical English; and, not least, he succeeded in developing within the Chilean university system considerable numbers of dedicated and professional colleagues, several of whom have gone on to establish reputations for themselves in their own right.

So far in this introduction I have concentrated on the main author of this Episode; it is now time to say something of the Latin American situation. In the larger Latin American countries, universities, both public and private, are numerous and quite a large percentage of young people embark upon a university education. The medium of instruction is Spanish (or Portuguese in Brazil) and English is seen very much as a 'library language'. Hence, many Service English Departments conceive their role as offering help to the students in their reading of recommended English-language textbooks and articles. The actual need of the students to read in English seems to be highly variable, but it is largely true that the more senior and more specialized the student the less likely he or she will be able to find references either written originally in Spanish or Portuguese or translated into those languages. As the English-language courses are typically scheduled for the first few semesters of the degree programme, it is easy to see that many ESP Departments are faced with a problem of motivation—the reading skills that they offer may not be immediately needed, but will only become so in their students' final years of study. The Latin American setting therefore is somewhat different to that of Thailand in the mid-sixties (Episode Three) where most of the textbooks were in English.

The Latin American ESP tradition is a reflection of the assumed primacy of the so-called 'receptive skill' of reading. Within that tradition there has been quite a strong emphasis on the grammar of English, and especially on identifying and teaching the grammatical structures typically found in scientific and other academic varieties of English. The main reason for this is that *vocabulary* is not seen as a major obstacle to developing a reading competence of a variety of technical English and, in turn, the reason for this is that much of technical vocabulary of English and Spanish is known to be of a common Romance origin or 'cognate'. The second contribution to this volume from Latin America is Episode Thirteen which illustrates some relatively recent materials that were developed in response to the characteristic Latin American insistence that ESP courses should be reading courses.

Further Notes is a clear successor to John Higgins' piece found in Episode Three. However, the scale of the work reported, the amount of research undertaken and most significantly the width of 'vision' as to the range of factors requiring attention in a properly-run ESP enterprise are all somewhat greater. Essentially, Ewer and Hughes-Davies report on the progress they have made in five areas. First, they describe their attempts to assess the role of English in Chilean academic and professional life. This attempt is somewhat crude by present-day standards—and indeed several new techniques were developed in Chile itself in later years—but it does give a lead where none existed before. The second area, the register of Scientific English, is so briefly described that on the evidence of this article alone, it merely consolidates findings discernible in the previous four Episodes. The third area, that of additional exercises, at times rather narrowly reflects characteristics of Professor Ewer's own Chilean experience and raises other difficulties that are discussed in the Commentary. The fourth is a progress report summarizing an aspect of ESP research that is closely associated with the two authors of this Episode—the study of Instructional English. Apart from Pittman, and possibly Louis Trimble, Ewer and Hughes-Davies were, I suspect, the first to scrutinize the language of training manuals and other instructional material. In the final section of the article, we find the first discussion in the ESP literature of particular problems that arise in 'converting' general English teachers to the ESP profession. In fact, this fifth area is also the first of a series of statements over the decade by Jack Ewer reporting his *first-hand* experience of teacher-training and, because Ewer was primarily a teacher-trainer rather than an ESP practitioner, his views in this area have a particular authority.

A final point. In the concluding paragraph the authors stress the value of establishing 'a close rapport between the English-teaching staff and their colleagues of the scientific and technological departments'. Although the importance of such working relationships is self-evident, the way ESP developed in many other parts of the world during the seventies tended to make the achievement of such 'rapport' more difficult than it might have been. Firstly, the emergence of independent 'Language Centres' or 'ESP Units' at times led to an unfortunate isolation from the rest of the institution. Secondly, the seventies saw the development of sophisticated procedures for analysing the English needs of students that could *only* be carried out by ESP specialists and this reinforced an isolationist tendency. Thirdly, the years subsequent to 1972 saw rapid increase in 'ESP Projects' that were often poorly integrated into the educational planning and educational expectations of their host institutions. However, the great common sense of the final paragraph of this Episode has in recent years become more widely recognized, and has indeed been taken well beyond the need for consultation between English-language and subject staff, as we shall see in Episode Twelve.

II

TEXT AND COMMENTARY

Further Notes on Developing an English Programme for Students of Science and Technology

by J. R. Ewer *and* E. Hughes-Davies
Department of English, University of Chile

In an article published in 1967, an inquiry into the main linguistic features of scientific literature and into the preparation of an introductory course for students of science at the
(a) University of Chile was described.[1] Further work in this field has since been carried out, and a brief account of this may be useful to the rapidly-growing number of teachers involved in this relatively underdeveloped branch of ELT.

Progress has so far been made in five directions:

1. The collection of local quantitative data on the importance of English in the professional training of scientists and technologists;
2. The acquisition of additional information on the principal points of divergence between the English of science and that of the other register to which the majority of students have been exposed, viz. the general or school course;
(b) 3. The provision of additional exercises and other material in order to reinforce and extend the scope of the basic course;
4. An investigation into 'instructional' English, and the development of didactic material based on the results;
5. The specialized training of teachers for scientific and technological ELT programmes.

Each of these projects is discussed briefly below.

The importance of English as a professional working-tool

At the end of 1967 a survey of foreign-language teaching was carried out in thirteen departments of the Faculty of Natural Sciences and School of Engineering of the University of Chile, a large complex attending to the needs of well over two thousand science and technology students. One of the principal objects of this survey was to evaluate the extent to which English and other foreign languages were necessary to students and teachers in their studies, and this was done by obtaining data on the following three aspects of their training: (a) the percentage of foreign-language textbooks in the required-reading assignments at all levels;

[1] J. R. Ewer and G. Latorre, 'Preparing an English Course for Students of Science', *ELT*, XXI, 3, 221–9.

(a) The published version is *A Course in Basic Scientific English* (Longman 1969) by the two authors referred to in the footnote. The 1967 article includes an appreciation of the extract chosen for Episode One:—

> Only recently (April 1966) did we come across a most interesting article by C. L. Barber . . . Although Dr Barber and his associates used a comparatively narrow sample, they did an extremely accurate word-by-word count which, making allowances for the differences in the samples, complements the work done here in a most delightful way.

(b) 'The basic course' refers to *A Course in Basic Scientific English*, and not to any 'general course'.

(b) the number of foreign teachers and visiting experts using languages other than the vernacular (Spanish) for the purpose of communication; (c) the number of scholarships for study abroad awarded to students and staff. The information received covered the three most
(c) recent years, and in some cases a projection for the current year was also given.

From the analysis of this data some points of considerable interest emerged. The first point was the overwhelming preponderance of English in both relative and absolute terms in all three of the aspects mentioned above. Thus the proportion of English-language textbooks in the total reading assignments (including Spanish) rose from an average of 44 per cent in the first years to 61 per cent in the fifth years of undergraduate study, and reached 65 per cent in the
(d) postgraduate courses; the numbers of visiting teachers and experts using English as a lingua franca—and these included Russians, Japanese, Czechs, Poles, and Israelis as well as native English-speakers—was rising steadily and steeply at nearly 20 per cent per year; finally, the numbers of fellowships awarded in countries where English is a medium of instruction shows a similar rate of expansion and involve numbers roughly equivalent to one out of every five of the final-year undergraduate population.

The second point of interest was the extremely minor role played by the other foreign languages for which courses had previously been provided (French, German, and Russian); this was a particularly important finding in a country where French and German have, for historical reasons, been traditional 'prestige' languages.

Lastly, and perhaps of greatest significance from the ELT point of view, was the fact that both scientific staff and language-teaching staff had greatly underestimated the central part played by English in professional training, and realization of the true state of affairs has now led to a fundamental reorganization of the language-teaching programmes in this particular institution. From what can be learnt of conditions elsewhere, there seems little doubt that this
(e) lack of awareness of precisely how important English is to scientists and technologists is widespread, and that further studies of this kind are urgently needed.

Differences between the English of science and that of the 'general' or school ELT course

The wide variations in lexis between the typical school course and that of the basic language of scientific literature has already been pointed out in the article referred to above (p. 225,
(f) footnote 2), and subsequent inquiry shows that discrepancies of a comparable degree also exist in grammar. Thus a comparison of the teaching items contained in three well-known 'general' courses with the structures typical of scientific literature reveals the following significant differences in kind and emphasis:

Group I: Items essential to basic scientific English but not presented and exercised in any of the courses:

-ing forms replacing a relative
Infinitive as substitute for longer phrases

(c) Ewer was a pioneer in this kind of analysis; and the advance on the much more informal and intuitive approach by Higgins in Episode Three is clear.

(d) Today we would be more likely to talk about 'English as a means of international communication' rather than 'English as a lingua franca'—as when, for example, Japanese and Arabs use English to conduct business.

(e) Presumably, *individual* scientists and technologists are well able to estimate how important English is to them personally and professionally; what is less well appreciated is the general or *institutional* recognition of the role of English in research and development.

(f) Ewer means by 'discrepancies' that the grammatical items given prominence in a structural General English syllabus are not necessarily those that should be given prominence in a Scientific English syllabus—and he goes on to illustrate a number of differences. He is not implying that the grammatical rules are different; only that different selections of grammatical structures are appropriate in each case.

(g) Words similar in form but with different meanings for the same function
Most prefixes and suffixes
Most structural and qualifying words and phrases.

Group II: Items essential to basic scientific English but not presented and exercises in two out of the three courses, or dealt with inadequately:
Compound nouns
Passives
Conditionals
Anomalous finites
(h) Cause-and-result constructions
Words similar in form but with different functions
Past participle usage
The prepositional (two-part) verbs common in scientific English.

It is therefore clear that any ELT materials for science students must place special emphasis on these items.

Supplementary material and teaching aids

These have been developed to deal with specific needs and include the following:
(a) *Remedial exercises and drills:* As it was known that the students' knowledge of English on entry to the scientific-English course might vary widely from institution to institution, the Teacher's Notes to the basic course[2] had included a number of suggestions for extra exercises and drills. This has proved even more important than was originally foreseen, since some of the students who have greatest initial difficulty with English are those with the greatest promise as scientists or technologists. It should be emphasized that in this branch of ELT, above all, care (i) of the 'backward' student is essential; hence a carefully-planned schedule of remedial work should be a built-in feature of the overall programme.

One of the first jobs was therefore to provide some of the extra materials required for this purpose. These consist mainly of conventional types such as completion, transformation and question-and-answer exercises, and substitution tables, and for the most part follow the suggestions given in the Teacher's Notes, with particular emphasis on the items referred to above in which the scientific register differs markedly from the 'general' ELT course. In this (j) latter area, the all-important structural and modifying words and phrases need special attention and are best exercised in concrete situations based on charts, diagrams, and simple kits such as the one described in the section on Instructional English below.

[2] Ewer and Latorre, *A Course in Basic Scientific English* (Longmans).

(g) The phrase 'words similar in form but with different meanings for the same function' is not at all clear from the text. It only makes sense when we read *A Course in Basic Scientific English* and understand that Ewer is using the term 'function' in a rather eccentric way. The following short extract comes from page 49 of the textbook:—

> A word may sometimes have more than one meaning though its function (ie whether it is a noun, an adjective, etc) remains the same. An example in the reading passage is the word *constant*, which in line 49 is equivalent to *unaltered*, whereas in line 62 its meaning is *continuous*.

(h) *Anomalous finites* are the auxiliary verbs, including modals. They are 'anomalous' because they require a special set of rules for negation and so on.

(i) Although we can all accept responsibility for making provision for the bright student with relatively poor English (particularly if relative weakness in English is partly explained by social disadvantage), Ewer's conclusion by no means follows. Indeed, in Episode Seven and elsewhere we shall meet a spirited attack on the appropriacy of 'going over' grammar that should have been learnt in school.

(j) 'Modifying words and phrases' will refer to such items as *somewhat*, *probably*, *seems to be* and so on.

Similar types of exercise have also been produced to deal with various difficulties which have emerged in the course of time. These are mostly of local origin and interest only, though some
(k) may be of more general application, such as false cognates, and rather less obvious ones such as shades of colours and the oral forms of numbers, letters of the alphabet, and symbols. The important thing here is to determine clearly which of the difficulties that students appear to encounter are significant—in other words, to discriminate carefully between 'acceptable' mistakes, i.e. those that do not interfere materially with communication between scientist and scientist,[3] and those that do: it is the latter that require the additional exercises. In this connection it is worth pointing out that a great deal of irreplaceable time can be lost by conscientious teachers who labour points which are not strictly indispensable for the learners' purposes; it may also be more difficult to eliminate this waste of effort than appears at first sight, since teachers naturally tend to deal thoroughly with points which they themselves have found difficult or which they may have a special facility for teaching, irrespective of whether or not they are appropriate to the students' requirements. This further underlines the need—discussed below—for a special training-course for teachers engaged in this type of ELT programme.

(b) *Other exercises:* 'Controlled' translation passages, containing only those items which have previously been exercised, have also been prepared, and a start made on the production of pronunciation and word-stress drills and exercises.

(l) (c) *'Listening' exercises:* One of the commonest problems of teaching scientific English is that the students have difficulty in following the long and often high-modified sentences characteristic of much of this register. This is by no means a purely linguistic problem, since experiment has shown that in the initial stages of their specialized course the students are almost equally incapable of following similar sentences in the vernacular and will also fail to follow a long instruction in even the simplest of English, though they will manage short instructions successfully. The reasons for this seems to lie mainly in the teaching methods used in the schools. Textbooks for all subjects are deliberately written in an artificially simplified language, and the questions appearing in them are characteristically short and uncomplicated. Since teachers tend to emulate this simplified manner of exposition and questioning, the students have little opportunity to bridge the gap between this 'artificial' school language and the language actually used by scientists to describe their work to each other, which is typically hedged about with reservations, modifications, comparisons, and extensions. As a result, students of the last year of a specialized school course or entering the first year of a university have had little training in following an idea through a series of rapid transformations even in their own language, and we have therefore found it necessary to produce special 'listening' exercises in order to develop this faculty. These are of several kinds:

(i) The teacher gives progressively more complicated oral instructions which the students have to carry out (these can involve the drawing of diagrams, the arrangement of objects, the solution of simple mathematical or logical problems etc., so that the results obtained can be quickly checked):

---

[3] An important qualification: people communicating a shared nexus of ideas (e.g. a biochemist talking about biochemistry to another biochemist) can 'guess' difficulties that arise far more easily than people communicating random sets of ideas (e.g. a biochemist talking to people he meets on a social occasion).

(k) 'False cognates' in this context are words that have a similar form in English and Spanish but differ in their meaning: *actually* and *actualmente* are such a pair. There continues a strong Latin-American ESP research tradition devoted to Spanish–English cognate vocabulary, mainly because the identification of English lexical items that are potentially 'transparent' to Spanish-speaking readers is an important input into reading course materials.

(l) Throughout this paragraph it is not clear that Ewer is making a sufficiently clear distinction between *oral* and *written* scientific explanation. It may well be true that spoken explanations tend to be 'hedged about' with reservations and qualifications, but it is less obvious that scientists speak 'in long sentences'.

(m) (ii) The teacher reads passages in which the sentences are progressively more complicated and then asks questions whose answers can only be obtained through simple deductions from the facts presented in the passage:
(iii) He reads progressively longer and more complicated sentences to the students, who have been issued with sheets containing from three to five statements about each, only one of which corresponds to the sense of the sentence which has been read, in spite of deliberate similarities in phraseology: the students have to mark the statement they judge to be correct[4].

Since these types of exercise will normally form a preliminary to the main scientific-English course, it may in some cases be necessary to use 'school' English or even the vernacular to begin with. As soon as possible, however, the vocabulary and structures of the basic language of science, including the language of instructions referred to below, should be employed. The content of the exercises should, as usual, reflect the professional interests of the students.

(d) *Extension Material:* This is designed to extend the scope of the basic course to cover individual disciplines in greater detail. The emphasis here is mainly on lexis (since the grammatical requirements are covered by the basic course and the additional exercises described above) and are centred on what are known here as catenized vocabulary units (CVUs). The vocabulary sections for these which have been prepared so far include mathematics and statistics, physics, chemistry, biology, geology and geomorphology, economics, sociology and computer science, as well as less purely scientific subjects such as the workshop, electricity, electronics, radiocommunications, general agriculture, mining and quarrying, industry, business, commerce and financial affairs, general technology, and building and construction. Others in process of completion are engineering, medical science and nursing, and agricultural science, animal husbandry, and forestry.

The terms incorporated in these vocabularies are the specialized terms which seem most important for an understanding of each subject, and in general correspond to those which occur most frequently in the relevant literature, as identified by visual scanning. They include not only nouns, but the related adjectives, verbs and phrases, and are arranged according to a
(n) development of the 'catenizing' principle suggested by Michael West,[5] which we have used for many years and found to add considerably to the speed and degree of retention of learning. Each catenized vocabulary is then checked by one or more experts in the subject before being printed in double-spacing (thus leaving room for the addition of vernacular equivalents and pronunciation, where necessary), and issued to the students. It may here be worth noting that, although the production of bilingual versions was begun, the results, surprisingly, were strongly counter-indicative. One of the main reasons for this failure seems to be that both teachers and students tended to assume that these versions relieved them of the conscious efforts of comparison and illustration which are such powerful aids to both understanding and memory; this particular experiment has therefore been discontinued.

---

[4] These exercises are based on those appearing in F. G. French's *New Oxford Course Supplementary Exercises* (Oxford University Press) and F. Millington-Ward's *Practice in the Use of English* (Longmans).

[5] Michael West, 'Catenizing (Chaining Words Together)', in *Learning to Read a Foreign Language* (Longmans).

(m) Although listening exercise *(i)* was an important and useful innovation, *(ii)* shows some confusion between the spoken and written modes. Today most ESP practitioners would not accept the practice of reading written passages aloud for listening comprehension work. Speech and writing have very different patterns of development reflecting the different properties of the ear and the eye. (See Activity 2 of Episode Three.)

(n) The 'catenizing' principle is based on idea-associations within a particular context. The end-product is a word-matrix. Here is one of Ewer's examples:—

Physics

Nouns	*Adjectives*	*Verbs*	*Associated words*
sub-atomic	(charged	(to emit	(mesons, pions, neutrinos;
particles	(uncharged	(to collide with	(scatter, collision, path

Each vocabulary is also being supplied with its own exercises—some of which are taped—and occasionally with visual aids, mainly roneoed pictures and diagrams; finally, the unit thus formed is completed by a 'projects' section designed to promote free oral or written production of the material, and based on the situational approach. This work is still in process of completion.

'Instructional' English

Another area of scientific and technological English in which progress has been made is that of the language used for instructions. Consideration of the lexis of this sub-register had in the main been omitted from the materials included in the original basic course, since it had been assumed that adequate coverage would be given by the various textbooks for technical English then beginning to appear. However, recent experience has shown that this is not so and an effort has therefore been made to establish an outline of this language and to produce appropriate teaching material.

The first step was to scrutinize a sample of typical 'instructional' literature (e.g. engineering
maintenance manuals, laboratory workbooks, textbooks on experimental physics, chemistry,
and biology, computer programming manuals, operational and maintenance handbooks for
various types of instruments, and textbooks for nurses, surveyors, and mechanical and electrical
technicians). This yielded about 60 frequently-occurring modifiers—almost all of which had in
fact been included in the original course—and about 280 verbs of high frequency and range
(o) (see Appendix). Although about a third of the latter also happened to have been included in
the basic course and a fair number of the remainder were pairs or groups of words with
approximately the same meaning, it was clear that for teaching purposes this basic instructional
language should be dealt with as a unit. The next step, therefore, was to devise a suitable
teaching-context, and here it was considered that in view of the highly practical purposes of the
sub-register, the best way of getting the students to master the material would be to put them
into situations where they would have to follow and carry out a series of interconnected
instructions, resembling as closely as possible those they would be likely to encounter in their
professional training. An obstacle immediately presented itself, inasmuch as in many cases it
was administratively impossible to use laboratory and workshop facilities for carrying out
appropriate operations during the hours of the English classes. A simple standard kit was
therefore designed for use in the ordinary classroom. This kit was made up of easily obtainable
(p) objects such as bits of wire, clothes-pegs, nuts and bolts, paper cups, etc., costing about one
shilling and sixpence ($.20 cents) at local prices. It is issued to individual students and is used
for carrying out a large number of operations and experiments in which the instructional
vocabulary is practised intensively.

(o) Unfortunately, there is no Appendix to the article published in *ELT Journal*. However, in a paper by the same authors entitled 'Instructional English' and published in *ELT Documents* 74/4 such a list is given. The list is broken into six operational groupings. Here is the group headed *Verbs associated with Controlling and Adjusting*:—

ADJUST	CORRECT	REGULATE
CHANGE	EXAMINE	SET (an instrument)
CHECK, VERIFY	INSPECT	TEST
CONTROL	OBSERVE	OVERHAUL
		WATCH

(p) We can see similarities and differences between Higgins's approach and that of Ewer and Hughes-Davies. Both use simple, cheap 'semi-scientific' realia in their classrooms, but Higgins uses such realia to generate experimental descriptions, whilst the authors of this Episode concentrate on comprehension. The difference is largely explained by the Setting, Ewer's primary objective being to develop in his students a useful understanding of scientific and technical English. The use of 'simple kits' for both purposes has been widely copied and adapted by other ESP practitioners.

The usual procedure is for the teacher to demonstrate a few items at a time (using part of the kit only); he then drills these items by giving appropriate instructions in both oral and written form and getting the students to give similar instructions to each other; finally, the students combine the various items by performing a small number of meaningful experiments, following both oral and written instructions. Hence at all stages of the process the instructional language being learnt is linked to the corresponding actions, and this has proved a highly effective method of teaching this essential material.

The specialized training of teachers

As indicated in the article already referred to,[6] the average teacher engaged in teaching English to science and technology students finds considerable difficulty in adjusting to a teaching situation very different from the one for which he was originally trained. On the one hand, there is the fact that he has been given little or no chance to become acquainted with the concepts and potentialities of modern science and technology, or with the ways in which scientists and technologists operate, and this leads to a series of disabilities which seriously impair his normal teaching efficiency. Thus, apart from the initial difficulty of mastering the specialized language itself, there is a real possibility that his previous literature-oriented education will have left him with an anti-science bias—conscious or unconscious—which is impossible to conceal from his students and which can ruin his relationship with them. Since, also, he himself has difficulty in following the concepts used in a scientific-English course, he naturally assumes that his students have similar difficulties and thus teaches at an unnecessarily slow pace,[7] or may become the victim of a most undesirable inferiority complex. On the other hand, the methodological demands on the teacher in this type of programme also differ in important respects from those for which he has been equipped. For example, the emphasis in his teacher-training course, as well as the teaching experience he has previously had, is likely to have been directed towards children of the ages 11–15; in an ELT programme for science and technology the students will be in a completely different age-group (17–20 or even older) and require a correspondingly different approach. Furthermore, the teacher of a school or even university English course does not usually have to prepare didactic materials, since there is a wide choice of well-established textbooks and other aids. This is not so in the relatively new field we are considering, and he will be obliged to try to remedy this lack for himself, though few teacher-training programmes prepare him to do so. Other difficulties, such as that mentioned under the heading of 'Remedial Exercises and Drills' above, have also to be considered.

(q) To alleviate these disabilities a special scheme has been introduced into the final year of the English-language course for teacher-trainees. In its present shape, each student chooses to specialize in one of two areas of 'special' English, viz. science, or technology and business (it is

[6] See note 5.

[7] In fact, our general experience has been that students of these courses have a tendency to learn *faster* than in the secondary school: one of the reasons for this is ascribed to their relative familiarity with the ideas being dealt with.

(q) As far as I am aware, Ewer was the first person to devise and teach an ESP component on an initial teacher-training programme. Although in later years Ewer was to develop his ideas for pragmatic teacher training very much further, this section of Episode Five underlines his innovative and pioneering role in the preparation of ESP teachers. Although there remains considerable uncertainty about the proper nature of ESP teacher training, we now have a number of possible inputs not available to Ewer right at the beginning of the seventies. Indeed, when we read Ewer's commentary on his course, we are struck by the complete absence of ESP readings as such; there are no textbooks to analyse, or ESP papers to study. He was forced to rely on 'primary' scientific and technical resources.

hoped that both areas will eventually be covered). The basis of study is formed by the catenized vocabulary units previously mentioned, complemented by (*a*) a programme of visits to scientific or industrial establishments, lectures (usually in the vernacular but sometimes in English) by experts in the various subjects, and other activities, which include (for the scientific-English candidates) the carrying out of laboratory experiments, instruction in the use of certain scientific instruments, and participation in field excursions; (*b*) a reading plan based on the cheap paperback literature now available. This consists, in the first place, of a rather simple set book giving a brief introduction to each area (those used so far are Halacy's *Nine Roads to Tomorrow* for technology, and either Berger's *Advances in Modern Science* or Lochspeich's *How Scientists Find Out* for science, all three published in the United States by Washington Square Press), and, in the second place, of the reading and discussion of three books chosen by each student individually from a list of over thirty—mostly 'Pelican' (U.K.) or 'Signet' and 'Mentor' (U.S.) editions—which cover important aspects of each area. Some of the most popular of these are currently Storer's *Web of Life* (ecology), Isaac's *Introducing Science*, Rachel Carson's classic *The Sea Around Us*, Sir Leon Bagrit's *Age of Automation*, *The Innovators* by Michael Shanks, *The World in 1984* edited by Nigel Calder, and S. Handel's *Electronic Revolution*; (*c*) the compilation by each student of a portfolio of visual and explanatory material relating to the area they have chosen to study; this not only helps the student to understand the different subjects himself, but also forms a valuable teaching aid which he can use in his later career; (*d*) the production by student teams or 'syndicates' of teaching exercises based on the CVUs.

Although the scheme means a great deal of work for everyone concerned, it has already begun to show its effectiveness. Several students from among the first groups of trainees to complete the scheme are now employed in teaching scientific and technological English, and it is clear that their preliminary training has gone a long way towards removing the most outstanding of the difficulties that beset their predecessors.

Conclusions

Although this is not the place to attempt a detailed analysis of all the implications of the projects outlined above, some broad conclusions of immediate interest may be briefly noted.

In the first place, the gathering of quantitative data on how, and to what extent, English is used as a professional tool in science and technology, has three applications of direct consequence to educational administrators: (*a*) it enables the importance of an ELT programme in this field to be estimated in a way that can reasonably be translated into practical resource-allocation terms (in our own case, for example, this has led to an extensive redeployment of resources); (*b*) legitimate projections can be used to give some indication of future requirements; and (*c*) it helps to determine the type of programme to be developed (in our own case, again, the fact that the local context involved appreciable numbers of visiting experts and overseas study-courses indicated that the courses should have a strong oral component).

In the second place, the further work done on the characteristics of the scientific register and the ways in which it differs from the 'general' ELT course, together with the additional material prepared, has led to a more effective organization of the programme and greatly enlarged its flexibility and scope. In this connection we should emphasize that, in the circumstances in which this type of teaching normally operates (students with varying levels of English at entry, and studying different disciplines; varying lengths of instruction-time allotted by different institutions), the provision of a flexible overall programme, made up of a master-course and a number of sub-courses capable of being combined in different ways, is of the utmost importance. The present full-length version in use here is in three overlapping stages, as follows:

Stage 1: Simple 'listening' exercises and 'instructional' English;
Stage 2: Basic course, with supplementary exercises for those that need them and advanced 'listening' exercises;
Stage 3: Specialized material for individual subjects.

Thirdly, the special training scheme has ensured a permanent supply of teachers who not only have a satisfactory command of scientific and technological English and the appropriate equipment of visual and other teaching aids, but who also appreciate the scientific point of view and the role of science and technology in modern society. Such training is in our view essential to the success of any ELT programme of this kind.

Finally, it will be obvious that the various projects described in the present article depended in innumerable ways on the active co-operation of members of staff of the specialist disciplines. We believe that no really effective language-course can be built up and maintained without this, and that the establishment of a close rapport between the English-teaching staff and their colleagues of the scientific and technological departments should therefore be a major consideration for those in charge of such courses.

III — ACTIVITIES —

(1) In the third paragraph the authors state that 'one of the principal objects of this survey was to evaluate the extent to which English and other foreign languages were necessary to students and teachers in their studies'. However, the three types of data the authors obtained would not seem to explore fully how necessary English was to Chilean academic staff. How would you discover this? Outline a scheme of your own.

(2) Give two examples each of the items listed in Group II (paragraph 8).

(3) In the section on 'Instructional English', comment *(o)* refers to the non-existent Appendix and then illustrates one grouping of *Instructional Verbs* taken from a different article by Ewer and Hughes-Davies.

Another grouping they give is *Verbs associated with Liquids and Mixtures.* There were 29 verbs in the *ELT Documents* list, including *boil, dilute, fill* and *stir.* What do you think the others were?

(4) In the final paragraph of the same section, a procedure is outlined for teaching the students to follow oral instructions. You have a 'kit' consisting of a box of matches for each student. Devise a suitable exercise and write it up so it can be used by another teacher. (Remember that it is much better if such 'idea-following' exercises have a useful result, i.e. they illustrate some fact or principle, rather than being some meaningless game.)

IV — EVALUATION —

In the introduction to the article, Ewer explains how progress has been made in the following five directions:—

1. The role of English
2. The register of Science
3. Additional exercises
4. Instructional English
5. The specialized training of ESP teachers

(1) In your estimation, in which of these areas do you think 'Further Notes' made a significant contribution to the development of ESP? In other words, how far do you agree with my assessment in the Setting and the footnotes?

(2) In your estimation, which of these areas will attract most interest in the years following the publication of this article? And why?

V

RELATED READINGS

The full background information to the lively ESP scene in Chile can be seen from reviewing the volumes of *EST/ESP Chile* of which the late Jack Ewer was the Consulting Editor. It has been announced that this Journal ceased publication with Issue 11 in March 1982, but at the time of writing there are rumours that it will revive. The journal secretary is Odette Boys (Casilla 16099, Santiago 9, Chile).

Issue 65 of *English for Specific Purposes* (see Episode Eleven) is a special tribute to J. R. Ewer's work; this issue contains a complete bibliography of his EST publications.

A similar bibliography can be found in *The ESP Journal* 2, 1, 1983 (see Episode Fifteen); the Journal is largely devoted to Jack Ewer's major statement of his views on teacher-training for EST, and to a number of responses to that statement.

EPISODE SIX 1972

John E. Lackstrom, Larry Selinker and Louis P. Trimble,
'Grammar and Technical English',
English Teaching Forum, X, 5, 1972.

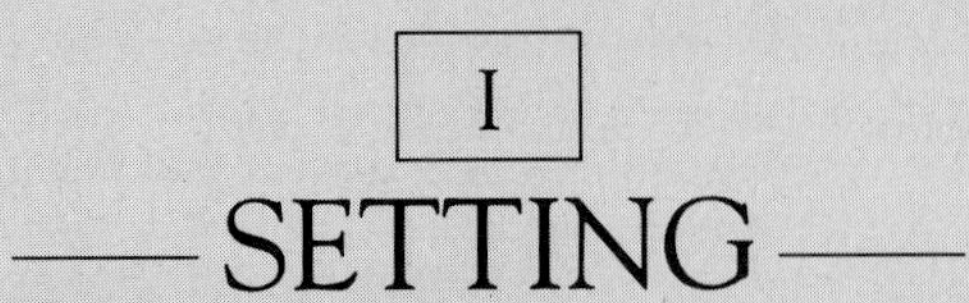

I SETTING

This article was originally published in 1970 and so, in a strict chronological sense, it should have been placed between Episodes Three and Five. However, the article only became widely known after it had appeared in *Forum* in 1972 (*Forum* being a US Government-aided journal with a considerable international circulation, especially in the Third World). I have therefore placed it here. I have also for the purposes of this volume chosen to include only the first third of 'Grammar and Technical English'; the original article is of considerable length, partly because it discusses with many examples four areas of English grammar as used in technical and scientific writing—tenses, the article system, the role of 'real' passives and statives, and the occurrence of nominalizations as opposed to passives. However, in each area the methods of argumentation adopted and the types of conclusion reached are really quite similar. I therefore feel that only a relatively small measure of injustice is being done to this important paper by cutting it short after it considers the uses of the present, the present perfect and the past tenses.

Episode Six must serve as an example of the publications (often joint) of Lackstrom, Selinker and Trimble. These three authors were the key figures in the American 'North-West' or 'Washington' school of EST and indeed, until comparatively recently, they were the only serious and influential protagonists of English for Science and Technology within the US academic world in general and within the numerous English Language Institutes attached to American universities in particular. The reasons for such a different state of affairs to those we have already seen (Episodes One and Two—Great Britain; Episode Three—South-East Asia; Episode Four—The Middle East; and Episode Five—Latin America) are several. Firstly, we can recognize that the very considerable power and prestige of general linguistics in the United States has had a considerable influence on the contrastingly underprivileged TESOL profession; and that, in the period covered so far by this volume, American linguistics was principally concerned with formal grammatical systems and was much given to decontextualized citations of 'constructed' rather than 'authentic' single sentences. Secondly, we can see that many 'orientation' programmes for overseas students were locked into the classifications imposed by the major examinations such as TOEFL and the Michigan Test, which are essentially measures of general English proficiency. Thirdly, the American TESOL community has been much exercised over the last two uncertain decades with finding a true 'caring and sharing' methodology. Although such a search is undoubtedly praiseworthy, it has tended to stress a sense of achievement within the class, rather than outside it, and so has tended to be dismissive of the tough *instrumental* motivation that often underpins ESP courses elsewhere. And fourthly, TESOL in America finds its ultimate justification in being part of a social service designed to help successive and continuing waves of immigrants to adjust to and integrate with the

American way of life. In recent years, there has been interesting work done on developing 'competency-based' courses and the designers of such courses are attempting increasingly precise and insightful identifications of the particular problems of particular groups. At times such courses do indeed become involved with English for Occupational Purposes, but this is rarely—and understandably—their major concern.

The 'Washington' school is no more. John Lackstrom has moved to the University of Utah, Larry Selinker to the University of Michigan, and Louis Trimble has retired. ESP has become much more widespread in the United States, but the North-West still exerts its influence; Karl Drobnic is at the University of Oregon (Episode Ten) and Elaine Tarone in Minnesota (Episode Fifteen).

Grammar and Technical English is a crucial paper in the development of EST and, with the work of Henry Widdowson (as represented in the following Episode), creates a new perspective of what an understanding of the language used in science and technology might involve. The differences that separate *Grammar and Technical English* from previous Episodes are quite marked. For one thing, we can see extensive use being made of standard linguistic techniques; in particular the careful commentary on pairs of sentences that differ only in the linguistic features under observation. Connected with this, we can see an advance on Episode Four in the level of confidence expressed by the researcher in ESP about the validity of his findings, even if those findings run counter to widely-held views about the proper explanation of certain features of English syntax. Another important departure is the emphasis the authors place on rhetorical considerations as determining grammatical choices. Such an emphasis began a movement towards developing more purposive and organization-oriented writing tasks and has led, especially in recent years, to a greater appreciation of the value of at least some of the recommendations in technical writing manuals designed for native speakers of English. (For many years, of course, such manuals were dismissed by ESP practitioners as being prescriptive rather than being based on descriptive analyses of actual linguistic data.) And a final beneficial influence of *Grammar and Technical English* was the way in which it held the door open to discourse analysis. Towards the end of the article, the authors write:—

> We have tried to show that when we begin to examine purely grammatical notions in relation to technical writing and communication, in an effort to help the student manipulate technical information in English, we are drawn from purely grammatical relationships to the attitudes and intentions of the writer and to the position of the sentence under discussion in its rhetorical relationships to the rest of the paragraph.

In the years following the *Forum* article, all three of its authors had important and interesting contributions to make to the rapidly-growing field of applied discourse analysis. But if *Grammar and Technical English* opened the door to 'rhetorical' explanation, it also half-closed the door of statistical analysis on surface grammatical features, such as we found in Episode One. In effect, it showed that frequency-work of the type undertaken by Barber and others could have descriptive validity but little explanatory force.

The main part of the following extract proposes a radical reinterpretation of the meaning and use of past, present perfect and present tenses in many Science and Engineering contexts. This was the part of *Grammar and Technical English* that caused particular excitement when it began to circulate and it still arouses lively controversy. Even if there have always been doubts about some of the authors' conclusions, this early paper by Lackstrom, Selinker and Trimble provided a major intellectual challenge to a growing band of ESP practitioners and did so from within the ESP movement.

II

TEXT AND COMMENTARY

Grammar and Technical English

by John E. Lackstrom, Larry Selinker *and* Louis P. Trimble

A common complaint about American approaches to the teaching of English as a second language holds that American ESL textbook materials and methodology—whether structurally or transformationally based—are sentence-oriented and lack important relationships to usage and content. 'Sentence-oriented grammar' provides explanations of grammatical choices in terms of syntax and semantics. By 'grammatical choice' we mean a decision to express a meaning in one linguistic form rather than in another, based on a judgment that one linguistic form of expression is more acceptable than another. If the judgment involves an appeal to grammatical facts only, then the judgment is syntactic. For example, a judgment to prefer sentence 1 to sentence 2 below is a syntactic choice only:

(a) 1. It is theorized that the energy of the absorbed quantum exceeds that of the chemical bonds.[1]

(b) 2. *The energy of the absorbed quantum is theorized to exceed that of the chemical bonds.

A judgment to prefer sentence 3 to sentence 4, however, is a grammatical choice determined by a semantic fact:

3. It is known that the energy of the absorbed quantum exceeds that of the chemical bonds.
4. *It is being known that the energy of the absorbed quantum exceeds that of the chemical bonds.

(c) The unacceptability of sentence 4 results from a constraint restricting the progressive aspect to verbs of process (non-stative verbs). Since *know* is semantically not a verb of process, it does not co-occur with the progressive aspect. Thus a grammatical choice, in this case, is determined by a semantic fact.

---

[1] All technical examples presented in this paper are representative of the English regularly found by the engineering student in his freshman and sophomore engineering textbooks and supplementary reading.

(a) The authors' footnote is significant. Their data is based on engineering textbooks and 'supplementary reading'. To what extent their findings might be applicable to other types of scientific writing, such as journals or technical reports, is an important matter to be taken up later.

(b) *Theorized* is not a common 'reporting-verb', and the syntactic unacceptability of 2 would be clearer with a more usual verb such as *suggested*—

2a* The energy of the absorbed quantum is *suggested* to exceed that of the chemical bonds.

(c) The argument here is somewhat swift. It is certainly true that *know* does not correctly occur in the present progressive tense or aspect. Given this, one could argue that 4 is unacceptable simply because 4 breaks this syntactic rule (just as *suggested to* breaks the arbitrary rule that *suggest* is followed by *that*). The authors, however, make the further claim that 4 is wrongly chosen for semantic reasons; but, as far as I can see, the difference between 1 & 2 and 3 & 4 is that for the latter pair we happen to have an explanation of why 4 is wrong whereas for 1 & 2 we are forced to concede that 2 is wrong because 'it just is'.

If we accept that semantics is concerned with meaning, we can perhaps better evaluate 4 in terms of its intended

Rhetorical considerations

Choices made on the basis of syntax or semantics can be made solely in terms of the single sentence. Choices made on the basis of rhetorical considerations, on the other hand, must refer to elements beyond the bounds of a single sentence. We understand 'rhetorical' considerations in technical English to include judgments concerning the order of the presentation of information, within the paragraph and within the total piece of which the paragraph is a part,
(d) and judgments on clarity and precision of exposition.[2] The following three sentences illustrate how a rhetorical judgment on clarity of exposition can affect grammatical choices. Consider first sentence 5:

5. The horizontal top surface of the burner emits a uniform flux of fuel gas at velocity U.

In a paragraph, sentence 5 may be followed by either sentence 6 or sentence 7.

6. Its temperature is maintained near ambient . . .
7. The temperature of this surface is maintained near ambient . . .

In sentence 6 *temperature* may be that of the surface or of the gas: the pronoun *its* is ambiguous. Sentence 7 is not ambiguous, since it specifies the element whose temperature is being maintained. The choice between 6 and 7 is neither syntactic nor semantic, since neither 6 nor 7 is anomalous either alone or in the context of sentence 5. Nevertheless, rhetorical considerations of clarity and precision cause us to prefer 7 to 6, as 6 is ambiguous and 7 is not. In this case, rhetorical considerations influence the grammatical decision to choose a phrasal construction rather than a pronominal one.

The effect that rhetorical considerations have on grammatical choices may not always be as direct as in the foregoing example. But rhetorical considerations often do determine the semantic structure of a given sentence, and the semantic structure thus required will in turn
(e) determine the grammatical choices the technical writer must make. Examples of such cases will be pointed out as they occur in the discussion.

[2] The reader is referred to Daniel Marder, *The Craft of Technical Writing* (Macmillan, 1960, pp. 5–6), wherein he defines 'rhetorical' as follows: '[In technical writing] rhetoric manifests itself in the techniques of organization and style that the writer employs. The organizational techniques are methods of solving various writing problems so that unity, coherence, and emphasis are maintained throughout the communications. These methods are used first to arrange the whole composition into related parts and then to arrange the parts for a total effect of clarity and forcefulness. . . . Style is the application of rhetorical principles to the smallest element of the composition—the sentence. It is the writer's manner of selecting words and combining them into the sentences that constitute the paragraphs. The paragraphs in turn are organized according to some technique or combination of techniques to make up the entire composition.'

interpretation. If the writer of 4 means 3 (i.e. 'it is generally known that . . .') then he will usually be misleading the reader and so his problem is indeed semantic. If, on the other hand, the writer of 4 means 4 (i.e. 'knowledge is growing') then 4 is semantically appropriate but syntactically unacceptable, and he should have written:

4a It is becoming known that . . .
or 4b It is being realized that . . .

I have discussed the use of the term 'semantic' at some length, because it has some importance in this paper. My advice in reading the paper is to concentrate on what Lackstrom, Selinker and Trimble have to say about the relationships between *rhetoric* and *grammar*, for this is where their important contribution lies; and the authors themselves are not always consistent in their inclusion of a semantic level.

(d) This is the first time in this volume that we find references to specialized English textbooks for native speakers. For many years, Americans in ESP have been involved in native-speaker work, typically because of the requirements in the US for *composition* or *rhetoric* courses. (In marked contrast, few British ESP practitioners have been so involved; however, this may now be changing, cf. *Common Ground—Shared Interests in ESP and Communication Studies* (ed. Williams, Swales and Kirkman, Pergamon, 1984).

(e) See (c).

We can see, then, that a sentence-oriented approach to grammar describes grammatical choices only in syntactic and semantic terms, without contextual references—a critical omission because it condemns the student to work with isolated sentences divorced from context and, very often, from content as well. This situation has probably developed from the American preoccupation with language teaching for oral communication. But, whatever the cause, the crucial roles of subject matter and rhetoric in the grammatical organization of sentences have been largely neglected by teachers and, to the best of our knowledge, ignored in the literature as well.

(f) The purpose of this article is to show that correct grammatical choices in a written medium cannot be taught apart from considerations of rhetoric and subject matter.[3] To support this claim we will examine several areas. We will show (1) that the choice of tenses in the written
(g) medium is dependent not on 'time lines', as most textbook presentations suppose, but on rhetorical and subject-matter considerations, (2) that specific grammatical choices involving definite and indefinite articles depend on rhetorical and subject-matter principles, and (3) that choices involving adverbs, aspect, agent phrases, and nominalization often demand contextual directives. In a sample paragraph of scientific writing, we will explore some additional aspects of the interpenetration of grammar and rhetoric.

The interpretation of technical English requires reading skills far beyond the scope of what is ordinarily covered in the usual EFL program. It is little wonder that students to whom English is a foreign language, especially those majoring in the sciences, find their academic subjects difficult, even though in all other respects they have the background and intellectual ability to do the work. An ordinary assignment seems unmanageable to students who cannot read rapidly with reasonable comprehension. It is not the subject matter *per se* but the complexity of
(h) scientific prose that constitutes their problem.

In the fall of 1967 we initiated at the University of Washington a program in technical communication to provide advanced work in English for foreign engineering students (FES).[4] From the beginning, we chose certain problems for intensive study, starting with a grammatical area known to be difficult—English tenses and their time relationships. We used the text *Mastering American English* (MAE), by Hayden, Pilgrim, and Haggard (Englewood Cliffs, N.J.: Prentice-Hall, 1956), as a point of departure.

Choice of Tenses

MAE makes a useful distinction between *tense* and *time* (p. 71): 'Tense refers to the form of the verb . . .'—which is an easy concept for the FES to master. *Time*, a concept left vague in the

[3] It is beyond the scope of this article to describe in greater detail the rhetoric of technical communication. By the term *rhetoric* we do not mean 'the art of influencing the thought and conduct of an audience.' There exists no book on technical rhetoric *per se*, but sections on certain aspects of technical rhetoric may be found in Marder, *op. cit.*, and in Herman M. Weisman, *Basic Technical Writing*, Merrill, 1962. The reader is referred to our (forthcoming) monograph entitled *Teaching Advanced Scientific and Technical Communication in English as a Second Language*.

[4] Although our approach is based on experience with FES alone, we believe that many of the principles presented in this article concerning grammatical explanations are applicable to foreign students in other scientific and professional areas as well.

(f) The authors here confirm that the aim of this investigation is to improve the teaching of scientific writing. Hence the main connection is with Episode Four.

(g) As indicated in the Setting, this Episode covers only the first of these.

(h) The three authors—and particularly Selinker—have often stressed the complexity of scientific prose, and the difficulties students may have in interpreting it. We need, however, to maintain a distinction between the complexity of the analysis and the complexity of the text. Sometimes texts appear 'complex' because they are not as clearly written as they might be; in other words, they offer to the *linguist* more than one possible and plausible interpretation. A further point is that scientific and technical writing typically has a simple and straightforward communicative purpose: such writing is designed to inform and/or to instruct. It is not designed to change political beliefs, affect moral behaviour, or to engender laughter or tears or sexual arousal.

book, is considered the governing factor in the choice of tenses. *MAE* emphasizes that one tense can express a large number of time concepts, and that one time concept can have several tenses. At the outset we believed the material on usage of tenses (Parts VII–IX) to be clear and useful. It seemed essential that the student master this material so that he could manipulate technical information in English well enough to prepare the necessary reports for his engineering courses. But we found this type of information and the practice exercises on it insufficient (for our purposes) on two counts: (1) the sentences are nontechnical in content, and (2) insofar as they are semantically and contextually isolated constructions, they are a paradigm case of sentence-oriented grammar presentation.[5]

(i) While it is true that in certain types of spoken discourse time relationships, as *MAE* insists, are the governing factors in tense-choice, an undue emphasis on time-tense relationships may obscure what are often more crucial factors. It may well be, for example, that paragraph
(j) organization will replace time as a governing factor in the choice of tense in a particular sentence.

The core idea

(k) A fairly rudimentary form of paragraph organization common in technical writing involves the statement of a *core idea* (thesis statement, topic statement, etc.) followed by the presentation of *supporting facts.* The core idea normally involves some claim that the author supposes the reader will not accept at its face value—that is, a claim that is not trivially true. Consider, for example, the sentence:

(a) A plant designed to consume a waste product from an operation found its supply of raw materials cut off.

A sentence of this form would hardly be considered material for a core idea, since it fails to make a claim that is worthy of support. A claim such as this could be false only if the author were lying. Technical writers, therefore, attempt to present core ideas that make nontrivial claims—if for no other reason than that they want to present some statement that they can support and hence provide detailed information about. A common way of making nontrivial claims is to state core ideas that, formally, are generalizations—as in the sentence:

(b) Unfortunate situations arise when plants designed to consume waste products from one operation find supplies of raw materials cut off or sharply curtailed.

(l) Although sentence **b** is closely related to sentence **a** in meaning, **b** does not make a trivial claim, whereas **a** does. As a core idea, **b** makes a statement that might be false even though the author is not lying. It is a sentence that requires some supporting facts.

The 'conceptual paragraph'

The convention of technical rhetoric whereby core ideas are stated in the form of generalizations develops not out of grammatical considerations but out of the organization

[5] We are not criticizing *MAE* specifically, but all textbook materials known to us.

(i) One might also expect this to be true of *narratives* as well.

(j) So far my comments on the authors' preparatory discussion have not been markedly enthusiastic. With this sentence, however, the authors begin to unfold their major and important hypothesis.

(k) Presumably 'a fairly rudimentary form of paragraph organization' is to be interpreted as a 'crude analytic description of paragraph organization' rather than as meaning that the paragraphs themselves are organized in a rudimentary way.

(l) By now we can see that the authors are attempting to understand the *rationale* of technical, expository prose.

(m) required for technical prose. This organization is fairly rigid in form, with the core of each conceptual paragraph being a generalization in relation to the specificity of the supporting facts contained within the paragraph. A 'conceptual paragraph' consists of (1) a core idea and (2) the material that supports this core directly or indirectly and relates the core to preceding and/or following ideas. A 'physical paragraph' is indicated by indentation or spacing and may not contain all of the elements necessary to make it a conceptual paragraph. If a core idea can logically be subdivided into units large enough to require development by supporting facts, each of these developed units might form a physical paragraph; if so, then the units share the core idea and each will form one part of the conceptual paragraph. In turn, each physical paragraph
(n) will have its own supported core; that is, a 'subcore' of the common core idea. Each subcore is both a generalization with respect to its supporting facts and a specific support with respect to the core that governs it (that is, the common core). All core ideas, therefore, are formally
(o) generalizations at one or another level of abstraction.[6]

In teaching technical communications to FES, it is essential to point out the rhetorical superiority of sentence **b** over sentence **a** as the statement of a core idea. But notice that in choosing **b** over **a** there is a concomitant choice of the present tense over the past tense. In grammatical explanations directed to the foreign student this choice is generally described as
(p) being related to time. However, we claim that tense-choice in this case is made on the basis of the notion *degree of generality*. In technical English the present tense means 'generalization'—and the present tense will occur where technical rhetoric requires the expression of this meaning. One of these places will be in the expression of the core idea. To say that the choice of the present tense is governed by the 'relatively permanent' time of the activity (*MAE*, p. 73) is to obscure the much more crucial relationship involving both the nontemporal meaning of the present tense and the rhetorical consideration governing the occurrence of this meaning in technical prose.

Three tense choices

Sentence **b** (unlike **a**), taken as the statement of the core idea of a paragraph, requires some supporting facts. The facts supporting a core idea can be given by the author in three distinct forms depending on the degree of generality the author wishes to claim for his information.

[6] A detailed discussion of these ideas may be found in the monograph mentioned in footnote 3.

(m) An approach to *teaching* the recognition of conceptual paragraphs is described by Drobnic in Episode Ten.

(n) The authors do not illustrate the relationships between *conceptual* and *physical* paragraphs. One very simple sort of relationship is diagrammed below:

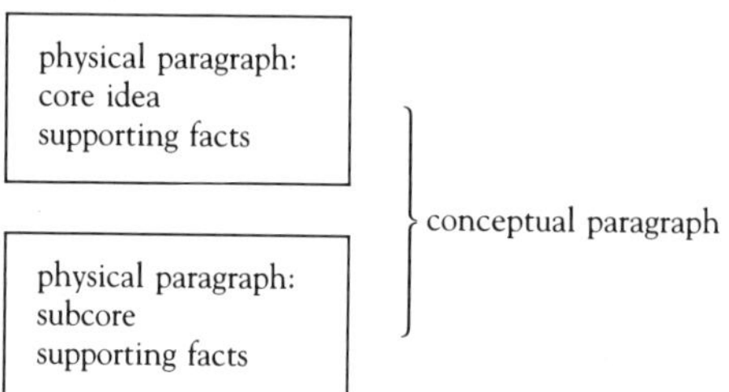

(o) The use of the adverb *formally* here is not very clear. It is unlikely that Lackstrom et al. mean that all core ideas have a typical linguistic form (in the way in which Allen and Widdowson in the next Episode will suggest that *generalizations* and *definitions* have different sentence structures); it seems more likely that we should interpret *formally* as meaning 'in terms of paragraph structure', i.e. *formal* at a discoursal rather than linguistic level.

(p) In this striking and well-argued paragraph the authors now offer their radical reinterpretation of tense usage in scientific and technical prose, and the remainder of the extract will develop their argument in exciting and original ways.

1. If the author wishes to claim no generality for the facts given in support of a core idea like **b**, he will present the information in the past tense:

(c) A plant to convert cellulose of pine sawdust into fermentable sugar and that into ethyl alcohol failed because a sawmill couldn't sell as much lumber as plans called for, and (q) **thereby curtailed the alcohol plant's raw material supply.**

2. On the other hand, the author may wish to convey to the reader the notion that, while the information given in support of the core idea is a good generalization about past events, he does not wish to commit himself with respect to future events. If this is the case, the present perfect tense would be an appropriate vehicle through which to present the information:

(d) Plants to convert cellulose of pine sawdust into fermentable sugar and that into ethyl alcohol have failed because sawmills haven't been able to sell as much lumber as plans have called for, and thereby have curtailed the alcohol plants' raw material supply.

Notice that in this last sentence the expression of the generalization involves not only the change in tense but also a change in the grammatical number of the noun phrases *plants* and *sawmills*. Without this concomitant change from singular to plural, the sentence in the present perfect would still express only a particular fact about the past.

3. If the author wishes to make an even more general claim about the information he is presenting in the form of supporting facts, he may use the present tense. Here, as in the use of the present perfect, the noun phrases must be pluralized to make sense:

(e) Plants to convert cellulose of pine sawdust into fermentable sugar and that into ethyl alcohol fail because sawmills can't sell as much lumber as plans call for, and thereby curtail the alcohol plants' raw material supply.

In the present-tense version of this sentence it is clear that the author claims the information to be correct not only for the past but also for the future. That is, he is claiming the information in (r) the supporting data to be some sort of universal truth about the world.

The point made concerning the choice of tense in the statement of a core idea must be emphasized again in relation to choice of tense in the presentation of supporting facts. The choice of the past, present perfect, or present tense in **c**, **d**, and **e**, respectively, is a choice based not on the time of the ethyl-alcohol-plant failures but on how general the author believes this phenomenon to be. To put it another way, the author will choose one or another of the tenses depending on how many instances of ethyl-alcohol-plant failures he knows about. If he has knowledge of a large number of cases he will use the present tense. If he knows of fewer cases, he will use the present perfect. If he knows of only one case, the past tense will be used. Here we have tense-choice based on semantic notions unrelated to time.

Rhetorical considerations will place constraints on the degree of generality expressed at (s) various points in the paragraph, and so play a role in the choice of tense. In technical prose, for example, there is a preferred progression from more to less general statements. So, if the author chooses statement **d** to express support for core idea **b**, he may wish to provide additional support for statement **d**. If he does provide subsidiary supporting statements, they will take the

(q) The use of the contracted form *couldn't* is somewhat surprising.

(r) The 'universal present' had, of course, been widely accepted as having particular relevance to scientific writing by all teachers and textbook writers for many years. One of the influential aspects of this article was its attempt to tie this use in with less 'universal' statements containing verbs in the perfect and the past.

(s) Having established a link between *tense* and *generality*, the authors conclude this most interesting section with some further hypotheses about the *ordering* of statements of different levels of generality. Although it would be unreasonable to expect that such a neat scheme would always be corroborated in actual texts, it did offer the ESP practitioner something to investigate, and something of a rhetorical rather than a linguistic nature.

form, roughly, of the sentences in **f**, below. Notice that these statements of additional or subsidiary support will invariably be in the past tense:

(f) **Plant A failed at such and such a time in such and such a place.**
Plant B failed at such and such a time in such and such a place.
Plant C failed at such and such a time in such and such a place.

The statements in **f** are in the past tense because they are less general than **d**—but they are less general because the rhetoric of technical English requires them to be so. A more general statement than **d**—like *Ethyl-alcohol plants on Long Island fail regularly for this reason*—could not provide support for **d** because it would violate the principle of progressing from the more to the less general statement. This example illustrates how a rhetorical consideration determines a semantic choice, which in turn governs a grammatical choice.

III
ACTIVITIES

(1) The *Conclusions* section of this article ends with this passage:—

> We do not know how widespread a phenomenon such grammatical–rhetorical dependencies are, but relatively unsystematic observation makes us lean toward the view that teachers of ESL have underestimated the complexities involved in teaching FES. It is common ESL practice to assume that an additional composition course will help the student overcome all his problems with technical English. However, our own research has shown that at the very least, *different*—not *more of the same*—training in English is necessary.

(a) What do you understand by 'grammatical–rhetorical dependencies'?

(b) How would you illustrate such a *dependency* from the area of choosing *active* or *passive*?

(c) Outline how you might develop a writing lesson that incorporates some of the main ideas in the extract.

(2) Consider these statements:

(i) *(a)* Chomsky disagreed with their conclusions.
(b) Readers disagreed with their conclusions.
(ii) *(a)* Chomsky has disagreed with their conclusions.
(b) Readers have disagreed with their conclusions.
(iii) *(a)* Chomsky disagrees with their conclusions.
(b) Readers disagree with their conclusions.

Discuss what you understand these sentences to imply. To what extent would they support Lackstrom, Selinker and Trimble's hypothesis? (Or would they suggest *time* and *generality* are more closely interconnected than the article implies?)

IV
EVALUATION

(1) *Grammar and Technical English* opened up the question of how best to approach tenses and other syntactic features in scientific and technical English. In this context, we should remember that Lackstrom, Selinker and Trimble based their analysis on engineering (first and second year) textbooks. It might therefore follow that other types of text might require *different* non-temporal explanations of tense usage. How would you explain the use of the *present* and *past* tenses in this abstract:—

> The foundations of the National Westminster Bank tower, London, one of the highest office blocks in Europe, *were instrumented* to monitor the performance of the piles raft foundation. Details of the instruments, their installation and the reading procedures

are given. The results *indicate* that at the completion of the main structure about 27 to 33% of the load *is directly carried* by the clay beneath the raft, and that there *are* two peaks in the raft/clay interface pressure at the outer edge of the core wall and towards the raft edge. Levelling studs, installed in the raft, *were surveyed* periodically and the observations *indicate* that a settlement of the order of 43mm took place at the raft centre. A centre to edge deflection of the raft of about 15mm *was estimated*. The technical note *sets out* the details, installation and reading procedures for the instrumentation installed, together with a discussion of the results obtained so far and conclusions reached. Recommendations, both contractual and technical, *are put forward* for future instrumentation contracts of this type.

(from *Geotechnical Abstracts* 9/1982 (C7)).

V
RELATED READINGS

The three authors of this Episode have gone their slightly different ways in the last ten years.

John Lackstrom's published work has been largely concerned with the description of linguistic and discoursal aspects of Scientific English and the pedagogical implication of such teaching. The following two references illustrate these interests:—

'Teaching Modals in EST Discourse' in *English for Specific Purposes, Science and Technology* (edited by Mary Todd Trimble, Louis Trimble and Karl Drobnic, Heinle & Heinle, 1978).

'Logical Argumentation: The Answer to the Discussion Problem in EST' in *English for Academic and Technical Purposes* (see Episode One).

Louis Trimble's papers—often co-authored with his wife—have tended to concentrate on technical English. There are several dealing with technical manuals (see Ewer and Hughes-Davies' discussion of Instructional English in Episode Five). Two similar papers are:—

'The development of EFL Materials for Occupational English', in the proceedings of the Paipa Seminar (see Episode Twelve for details);

'The development of EFL Materials for Occupational English: The Technical Manual' in *English for Specific Purposes, Science and Technology* (op. cit.).

Selinker's work in EST has continued to stress the importance of the structuring of rhetorical information. For instance:—

Selinker *et al.*, 'Presuppositional Rhetorical Information in EST Discourse', *TESOL Quarterly*, 10, 3, 1976.

Selinker *et al.*, 'Rhetorical Function-Shifts in EST Discourse', *TESOL Quarterly*, 12, 3, 1978.

Selinker's growing concern with specialist informants is referenced in the Related Readings of Episode Fifteen.

EPISODE SEVEN 1974

J. P. B. Allen and H. G. Widdowson, 'Teaching the Communicative Use of English', *International Review of Applied Linguistics*, XII, 1, 1974, pp. 1–20.[1]

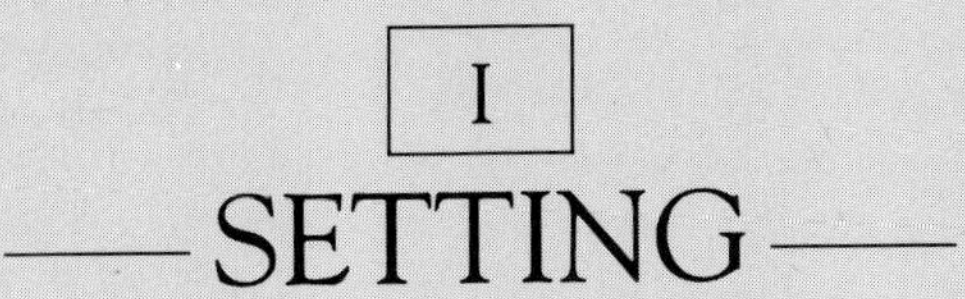

I SETTING

If there is a central Episode in this volume, it is this one. For one thing, the article introduces the thinking of Henry Widdowson, who has been the single most influential voice in the development of English for Science and Technology over the last fifteen years. It also offers comprehensive illustration and commentary on the first of the volumes in the *Focus* series, of which the two authors of this Episode were the general editors. 'Teaching the Communicative Use of English' thus sets the scene for a period lasting until about 1980 in which we saw the publication of considerable numbers of subject- and discipline-specific ESP textbooks. Thirdly, this Episode—and the following one—are, in many ways, a culmination of the first era of ESP. The first eight Episodes represent, for all the differences that have been noted between the positions of individual authors, a gathering consensus of what the teaching of scientific English should involve, of how investigations into the characteristics of scientific English might be conducted, of what appropriate teaching materials might look like, and of what sorts of methodology might be successful. However, as the later Episodes will demonstrate, the closing years of the decade saw the collapse of this consensus in the face of enterprising and experimental solutions to the problems presented by particular ESP situations. And the textbook publishers were, to some extent, trapped by their extensive forward planning: as they were lengthening their lists of subject-specific ESP textbooks, the rationale for their adoption was being increasingly undermined. The three key features of the Setting of this Episode will now be taken up in turn.

Some attempt to summarize and explain the position Henry Widdowson had reached by about the time this article was published is clearly necessary, because 'Teaching the Communicative Use of English' is part of an extended and evolving series of statements about EST that began with the publication of his Edinburgh Diploma in 1968. However, if I succeed in communicating something of the substance of his thinking at that time, I fear I will fall short of the stylistic elegance for which Widdowson is justly admired.

As a preliminary, it is well to recognize that Widdowson is essentially an applied linguist, although one with a considerable involvement in the advanced training of experienced EFL teachers and lecturers. Like Ewer, he is not an ESP practitioner as such. In that sense he shares academic interests with people like Barber, Lackstrom and Selinker, and has had a somewhat different professional life and somewhat different professional responsibilities to British Council Officers like Herbert and Higgins or ESP practitioners like Swales, Bates and Dudley-Evans. Further, Widdowson's views on applied linguistics are themselves important. In the Introduction to his Selected Papers, *Explorations in Applied Linguistics* (1979), he states, 'Applied Linguistics, as I conceive of it, is a spectrum of inquiry which extends from theoretical studies of language to classroom practice . . . considerations of theory are linked to pedagogic relevance and demonstrations of practical teaching procedures are linked to theoretical principles'. This firm commitment to the interpenetration of theory and practice (although, interestingly, not to experimental validation of either theoretical principles or practical teaching activities) is in turn related to a fairly consistent—and highly articulate—scepticism of the relevance of much of the work of theoretical linguists. In his seminal 1971 paper he quotes with approval the following observation made in 1970 by the distinguished American sociolinguist William Labov:—

> It is difficult to avoid the common-sense conclusion that the object of linguistics must ultimately be the instrument of communication used by the speech community; and if we are not talking about *that* language, there is something trivial in our proceeding.

Widdowson therefore does not accept that 'theoretical studies of language' should be confined to syntactic analysis of decontextualized single sentences, as in much of transformational grammar, but should be concerned with communication. In the early seventies Widdowson was also rejecting the traditional British approach to varieties of English. In Episode One and elsewhere we have seen the concept of a variety or 'register' of Scientific English, and we have seen that Barber, following Halliday, attempted to identify the formal (i.e. syntactic and lexical) characteristics of Scientific English. In order to see why Widdowson should take the position that register-based ESP materials can serve only some of the needs for which they are intended, it is now necessary to consider some of the binary distinctions for which he is particularly well known.

In the 1971 paper already referred to, he makes a distinction between the *usage* of language to exemplify linguistic categories and the *use* of language in the business of social communication. When the teacher says 'This is a chair' we have an instance of language *usage* because it exemplifies but does not communicate. 'This is a chair' is meaningful, but only because it indicates the *signification* of a linguistic item. In contrast, when the teacher says 'Come here' or 'Sit down' we have language *use* because what has been said has communicative *value*. A register approach is therefore concerned only with *usage*; if we analyse the grammatical and lexical features of samples of Scientific English we are treating those samples as exemplifications of the language system. We are treating the language as a *text* rather than as a *discourse*. It is only when we concern ourselves with the particular and different communicative purposes of those samples that we are concerned with *use* and *value*; and only then will we be conducting an analysis of *discourse* rather than a *textual* analysis. For Widdowson, as for Labov, the object of linguistic investigation must be how language operates as an 'instrument of communication'.

Having established the need to consider *use* as well as *usage* or linguistic form, Widdowson then needed to establish an approach to *use* that would be of benefit to students of English for Science and Technology. It seemed clear that rules of use would be something like rhetorical rules and could be identified via a study of the rhetorical functions of sentences in ways broadly similar to those adopted by Lackstrom, Selinker and Trimble in Episode Six. Towards the end of the 1971 paper, Widdowson suggests that such a rhetorical/functional approach is particularly suitable for the preparation of EST teaching materials; and he observes that 'scientific discourse can be seen as a set of rhetorical acts like giving instructions, defining, classifying, exemplifying, and so on, but the manner in which these acts are related one with the other and the manner in which they are linguistically realized may be restricted by accepted convention'. And, further, as Widdowson was to make clear in an article published the same year as 'Teaching the Communicative Use of English' the accepted conventions could well be considered as reflecting the standard modes of thought and practice adopted by scientists all over the world. 'We should think of "Scientific English" not as a kind of text, that is to say a variety of English defined in terms of its formal properties, but as a kind of discourse, that is to say a way of using English to realize universal notions associated with scientific inquiry.' Given that university students of science and engineering will already be familiar in their first language with how scientific communication is carried out, it follows that the EST teacher's task is to provide an alternative and *English* way of communicating the knowledge of science they already have, and to provide access to texts written in English but structured in terms of communicative units with which they are also familiar. The final stage of the argument belongs to the period after 1974, but we can note here that Widdowson will go on to argue for a methodology for teaching Scientific English that is modelled on standard methodologies for teaching science, for this will not only build further on the educational familiarities already stressed, but also integrate the science and language and so maintain a proper attention to *use*. Thus, the circle is complete.

I hope I have managed to convey something of the substance of Widdowson's impressive argumentation as it stood by about 1974. I also hope that I have succeeded in indicating that he was already achieving sufficient stature to be able to protect what he considered to be the correct application of linguistics to the teaching of EST from the rapidly-shifting interests and attitudes of linguistics itself—and by extension (and however unknowingly) offering encouragement to those ESP practitioners who themselves felt that academic linguists were not providing answers to the sort of questions that they had about the nature of Scientific English. In short, I hope that I have succeeded in identifying Henry Widdowson as something of a champion of the ESP profession (even if in the eighties he is reconsidering his position) because I would now like to make one or two observations that are not fully supportive of his basic orientation. First, although even in 1971 he was making observations like 'there are many ways of linking different acts to compose larger communicative units like, for example, a report or an exposition or a legal brief', he himself has left the investigation of the relationship between communicative purpose and the composition of larger communicative units to others; and this lack of interest in particular discourses within particular disciplines as opposed to discourse in general had perhaps unwelcome consequences for the *Focus* series.

A second criticism would be one that Henry Widdowson might be one of the first to accept—the binary distinctions, despite their very considerable importance for the development of a communicative approach to language teaching, are too black-and-white. There is much going on in contemporary English language classrooms that is neither pure *usage* ('I am now opening the window') or pure *use* ('open the window please—it's hot in here'). Widdowson, I think, might answer this objection by claiming that it is overall *intention* which is important. However, even here many experienced classroom teachers often intend to express and generate stretches of language that serve simultaneously as both *usage* and *use*.

More important, however, is the question of the universality of science. If Widdowson is right—and the question does seem an empirical one open to pragmatic investigation—then it seems to me that Widdowson's argument is ultimately contradictory. If scientific discourse is the same in every scientific speech community—if scientific textbooks, papers and lectures are organized on the same rhetorical principles in China, India, the USSR, Brazil and the United States—then the argument for paying particular attention to *use* rather than *usage* is decidedly undermined. If science and engineering students and researchers are acquainted with the universal rhetorical organization of the text-types in their discipline they are faced with a simple problem of *usage*, i.e. they are essentially faced with a problem of linguistic translation. Such non-native speakers of English do not apparently need to be taught how scientific textbooks, papers or lectures are constructed in English; all they need to be taught is the English language (the correct uses of English tenses etc) that will transform their first-language scripts into a foreign language. But is Widdowson right?

My own guess is that Widdowson's position may be valid as far as scientific research is concerned, but is probably untenable in terms of scientific education. ESP practitioners who have worked for several years in particular tertiary institutions around the world are often struck by the peculiarities of study modes, teaching styles and of general educational expectations within those particular institutions (as a reading of *ELT Documents 109* demonstrates). After all, the fact that a particular science textbook is used in a number of different institutions around the world by no means implies that it is used in the same way; its role and purpose may vary from being the revealed truth to that of an object of continued (and educationally valuable) criticism. If EST is largely concerned with teaching undergraduates in their first two years, then I think it would be difficult to argue that, as far as that clientele is concerned, their scientific activities are part of universal scientific culture, rather than being influenced by national, social, cultural, technical, educational and religious expectations and inspirations. However, there are paradoxical implications here. If Widdowson is wrong about the facts of scientific education, then the stress he puts on *communicative value* becomes more important, more relevant and more valuable rather than less so. This is because in cross-cultural situations we have again to take up the matter of 'teaching' in some way the rationale of scientific communication in English. On the other hand, we have to abandon Widdowson's hope of using a methodology based on the teaching of science in the first language because that is now recognized to be a local phenomenon.

The other two areas of useful background information I mentioned in the opening paragraph can be covered more quickly. First, the *English in Focus* series—and here the co-author of this *Episode*, Patrick Allen, comes into greater prominence, for he was not only the series editor with Henry Widdowson, but also played a major part in the writing of two of the volumes. There were nine volumes in all: *Physical Science* (1974), *Mechanical Engineering* (1973), *Workshop Practice* (1975), *Basic Medical Science* (1975), *Education* (1977), *Agriculture* (1977), *Social Science* (1978), *Biological Science* (1978), and *Electrical Engineering and Electronics* (1980).

Some of the principles underlying the series will have become clear from the preceding discussion of the academic writing of Professor Widdowson. In short, the series aims to exploit both the scientific knowledge of the learner and his or her first-language knowledge in an approach that engages the students' intellectual capacities and at the same time breaks with their past English language learning experience. The teaching material is designed to reveal the communicative character of scientific writing and therefore the *communicative value* of linguistic forms is to be stressed. As this aim can easily be obscured by the linguistic idiosyncracies of 'authentic' texts, the reading texts are simpler accounts which emphasize standard features of scientific discourse. The purpose of such reading work is 'to draw the reader's attention to the process by which a piece of language is interpreted as discourse' and not simply to test comprehension. Finally, the fact that scientific textbooks typically communicate by visual as well as verbal means is exploited to create challenging and communicative 'information transfer' exercises.

Despite its impressive theoretical underpinning, and the linguistic expertise and teaching experience of the individual authors, the *Focus* series itself has neither been a great critical nor a great commercial success. There was perhaps a certain rigidity in the format, particularly in the structuring of the Units and in the exercise types, that failed to take sufficient account of teachers' experience. It was only with the appearance of one of the last volumes, Ian Pearson's *Biological Sciences*, that the mould was broken to such an extent that the EST teacher gets an impression that the book has been designed from 'inside' the subject and from inside the teaching of the English of Biology. Perhaps it is not surprising that ESP practitioners producing revised versions of trialled materials have been able to translate pedagogical principle into pedagogical practice with greater success—and some indication of this is given in the next Episode.

One final point. Widdowson and Selinker were the principal architects of the framework of a rhetorical–communicative approach towards EST language learning (whatever debt may be owed to Wilkins's work on general notional syllabuses). But if the last two *Episodes* represent a communicative approach, it is certainly one that is articulated through a cognitive and teacher-directed methodology. Alternatives to this view of the learning environment will emerge.

II

TEXT AND COMMENTARY

Teaching the Communicative Use of English

by J. P. B. Allen, *University of Manitoba and*
H. G. Widdowson, *University of London Institute of Education*

1 Introduction

In recent years, English language teaching overseas has taken on a new character. Previously it was usual to talk about the aims of English learning in terms of the so-called 'language skills' of speaking, understanding speech, reading and writing, and these aims were seen as relating to general education at the primary and secondary levels. Recently, however, a need has arisen to specify the aims of English learning more precisely as the language has increasingly been required to take on an auxiliary role at the tertiary level of education. English teaching has been called upon to provide students with the basic ability to use the language to receive, and (to a lesser degree) to convey information associated with their specialist studies. This is particularly so in the developing countries where essential textbook material is not available in the vernacular languages. Thus whereas one talked previously in general terms of ELT, we now have such acronymic variants as ESP (English for Special Purposes) and EST (English for Science and Technology).

This association of English teaching with specialist areas of higher education has brought into prominence a serious neglect of the needs of intermediate and advanced learners. Most of the improvements in language teaching methodology brought about during the last two decades have concentrated on the elementary syllabus. The reason for this is fairly clear: in any attempt to improve language teaching materials the logical place to start is at the beginning. Moreover, this approach ensures that the problems of organizing language data are reduced to a minimum, since the course writer has a comparatively small number of words and structures to deal with in the early stages. The large amount of time and money that has been spent in developing elementary language teaching materials has produced impressive results, and a wide range of courses is now available to cater for the needs of students who are still in the process of acquiring a stock of basic vocabulary and simple grammatical structures. The teaching method which has proved most effective for this purpose contains two main ingredients: a step-by-step technique of structural grading, and a battery of intensive oral drills. Both features are based on the behaviourist doctrine that language learning consists primarily in establishing a set of habits, that is, a set of responses conditioned to occur with certain stimuli which may be either situations or words in a syntactic frame. Unfortunately, however, the generous provision of basic courses has coincided with a striking lack of new material specially designed for intermediate and advanced students. As a result, students who have become accustomed to an orderly progression of graded materials, simple explanations and easily-manipulated drills during the first two or three years of language learning find that these aids are suddenly withdrawn when they reach the end of the basic course, and that they are left to fend for themselves with little or no guidance at a time when the language is rapidly becoming more difficult. On the one hand we have an abundant supply of basic language courses, and on the other hand we have advanced teaching techniques (essay writing, report making, comprehension of complex reading material, etc.) designed for students who have a near-native *(a)* competence in handling the target language, but there are virtually no materials to help the learner effect an orderly transition between these two extremes.

The general English instruction which is provided in secondary schools has in most cases proved to be inadequate as a preparation for the use which students are required to make of the language when they enter higher education. In consequence, many technical institutions and universities in developing countries provide courses with titles like 'Functional English', 'Technical English' and 'Report Writing', the purpose of which is to repair the deficiencies of secondary school teaching. However, such courses seldom recognize that a different approach may be needed to match the essentially different role which English assumes in higher education. They continue to treat English as a subject in its own right. It is true that there is some recognition of the auxiliary role it now has to play in that the selection of grammatical structures and lexical items to be taught are those which are of most frequent occurrence in the specialist literature with which the students are concerned. But the emphasis is still squarely on separate grammatical structures and lexical items, and such courses do little more than provide
(b) exercises in the manipulation of linguistic forms. The approach to English teaching is basically the same as that of the schools, and the assumption seems to be that it is likely to be more effective only because it is practised more efficiently. In fact, there is little evidence that such
(c) remedial courses are any more effective than the courses which they are intended to rectify.

The purpose of this paper is to suggest that what is needed is a different orientation to English study and to outline an approach which departs from that which is generally taken. Broadly, what is involved is a shift of the focus of attention from the grammatical to the communicative properties of the language. We take the view that the difficulties which the students encounter arise not so much from a defective knowledge of the system of English, but from an unfamiliarity with English use, and that consequently their needs cannot be met by a course which simply provides further practice in the composition of sentences, but only by one which develops a knowledge of how sentences are used in the performance of different communicative acts. The approach which we wish to outline here, then, represents an attempt to move from an almost exclusive concern with grammatical forms to at least an equal concern with rhetorical functions.

One might usefully distinguish two kinds of ability which an English course at this level should aim at developing. The first is the ability to recognize how sentences are used in the performance of acts of communication, the ability to understand the rhetorical functioning of language in use. The second is the ability to recognize and manipulate the formal devices which are used to combine sentences to create continuous passages of prose. We might say that the first has to do with the rhetorical coherence of *discourse*, and the second with the grammatical cohesion of *text*. In practice, of course, one kind of ability merges with the other, but in the form and function approach we are presenting here we focus on each of them in turn, while at the same time allowing for peripheral overlap.

2 The Use of Language in Discourse

Language considered as communication no longer appears as a separate subject but as an aspect of other subjects. A corollary to this is that an essential part of any subject is the manner in which its 'content' is given linguistic expression. Learning science, for example, is seen to be not merely a matter of learning facts, but of learning how language is used to give expression to certain reasoning processes, how it is used to define, classify, generalize, to make hypotheses, draw conclusions and so on. People who talk about 'scientific English' usually give the

(a) A reader of the previous Episodes might well conclude that Allen & Widdowson's dismissal of earlier work in EST is exaggerated.

(b) The author of Episode Four (as one of several) might wish to dispute this.

(c) A good point. Educational success is rarely built directly on educational failure, but seems to require different strategies and approaches.

impression that it can be characterized in formal terms as revealing a high frequency of linguistic forms like the passive and the universal tense in association with a specialist vocabulary. But to characterize it in this way is to treat scientific discourse merely as exemplification of the language system, and does little or nothing to indicate what kind of communication it is.

The first principle of the approach we propose, then, is that the language should be presented in such a way as to reveal its character as communication. Let us consider how this principle might be put into practice. We will suppose that we are to design an English course for students of science in the first year of higher education.* We make two basic assumptions. Firstly, we assume that in spite of the shortcomings of secondary school English teaching the students have acquired considerable dormant competence in the manipulation of the language system. Secondly, we assume that they already have a knowledge of basic science. Hitherto, these two kinds of knowledge have existed in separation: our task is to relate them. We do this by composing passages on common topics in basic science and presenting them in such a way as to develop in the student an awareness of the ways in which the language system is used to express scientific facts and concepts. The passages are composed rather than derived directly from existing textbooks for two reasons. Firstly, we are able to avoid syntactic complexity and idiosyncratic features of style which would be likely to confuse students fresh from their experience of controlled and largely sentence-bound English instruction in schools, and/or deflect their attention from those features of use which we wish them to concentrate on. Our intention is to make linguistic forms as unobtrusive as possible. At the same time we wish to make their communicative function as obvious as possible, and this is the second reason for composing passages: we are able to 'foreground' features of language which have particular communicative value. It might be objected that the passages are not therefore representative of scientific writing. The answer to this is that they are representative of what we conceive to be certain basic communicative processes which underlie, and are variously realized in, individual
(d) pieces of scientific writing, and that they have been designed expressly to bring such processes more clearly into focus.

Each passage is provided with comprehension questions, but since we want to bring the student's attention to bear on his own reading activity as a process which involves a recognition of how language functions to convey information, the questions are not given at the end of the passage, as is the common practice, but are inserted into the passage itself. Furthermore, to ensure that the student is made aware of how the functioning of the language and his own understanding are related, solutions are provided for each comprehension question. These solutions are explanations in the sense that they make overt the kind of reasoning which underlies the ability to give the correct answer to the comprehension questions with which they are associated. Reasoning procedures such as are represented in these solutions might be said to be an essential element in any area of scientific enquiry, and their use here is intended to show the relevance of language to the study of science and to make appeal to the particular cognitive bent of science students.

The following is a sample of a passage composed and presented as described above. The sentences are numbered for ease of reference in the solutions, and in the exercises, which we shall discuss directly.

Matter and Volume

[1]Matter is the name given to everything which has weight and occupies space. [2]It may usually be detected by the senses of touch, sight or smell.

---

*The examples of teaching material which appear in this paper are from a draft version of *English in Physical Science*. The *English in Focus* Series is published by OUP.

(d) This interesting and persuasive justification for re-written texts has been put forward (with some variations) by Widdowson on a number of occasions. However, response has always been mixed, and in Episode Nine Phillips & Shettlesworth make a spirited defence of 'authentic' materials.

[3]Matter may exist in three states: solid, liquid and gas. [4]All substances, except those which decompose when heated, like wood, may be changed from one state into another. [5]A substance in the solid state may be changed into a liquid substance, and one in the liquid state may be changed into a gaseous substance. [6]Conversely, changes can take place in the reverse order: gases may be changed into liquids and liquids into solids. [7]A solid substance such as ice may be changed into the liquid state, or liquefied, to become water; and this may be changed into the gaseous state, or evaporated, to become steam. [8]Steam may also be converted into water and water into ice.

(a)	Matter can usually be seen, smelt or touched.
(b)	Matter can be seen, smelt and touched.
(c)	All substances can be changed from one state into another.
(d)	A liquid can be changed either into a gas or into a solid.

SOLUTIONS

(a) may = can
may usually be detected by the senses of touch, sight or smell. (2)
= can usually be touched, seen or smelt.

∴ | Matter can usually be seen, smelt or touched. |

(b) touched, seen or smelt.
= *either* touched *or* seen *or* smelt.
i.e. Some matter can be seen but not touched (e.g. visible gases)
Some matter can be smelt but not seen (e.g. some invisible gases), etc.
Matter can be seen, smelt and touched.
= *All* matter can be seen *and* smelt *and* touched.
∴ *It is NOT TRUE that matter can be seen, smelt and touched.*

(c) All substances, *except those which decompose when heated*, may be changed from one state to another. (4)
∴ Some substances cannot (= may not) change from one state to another.
∴ *It is NOT TRUE that all substances can be changed from one state to another.*

(d) A substance in the liquid state may be changed into a gaseous substance. (5)
i.e. A liquid can be changed into a gas.
Gases may be changed into liquids and liquids [may be changed] into solids. (6)

∴ | A liquid can be changed *either* into a gas or into a solid. |

The purpose of the comprehension 'check' questions and the solutions is to draw the reader's attention to the process by which a piece of language is interpreted as discourse. The notes are meant to relate surface language forms to logical operations, and so to point to their communicative function in the passage concerned. It is likely that the student will know the meanings of such forms as elements of the language code: this kind of meaning, which we will call *signification*, can be exemplified by isolated sentences and is usually learned by pattern practice. What the student is less likely to recognize is the *value* which such items take on in utterances occurring within a context of discourse. For example, in the case of the passage just quoted, the student may know the signification of items like the articles, the quantifier *all* and the adverb *usually*. What the comprehension questions and solutions are intended to draw out is the value such terms have in the making of statements of different kinds: generalizations, qualifications and so on, which set up implicational relations with other parts of the discourse. When a qualification is signalled by the use of *usually*, for example, we need to recognize not only that the sentence in itself has a particular rhetorical value, but also that it has a rhetorical relation with preceding and succeeding sentences. *(e)*

This focus on communicative value is also a feature of the exercises which follow the notes. The first of these draws the student's attention to anaphoric devices. Such devices, of course, are capable of a very wide range of values. The so-called 'demonstrative pronouns' *this* and *these*, for example, are generally given an 'ostensive' signification which associates them with singular and plural noun phrases: in the early lessons of an English course they occur in sentences such as 'This is a book' 'These are books' and as pro-forms they usually make no further appearance in the course. In actual discourse, however, it is not always easy to recognize which noun phrase, or phrases, such pro-forms are to be related to since they do not appear in neat equative sentences such as are presented in the early English lessons. The reader has to select the appropriate value from a number of alternatives, all of which are grammatically possible. Furthermore, it commonly happens that *this* does not relate to a noun phrase at all, but to some superordinate notion which is not given overt expression as such in the course. Thus, it may take on the value 'the fact X', 'the set of facts X, Y, Z', 'the idea X', 'the set of ideas X, Y, Z', 'the argument X', 'the set of arguments X, Y, Z' and so on, where X, Y, Z are elements in the preceding discourse. To recognize the value of *this* in such cases the reader has to understand the communicative intention expressed through the choice of particular surface forms.

The passage cited above would be an early one in the course we have in mind and so contains no instance of the use of *this* to refer to a superordinate notion. It is better to lead up to the 'superordinate' use of *this* by getting the student to recognize first the simpler operations of anaphora. One way of doing this (where *this* = 'the ability to recognize the simpler operations of anaphora'!) is by drawing the student's attention directly to features of anaphora in the passage by means of an exercise of the following kind: *(f)*

EXERCISE A: PRONOUN REFERENCE

1 In sentence 2, *It refers* to:
   (a) Weight
   (b) Space
   (c) Matter

2 In sentence 5, *one* refers to:
   (a) A substance
   (b) A substance in the solid state
   (c) A liquid substance

3 In sentence 7, *this* refers to:
   (a) A solid substance
   (b) Water
   (c) Ice

(e) It may also, of course, relate to the world of knowledge outside the text. In this case, for instance, the text does not give an example of a substance that *cannot* be detected by the senses (such as oxygen as a gas). The authors tend to ignore opportunities to get the students to *think about* the reading passages in this kind of way.

(f) This kind of exercise was an important innovation and has become a regular part of many ESP reading courses. We still lack, however, hard evidence that anaphoric reference is a foreign language learning problem (see Activity 1 of Episode Two). Certainly at times, native speakers are uncertain about pronoun references, thus suggesting that the real problem lies sometimes in the ambiguity of the text. The reference to the 'superordinate' use of *this* is also interesting, especially as academic and expository texts can have a surprising number of sentences that begin with **this** + *Noun Phrase* (as in note *(d)* above). And what is particularly interesting is the superordinate nouns for these are often precisely the vocabulary items that cause learners difficulty. If we refer back to *(d)* again we can see that I might have written any of the following, and the advantages and disadvantages of each are complex:

This . . . justification for . . .
argument for . . .
defence of . . .
support for . . .

Another difficulty which learners have in understanding discourse is in recognizing when different expressions have equivalent contextual value. Learners may have their attention drawn to the way different forms function as expressions in a particular passage by means of an exercise of the following kind:

EXERCISE B: REPHRASING

Replace the expressions in italics in the following sentences with expressions from the text which have the same meaning.

1 A *substance in the solid state* may be changed into *a liquid substance.*
2 *Gases* may be changed into *liquids* and *liquids* may be changed into *solids*.
3 A solid may be *changed into the liquid state*.
4 A liquid may be *changed* into a gas.

So far we have been principally concerned with getting the learner to recognize the communicative value of expressions which correspond with sentence constituents. We may now introduce exercises which focus on the way sentences themselves function as communicative acts within the discourse. Our interest now is in the illocutionary force of the sentences which are used. (Austin, 1962; Searle, 1969). We want to get the learner to see that understanding a passage of English involves the recognition of what illocutionary acts are performed in it. One way of doing this is to ask him to insert expressions into the sentences of the passage which make explicit what their illocutionary function is. Thus in a sentence which is being used as an illustrative statement, *for example* can be inserted; in one which serves as a classification, one can insert the performative verb *classify*, and so on. An exercise of this kind based on the passage given might be as follows:

EXERCISE C: RELATIONSHIPS BETWEEN STATEMENTS

Place the following expressions in the sentences indicated. Replace and re-order the words in the sentence where necessary:

(a) can be defined as (1)
(b) for example (4)
(c) thus (5)
(d) also (6)
(e) thus (6)
(f) for example (7)
(g) then (7)
(h) conversely (8);

The three types of exercise which have been proposed are graded in the sense that they are designed to make increasing demands on the learner's own writing ability. Exercise A, like the comprehension check questions, involves no writing at all. Exercise B is a simple copying exercise, the purpose of which is to reinforce the reader's perception of certain discourse functions. Exercise C requires the reader to use his knowledge of the language productively: he has to insert the given expressions in the correct places and to make structural alterations where
(g) necessary in the sentences concerned. This grading is intended to effect a gradual transfer from receptive awareness to productive ability.

We may now continue to provide writing practice based on the reading passage. But we wish to do this not as a meaningless manipulation of sentence patterns, but as a use of English in the performance of different communicative acts relevant to the learner's special subject of study. We want to preserve the rhetorical orientation we have adopted, and keep the learner's

(g) Teachers of *English in Focus* have often found Exercise C very 'bitty' and somewhat laborious. Many teachers prefer to get their students to insert the explicit markers in a more open way and without telling them what to put in each sentence.

attention focused on language in use. In Exercise C our purpose was to get the learner to make acts like defining and illustrating explicit. Now we want to get him to perform such acts himself. This might be brought about by an exercise of the following kind, which combines control with the sort of scope for mental activity which might be expected to appeal to the kind of learner we are concerned with, and which brings the language being learnt into close association with the subject for which it serves as medium. The exercise is based on the continuation of the reading passage quoted above, which provides the information necessary to complete the diagram.

EXERCISE D: STATEMENTS BASED ON DIAGRAMS

1 Write out a complete version of the following diagram by filling in the spaces.

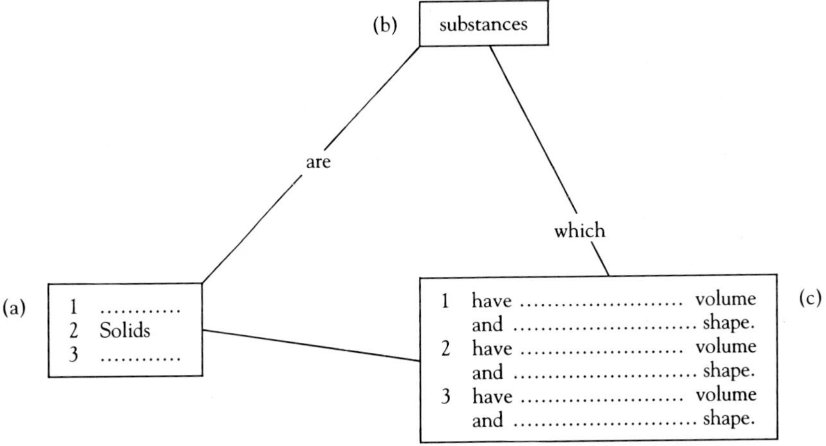

2 Use the completed diagram to:

(i) Write definitions, by using boxes (a), (b) and (c)
EXAMPLE: Solids are substances which have a definite volume and a definite shape.

(ii) Write *generalizations*, by using boxes (a) and (c)
EXAMPLE: Solids have a definite volume and a definite shape.

Exercise D reflects the importance we attach to the presentation of language as an essential aspect of the scientific subject which the learner is studying. The purpose of the approach we are illustrating here is to get the learner to recognize how the language and 'subject matter', commonly considered in isolation, are interrelated in acts of communication. We may promote (h) this purpose further by following up Exercise D with exercises which present a problem requiring reference to knowledge of both language and of 'subject matter' for its solution. One might, for example, get the learner to produce definitions and generalizations relating to another content area by asking him first to reduce the essential information to tabular form. Again, one could get him to draw a simple diagram of a machine, or a flow-chart of a process as a preliminary to providing a verbal description. Given any scientific or technical field, it is not difficult to think of relevant problems which would serve to integrate the student's knowledge of language and 'subject matter', and which would be a logical extension of exercises based on reading passages.

So far our business has been to draw the attention of the learner to the way English is used to communicate. We have been concerned with rhetorical function, although this has naturally

(h) It is up to the teacher to decide whether the students can also produce their own definitions outside the tight content frame.

involved consideration of the formal operation of language. We now shift our emphasis from discourse to text, and focus on the formal properties of language in use. We assume, of course, that the previous exercises will have provided the learners with a meaningful communicative framework to which they will relate their learning of the way language forms combine in the composition of texts.

3 The Use of Language in Text

In considering the formal properties of language in use, we must first decide on what attitude to adopt to the teaching of grammar. What factors do we have to take into consideration in designing a model of grammar for advanced or remedial language teaching? We may assume, firstly, that a pedagogic grammar for advanced learners must provide the student with fresh and stimulating material. As was suggested earlier in this paper, there is no point in presenting a remedial English class at the University level with a speeded-up version of the secondary school syllabus, for the class will rapidly become bored and resentful even if they show evidence of not having fully mastered the material. The rejection by students of the rapid repeat technique of remedial teaching is a familiar experience in higher education, and should occasion no surprise. Not only do advanced learners have a natural reluctance to cover familiar ground for the second or third time, they have, in fact, reached a stage in their studies when they may no longer be able to benefit from the oral, inductive type of teaching employed at a more elementary level. As was pointed out earlier, it is this fact that prompts us to propose an approach which gives recognition to the real needs of advanced students. It must be stressed that the task for the advanced learner is not simply to experience more language material, but to develop a complex set of organizational skills over and above those which he needed to cope with the elementary syllabus, and to learn to put these to use in serving a variety of communicative purposes. One difference between elementary and advanced courses lies in the fact that students at an advanced level have had a good deal of instruction in grammar and, as was suggested earlier, are likely to possess considerable dormant competence in English. It follows that one of the principal aims of advanced language teaching should be to activate this competence, and to extend it, by leading the student to relate his previously acquired linguistic knowledge to meaningful realizations of the language system in passages of immediate relevance to his professional interests or specialized field of studies.

A second consideration is that the information in a pedagogic grammar must be relevant to a learner's needs. In order to ensure this we must insist on a clear distinction between linguistic and pedagogic grammars. A linguistic grammar is concerned with a specification of the formal properties of a language, while the purpose of a pedagogic grammar is to help a learner acquire a practical mastery of a language. There is no reason for supposing that the two types of statement
(i) will bear any overt resemblance to one another. It is particularly important that this principle should be clearly stated at a time when many teachers and textbook writers are turning to linguistics as a source of ideas about how to handle language in the classroom. In general, we expect that a knowledge of linguistic grammars will provide teachers with pedagogically useful insights into language structure, but we do not expect that the content of a linguistic grammar will be reflected in any direct or systematic way in a pedagogic grammar based on it. A further principle is that pedagogic grammars are typically eclectic. By this we mean that the applied linguist must pick and choose among formal statements in the light of his experience as a teacher, and decide what are pedagogically the most appropriate ways of arranging the information that he derives from linguistic grammars. Thus, we expect that the insights incorporated in a pedagogic grammar will be drawn from a number of linguistic models, and that the teaching materials will be judged solely in terms of whether or not they promote quick and efficient learning in the student.

As already stated, we assume that the students have some knowledge of how the language works, which derives from pedagogic grammar. We also assume that this knowledge will be

(i) This paragraph is a nice example of the 'detached stance' towards linguistics referred to in the Setting.

consolidated as the students experience language used in meaningful contexts. For these reasons we have not attempted to provide a detailed review of English grammar. Instead, the grammar exercises are designed to focus on points which are particularly important in scientific writing, especially those which may represent continuing 'trouble spots' for many students. Wherever possible we aim to avoid the more mechanical types of substitution drill. The whole approach we adopt in this paper is based on the assumption that the students will be people whose minds are directed towards rational thought and problem-solving, and the grammar exercises are designed to take this fact into account. Wherever possible, we have here, as elsewhere, used exercises which we hope will require the same kind of thinking that science students would naturally be engaged in as part of their specialist studies. The following examples show how we have attempted to provide grammar practice in a meaningful way, and without losing sight of the natural communicative use of language.

EXERCISE E: DEFINITIONS IN SCIENTIFIC DISCOURSE

Definitions in scientific discourse often take the following forms:

(a) A {is/are | may be defined as} B which C

E.g. A thermometer *is* an instrument *which* is used for measuring temperatures.
A thermometer *may be defined as* an instrument *which* is used for measuring temperatures.

(b) B which C {is/are called | is/are known as} A

E.g. An instrument *which* is used for measuring temperatures *is called* a thermometer.
An instrument *which* is used for measuring temperatures *is known as* a thermometer.

Expand the following into full definitions. Write each sentence twice, using any of the
(j) patterns illustrated above.

1 Metamorphosis/the physical transformation/is undergone by various animals during development after the embryonic state.
1 Metals/the class of chemical elements/are characterized by ductility, malleability, lustre and conductivity.

EXERCISE F: FORMATION OF THE IMPERSONAL PASSIVE

Write down the passive version of all the active sentences. Then combine the passive sentences, following the clues provided in the box.

Active: we may show the expansion of a gas
Passive: the expansion of a gas ....
Active: we heat the gas
Passive: the gas ....
Active: we demonstrate an apparatus in Figure 41
Passive: an apparatus .... in Figure 41

The expansion of a gas when it .... may .... by the apparatus in Figure 41

(j) I have argued elsewhere that (a) and (b) type definitions may well have the same *signification* but equally they may well have different communicative *value*. If this is so, then students need to appreciate this and should not be asked to produce (a) and (b) versions as if they were the same. Indeed, as far as I can see, students will need to produce the (b) type only very rarely, although both types will occur in their reading.

(k) (i) Rewrite the sentences, selecting one of the time expressions and putting it at the beginning of the sentence. The time expression you select should be the one which corresponds most closely to the meaning of the words in italics, which should be omitted.

1 The water vapour condenses to water *as a result* it is able to fall downwards as rain or snow (when, before).

2 The aluminium is in the measuring cylinder *during this time* we may measure the volume of water displaced (as soon as, while)

3 *First* the water is forced out of the ballast tanks by compressed air *before this* the submarine is not able to rise to the surface (until, when)

(ii) Compare the following sentences with your answer in Part (i). If the sentences have approximately the same meaning, put a tick in the box; if not, put a cross.

1 Water vapour can fall as rain or snow but the vapour must condense to water first. ☐

2 A volume of water is displaced and as a result we can put the aluminium in the measuring cylinder. ☐

3 A submarine is not able to rise to the surface while the ballast tanks are full of water. ☐

It may seem to some that exercises based on a surface structure approach constitute a return to outmoded principles. There is an important issue at stake here, which we touched on earlier in our discussion of the distinction between linguistics and pedagogic grammars. A number of recent publications have shown a tendency to assume that the latest developments in linguistic theory should at all costs be reflected in language teaching materials. But it is not always the latest linguistic model which provides the most satisfactory basis for the preparation of teaching materials. For example, the relevant treatment of transformations for our purpose appears to be that of Zellig Harris rather than Chomsky. For Harris, transformational analysis is a logical extension of constituent analysis, and is based on the same criteria of form and distribution.
(l) Transformations are set up formally as a relation between text-sentences, and not in the form of instructions for generating sentences, as in Chomsky's theory. A pedagogically useful consequence is that we can distinguish well-established transformations from those which are barely acceptable or used only in particular linguistic environments. Moreover, Harris's transformational rules are relevant to the notion of communicative competence, and therefore seem to be a more suitable basis for teaching material than Chomsky's transformations, which operate without reference to context.

4 Methods of Teaching the Writing Skill

In the classroom it is not always easy to devise situations which call for genuine written communication, so that students can express themselves in a natural way in response to a real need. One method of making writing meaningful is to get the learner to 'talk to himself' on paper. This approach, generally known as 'creative writing' has been widely advocated in L_1 teaching situations as a substitute for formal essays which fail because the task is boring and artificial. Creative writing clearly has a general educational value, but its usefulness is limited in that it tends to produce an intensely personal style, in fact a type of literature, which has little or no social function. Advocates of this approach believe that the skill developed in creative writing carries over into institutional writing without the need for further instruction, but this claim is not substantiated by the evidence so far available. On the face of it, it seems unlikely that a student who has been encouraged to express himself through the medium of prose poems

(k) As so often in ESP materials, the instructions to the students have a tendency towards complexity.

(l) The study of the relations between sentences has now advanced well beyond Harris's work in the late fifties, and the reader today need not concern himself with this discussion.

will be able to turn his hand readily to the production of business correspondence or an academic treatise, without some explicit instruction in the conventions which govern these particular styles of writing. A second limitation is that the creative writing approach is restricted to an L_1 learning situation. If an L_2 student wishes to express himself 'creatively' he will normally turn to his mother tongue. He needs the target language in order to read textbooks, write summaries and reports, and participate in routine professional or social conversations, all of which are examples of the institutional use of language, which require a mastery of the appropriate conventions.

A variation of the creative writing approach is found in many American textbooks designed for use with freshman composition classes. These books devote much space to the discussion of such traditional principles of rhetoric as coherence, unity and emphasis, the classical structure of the oration and an analysis of the various types of discourse (exposition, argument, description, narration, etc.). The authors of some composition handbooks include the rudiments of formal logic, in the belief that patterns of proof can be used as an aid in the organization of paragraphs and in checking for weak points in an argument once it has been written. Such books are based on the assumption that it helps a learner if he understands the potentialities of written language and is familiar with some of the rhetorical devices that fluent writers habitually use. However, it is doubtful whether an *analysis* of other people's writing can in itself produce fluent writers. What the learner needs, especially in an L_2 situation, is a form of exercise which will help him to achieve a *synthesis* of many disparate grammatical and lexical elements in the form of a coherent composition of his own. One problem in achieving this type of synthesis in the classroom is to find the right combination of freedom and control: enough control to ensure that the student's composition does not degenerate into a mass of mistakes,
(m) and enough freedom for the student to exercise his own judgment and thereby to learn something instead of merely copying. Various attempts have been made to provide guided practice developing into free composition. The materials available fall into four main categories, and we will examine a representative example from each category.

SUBSTITUTION IN FRAMES

Example: K. W. Moody (1966). Moody's frames are akin to the familiar substitution table in which interchangeable elements are grouped in columns, but whereas most substitution tables represent the structure of a single sentence, in this case the frames are arranged in a series, so that a succession of choice from left to right will result in a paragraph, letter or short composition. The selection of alternatives is not entirely automatic; the structural patterns are fixed but the choice of lexical items is determined by the student. When he begins this series of exercises the student does not have to worry about the choice of grammatical patterns or the way in which sentences interrelate, but he has to think about the meaning of what he is writing and he must ensure that his lexical choices produce a composition that makes sense. The exercises are arranged in four stages to give the student progressively more freedom of choice. At the first stage the sets of alternatives in the frames are written out in full, and the student's problem is mainly one of lexical collocation. Each exercise at Stage 1 is matched with a Stage 2 exercise in which the frame is repeated but with a number of blanks. The purpose of this is to give the learner some opportunity of using his own choice of words, once he has achieved control over the structural patterns of the paragraph. At Stage 3 the student has even more freedom of choice, since only a few words are retained from the original frame. At Stage 4 he is asked to write a paragraph of his own, along the lines suggested by the earlier exercises, but without the frame to guide him. At the final stage, therefore, the student has a free choice of words and structures, but he has been led into free composition gradually and he should retain a clear idea of the paragraph outline from earlier stages of the practice.

(m) A very useful discussion of teaching writing and we can perhaps carry forward the authors' remarks about 'the mastery of the appropriate conventions' and about the difficulty of balancing *freedom* and *control*.

SAMPLE COMPOSITION WITH SELECTIVE STRUCTURE PRACTICE

Example: T. C. Jupp and John Milne (1968). As in the case of Moody, the aim is to provide students who are learning composition writing with detailed guidance in language and subject matter, but at the same time to leave them with the opportunity for personal expression. With this second approach, however, the element of control is more relaxed and the student is encouraged to make his own selection of words and structures throughout the practice. The Jupp and Milne sequence is arranged in four stages. Stage 1 consists of a statement of the subject of the composition, e.g.: 'Write about a very important examination, interview or meeting which you once went to. Carefully describe your feelings and thoughts, and say what happened.' Stage 2 consists of oral and written structure practice, the aim of which is to make students proficient in the use of those structures which he is likely to need in order to write about the set topic. A few new patterns are introduced in each unit, but most of the structure practice consists of a revision of patterns which have been previously learned. It is a feature of this material that the structures practised are grouped according to topic rather than being determined by an abstract linguistic scheme of grading. At Stage 3, having been well primed by class discussion and by structure drills, the student reads a sample composition in which the set topic is handled in a context familiar to the authors (in this case, an account of an entrance examination at Cambridge). The structures that the students have been practising are exemplified in the sample composition. Finally, at Stage 4, the student is instructed to (a) write down some sentences from the structure practice; (b) carefully re-read the sample composition, noting examples of relevant structures; (c) write a composition of his own, referring if necessary to the sample composition and making sure that he uses examples of the practised structures; (d) give the finished composition to a friend to read.

MODIFICATION OF MODEL PARAGRAPHS

Example: Dykstra, Port and Port (1966). These materials consist of a collection of 42 passages all concerned with the adventures of Ananse the spider, a character in West African folklore. Using these passages as a basis, the student is required to perform a series of operations, including structural modification and lexical insertion, in a series of graduated steps, beginning with relatively mechanical operations and proceeding as quickly as possible to the most advanced steps, which represent free creative composition. The materials are arranged in such a way that they represent a roughly programmed course which can be useful to students who have attained different levels of control over writing in English. The following instructions, all quoted from the text, show the types of activity involved. The numbers indicate grading in difficulty on a scale 1–58. The operations listed can be performed on any of 42 passages, and usually more than one operation is performed on a single passage.

1 Copy the passage.
4 Rewrite the entire passage changing *Ananse* to *the spiders*. Change the pronouns where necessary.
14 Rewrite the entire passage in the active voice.
36 Rewrite the entire passage adding adjective clauses beginning with *who*, *which* or *that* after the following words: *young man*, *mother*, *village*, etc.
58 Create a folktale of your own about Ananse the spider. Use between 100 and 150 words in your tale.

The three types of guided composition exercise summarized above are all based on the notion of parallel texts. This approach is successful so long as the student's writing is restricted to short letters, folktales, personal histories or other stereotyped formulas. However, the parallel text approach tends to break down if the student has to handle scientific subjects, since in this type
(n) of writing the arguments are highly specific and each text must be regarded as unique. The

(n) The reasons for the rejection of the parallel text approach come as a considerable surprise. After all, Allen and Widdowson have been talking of the conventions and the routines of scientific writing. Certainly in the types of writing first-year students might be engaged in, such as reports of laboratory experiments, to claim that 'the arguments are highly specific and each text must be regarded as unique' seems decidedly far-fetched.

guided composition method discussed below involves the intensive study of a single text, and is suitable for use in the context of scientific writing where parallel texts are difficult to devise.

GUIDED PARAGRAPH BUILDING

The exercise is done in four stages. At the first stage the student examines various groups of words and combines each group into a sentence by following the clues provided. Some sentences are easy to write, some are more difficult; this reflects the situation in actual writing, where simple sentences alternate with more complex structures according to the nature of the message the writer wishes to convey. At the second stage the student creates a coherent paragraph by rewriting the sentences in a logical order, adding various 'transitional' features where necessary. Thirdly, the student checks his work against a version of the paragraph incorporated into a free reading passage elsewhere in the book. The paragraph writing is designed to allow some scope for the student to exercise his own judgment, so there is no reason why the student's version should be identical to the one in the book. If the paragraphs differ, the student should try to evaluate the relative merits of the two versions. At the fourth stage the student writes the paragraph again in a free style of his own devising, based on a set of notes which are similar to the rough jottings made by an author when he is sketching out a plan for a paragraph. Thus the student is led by stages to the point where he should be able to write a paragraph of his own, in a way which seeks to imitate some of the processes of real-life composition.

The following paragraph writing exercise illustrates this procedure.

A Join each of the groups of words below into one sentence, using the additional material in the box. Words in italics should be omitted. Number your sentences and begin each one with a capital letter.

1 an acid will *affect* litmus
an acid will react with washing soda
it will give off carbon dioxide

turn/red/and/it/,/giving

2 the metal disappears
hydrogen is liberated

and

3 one class of basis *is* called alkalis
they will dissolve in water
they will form solutions
they will *affect* red litmus

special/,/,/and/which/turn/blue

4 an acid is a compound
it will attack some metals
it will liberate hydrogen
magnesium is dissolved in it

containing hydrogen/which/and/when

5 alkalis form solutions
they feel soapy
they will dissolve substances
they are used in various cleaning processes

which/and which/oily and greasy/,/and for this reason/frequently

6 acids *burn* substances
wood paper cloth human skin

have a burning effect on/like/,/,/and

B Create a coherent paragraph by rewriting the eleven sentences in a logical order.* Before you write the paragraph, add the following material to the sentences.

2 in the latter case 6 a further characteristic of acids is that they

C When you have written your paragraph, re-read it and make sure that the sentences are presented in a logical order. Give the paragraph a suitable title. Check with the version given in the back of the book and correct if necessary. (It is possible to write this paragraph in more than one way.)

D Read through the paragraph again. Make sure you know all the words, using a dictionary if necessary. Without referring to your previous work rewrite the paragraph using the following clues:

compounds – divided – acids – bases – salts
acid – compound of hydrogen – attack metals – liberate hydrogen – magnesium dissolved
acid – litmus red – washing soda – carbon dioxide
burn substances – wood, paper, etc.
base – oxides, hydroxides – neutralize acids – salt-like substances
alkalis – solutions – soapy – dissolve oil – grease – cleaning
salt – product, acid neutralized – metal dissolved
metal disappears – hydrogen liberated
salt – substance – metal takes place of hydrogen

5 Conclusion

In this paper we have suggested an approach to the teaching of English which recognizes that the acquisition of receptive and productive knowledge of a language must involve the learning of rules of use as well as rules of grammar. Many students who enter higher education have had experience only of the latter and are consequently unable to deal with English when it is used in the normal process of communication. What we have attempted to do is to show how rules of use might be taught, both those which have to do with the communicative properties of discourse and those which have to do with the formal properties of texts. We make no claim that the kind of exercises which we have illustrated here are in any sense definitive: other, and no doubt more effective, exercises might be devised. We believe, however, that such exercises should take into account the needs of the students and the nature of the abilities which must be developed to meet them, and be related therefore to the kind of theoretical considerations within the context of which we have placed the exercises presented here. There are signs that

* Five groups of words have been omitted.

linguists are now turning their attention to the communicative properties of language and the functioning of language in social contexts. We have said that it is a mistake for the language teacher to assume that he must automatically adjust his pedagogy to conform to the latest linguistic fashion, but in this case it is necessary for the language teacher to emulate the linguist by considering communicative functions as well as, and in relation to, linguistic forms. Such a (o) shift in focus is warranted not by the practice of the linguist but by the essential needs of the language learner.

References

Austin, J. L., *How to Do Things with Words*, Oxford: The Clarendon Press, 1962.

Dykstra, G., Port, R. and Port, A., *A Course in Controlled Composition: Ananse Tales*, New York: Teachers College Press, 1966.

Jupp, T. C. and Milne, J., *Guided Course in English Composition*, London: Heinemann, 1968.

Moody, K. W., *Written English Under Control*, Ibadan: Oxford University Press, 1966.

Searle, J. R., *Speech Acts*, Cambridge: Cambridge University Press, 1969.

(o) The concluding paragraph will serve as an excellent example of the logical and literary qualities of Allen and Widdowson's prose.

III — ACTIVITIES —

(1) Look again at the *Matter and Volume* passage and associated exercises.

- *(a)* List the features of Scientific English that you think are 'foregrounded' in the passage.
- *(b)* What do the authors consider to be the 'difficulties' of this passage?
- *(c)* Are their views the same as those in Episode Six?

(2) What objections can you make to Allen and Widdowson's view on 'authentic' passages?

(3) Work carefully through the four stages of *Guided Paragraph Building.*

- *(a)* Attempt D.
- *(b)* Consider this quotation from the article:—

  Our problem in achieving this type of synthesis in the classroom is to find the right combination of freedom and control: enough control to ensure that the student's composition does not degenerate into a mass of mistakes, and enough freedom for the student to exercise his own judgment and thereby to learn something instead of merely copying.

  Do you consider that Allen and Widdowson have found the right combination? (Bearing in mind that the work quoted is taken from Unit 1 of the textbook.)
- *(c)* How is the approach to writing in Episodes Four and Seven similar and different?

IV — EVALUATION —

(1) 'The theory is exciting but the application of that theory is disappointing.' Do you consider this an over-critical evaluation?

(2) The article is entitled *Teaching the Communicative Use of English.* How far do you think Allen and Widdowson's proposals achieve such teaching?

V

RELATED READINGS

Reference has already been made to *Explorations in Applied Linguistics* (see Episode One/V for bibliographical details), so there is no need to re-emphasize its relevance here.

With regard to the debate on *specific* versus *general* study and research habits, the most accessible source of opinion is *ELT Documents 109 – Study Modes and Academic Development of Overseas Students*, The British Council, London, 1980. One of the aims of the volume is to investigate similarities and differences between educational arrangements and learning styles in various countries on the one hand and in the United Kingdom on the other, and to evaluate the practical problems that any such differences can present. It is worth noting that of the four papers offering specific cultural profiles three tend towards the position that cross-cultural differences are profound, whereas one (Roger Bowers on the Indian subcontinent) admits to only essentially superficial differences.

I know of two reviews of *English in Physical Science*. One is fairly critical (Phil Skeldon—*ESPMENA* 4, 1976) (see Episode Ten); the other by Michael Long (*Language Learning* 28, 2, 1978) is guardedly approving. The latter ends 'Although EPS is occasionally frustrating in its failure to exploit its own imaginative ideas, it is still a considerable improvement over most ESL reading texts, and there is no reason why other more general reading comprehension materials for ESL students should not profit from the original contributions it makes to this area of applied linguistics'.

EPISODE EIGHT 1976

Martin Bates and Tony Dudley-Evans, *Nucleus General Science* (pp. 67–73), Longman, London, 1976.

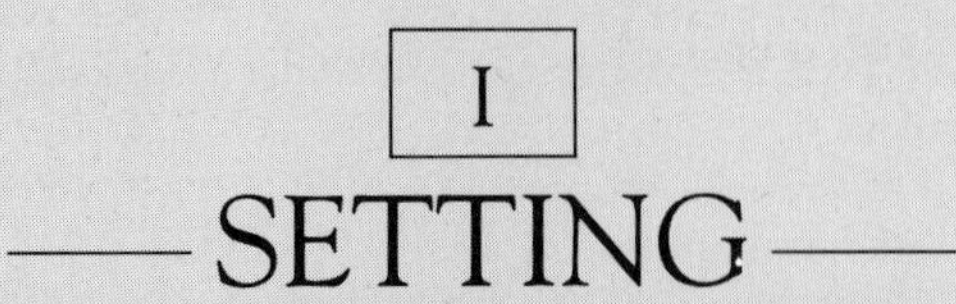

I — SETTING —

Less than two years after Oxford University Press had launched the *English in Focus* series, Longman, its great rival in British EFL publishing, introduced the *Nucleus* series. Like *Focus*, there were two general editors and these editors were also the authors of the first volume. However, the first volume of the *Nucleus* series (General Science) had a different relationship to its successors than in the case of *Focus*. *General Science* was an introductory 'core' course designed to introduce students to the main ways in which essential scientific concepts are expressed in general scientific English. The later volumes in the series were more specific (and a little less introductory) and applied the same scientific concepts to different branches of science and technology. In the four years after the appearance of *General Science* in 1976, six titles appeared: *Biology*, *Engineering*, *Geology*, *Nursing Science*, *Mathematics* and *Medicine*. Two more are promised (*Agriculture* and *Architecture and Building Science*) but at the time of writing have not yet been published.

All the volumes have a basic 12-unit structure (plus three shorter revision units) and all follow the same concept-based syllabus. The extract following this introduction is the first half of Unit 8 of *General Science*. The Unit is entitled *Process 3 Cause and Effect*. The seven preceding Unit headings of this volume (and of all the others) are as follows:

Unit 1 Properties and Shapes
Unit 2 Location
Unit 3 Structure
Unit 4 Measurement 1
Unit 5 Process 1 Function and Ability
Unit 6 Process 2 Actions in Sequence
Unit 7 Measurement 2 Quality

Thus it was that Bates and Dudley-Evans opted for a concept-driven syllabus design, whereas Allen and Widdowson structured the textbooks in their series along rhetorical–functional lines. Given that both parties had the same communicative orientation towards the teaching of ELT, we now need to consider why the two major series of ESP textbooks differ in their basic structure and organization.

One possible line of exploration would be the fact that the *Nucleus* series originated at the University of Tabriz (now Azerabadegan) in north-west Iran, and that the published volume owed much to the educational environment that shaped the original classroom materials. Of that environment it is now only necessary to observe that:—

(a) the standard of English at entry was rather low;
(b) the medium of instruction at the University was rarely English;
(c) students could rarely cope with their English-medium textbooks and, as a consequence, their main method of study was to memorize the lecturers' handouts.

Even from this extremely sketchy description of the situation facing the service English team we can see that it looks highly typical of much of the Middle and Far East. Thus, the originality of the *Nucleus* scheme does not lie in original features of the teaching situation. However, that teaching situation does largely explain the methodology. According to Bates, the leaders of the Tabriz team concluded that 'the material had to be attractive to the students both by being clearly related to their academic needs and by containing interesting learning activities'. And one consequence of this recognition of the importance of motivation was the decision that 'at the early stages there should be plenty of active use of English, encouraging students to participate, giving them confidence and a feel for the communicative value of the language, which would lead into "passive" reading and listening exercises. Hence the decision to precede texts with rapid productive exercises preparing the students to handle the key concepts contained in them.'

Even if we can now account for the approach to classroom activities, we have yet to explain the genesis of the syllabus design. We might now suppose that Tabriz was not only geographically isolated but also cut off from professional developments in ELT; and that in the climatically-extreme mountain fastnesses of Azerabadegan an entirely new approach to ESP was being born. Although Martin Bates has stated that at the beginning of the project in 1972 'ideas about *functional* and *communicative* language-teaching and the rhetorical dimension of language use were only just beginning to filter through to Tabriz', in 1972 such ideas had still to be heard of in most countries of the world. In fact the first collection of ESP papers (which included the influential paper by Widdowson discussed in the previous Episode) had only been published the previous year. Moreover, Bates goes on to say 'the fact that two of us had recently studied at Edinburgh and come into contact with the ideas of H. G. Widdowson was an important influence'. Clearly, the 'argument from isolation' will also not work.

In my view, the key to the brilliant and ambitious scheme developed at Tabriz lies in the perceived need to produce intermediate and introductory courses; more particularly, it lies in the course designers' decision to limit themselves mainly to the language of *observation* and *description*. Given such a limitation, the opportunity to structure around an evolving series of rhetorical functions along the lines proposed by Selinker and Widdowson was inevitably denied. However, the central and relatively simple descriptive scientific statements needed to be categorized in some way; they needed to be ordered, and needed to be blocked into manageable teaching Units. If syntactic complexity was no longer acceptable as the major criterion because it could not be identified with the communicative approach to language teaching, and if rhetorical function was insufficiently differentiated at the level of material Bates and Dudley-Evans were concerned with, what was left?

According to Bates and Dudley-Evans, the remaining organizing principle would lie within the basic scientific concepts, such as *structure*, *function* and *causation*, extractable from descriptive scientific statements. This imaginative and innovative decision to adopt a concept-based syllabus design (although it probably owes something to Price's *A Reference Book of English Words and Phrases for Foreign Science Students*, Pergamon Press, 1966) had a number of considerable benefits.

First, *concept* was not tied to either discipline or subject matter; the concept of *structure* could be applied equally well to the cell in biology and to the atom in the physical sciences. This, in turn, meant that a single syllabus outline could be produced which could then be applied (with a little luck and a certain amount of juggling) to a whole range of scientific and technological disciplines. Second, a *concept* would have a wide range of linguistic realizations and these could be selected and ordered (and interconnected with the realizations of other concepts) as seemed most appropriate. Thirdly, the key concepts had within them features that lead to their sequencing in a more or less convincing way: some seemed logically prior to others; some appeared to require more elaborate language than others; and some were more self-evident than others. Here is Bates again:—

> Our arrangement of basic concepts with associated language forms also enabled us to produce a 'cyclical' course with a cumulative learning effect. Thus Unit 1 provided ways of describing properties, Unit 2 ways of describing both the properties and location of parts of a system, Unit 3 the overall structure of a system including properties and locations, Unit 5 introduced ways of specifying the functions of parts of a system which in natural texts would often collocate with its structural description and so on.

Nucleus General Science has been by far the most successful ESP textbook so far published. Total sales exceed one million, even though a major contribution to this astonishing figure is provided by the special edition used in Egyptian technical secondary schools. The reasons for its wide acceptability and adoption are several. Firstly, it is 'teacher-friendly': in particular, it is an introductory text on which the teacher can easily build. Secondly, the material has a considerable degree of inventiveness, especially in the use of visual prompts. Thirdly, there remains tight structural control within the conceptual and notional frames. Fourthly, the lay-out is much more attractive—especially to the less highly-motivated learner—than that of three textbooks we have illustrated so far in Episodes Two, Four and Seven. These qualities can be seen in the half-Unit that follows.

Nevertheless, there have been dissatisfactions too. One common complaint is that there is insufficient reading material and, further, that the approach to reading is not as sophisticated or discourse-oriented as in the *Focus* series. Another is that the subject-specific volumes are variable in quality, both reflecting the different levels of material-writing skills of the authors but also reflecting differences in the appropriateness of 'conceptual fit' between the core course and the satellite subject-specific texts. A third disappointment relates to communicative *value*, and the feeling that *Nucleus*, like *Focus*, does not quite live up to its promises in this area. Although, for instance, the following extract imaginatively presents and practises varieties of expression usable in statements of cause and effect, there is no attempt to indicate where and when a particular type of statement is or is not communicatively appropriate.

Commentary for (a) on opposite page.

(a) There are a number of things to notice about this first exercise:—

(i) it is not called an exercise;
(ii) the instructions are simple;
(iii) the teacher can easily *perform* the actions if he or she should so wish;
(iv) the Unit starts with the 'ordinary language' or 'General English' expression of result (*so that*) and then moves on to forms more typical of Scientific English;
(v) the exercise runs into trouble in the second half. 'A match is dropped on the surface of water so that it floats' is a rather strange utterance. This is not the place to enter the tangled area of *effects*, *consequences* and *results*, but a more plausible result might be:—

> A piece of wood is dropped on the surface of the water so that the water does not spill so easily.

II

TEXT AND COMMENTARY

Nucleus General Science

by Martin Bates
and Tony Dudley-Evans

Unit 8 Process 3 Cause and Effect

Section 1 Actions and results

1. Look at this example:

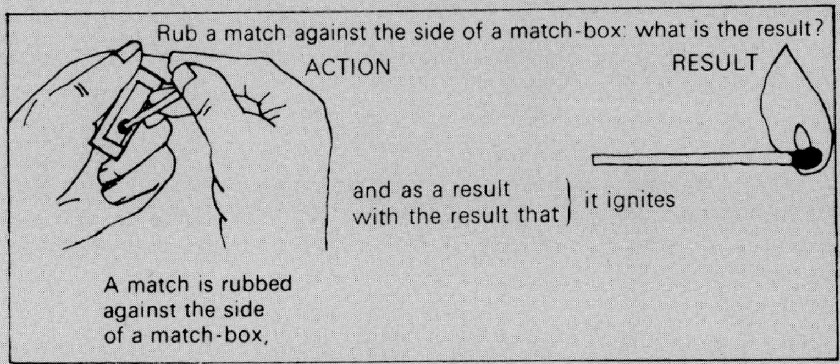

Rub a match against the side of a match-box: what is the result?
ACTION
FIRST ACTION
RESULT
The burning match is inverted
The match is held
pointing upwards
and as a result
with the result that
it ignites
A match is rubbed
against the side
of a match-box,

Now make similar statements about the actions and results below:

(a)

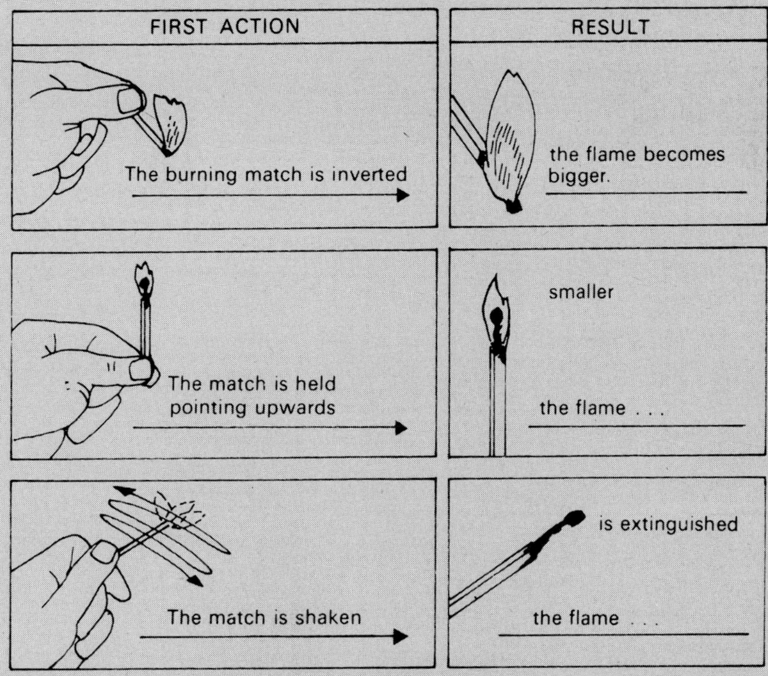

The match is shaken
is extinguished

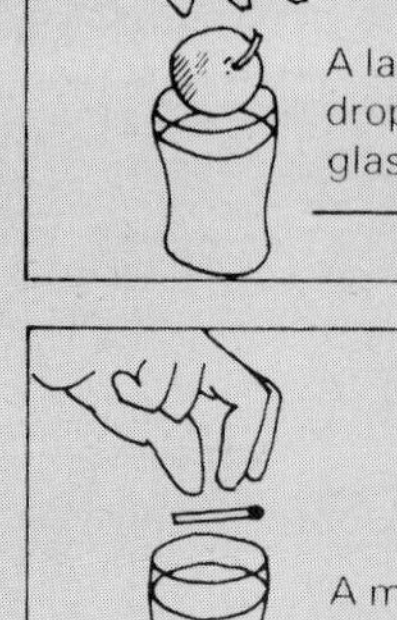

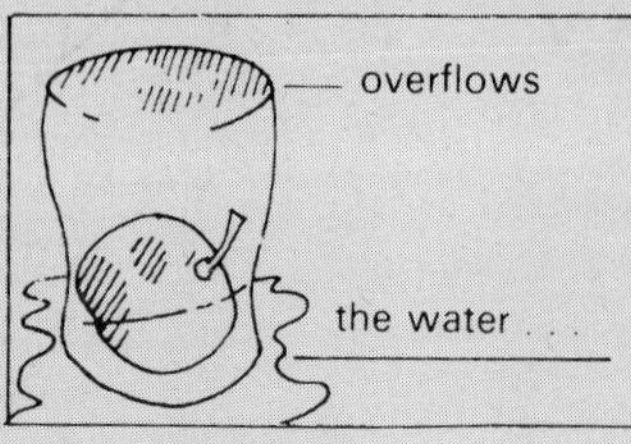

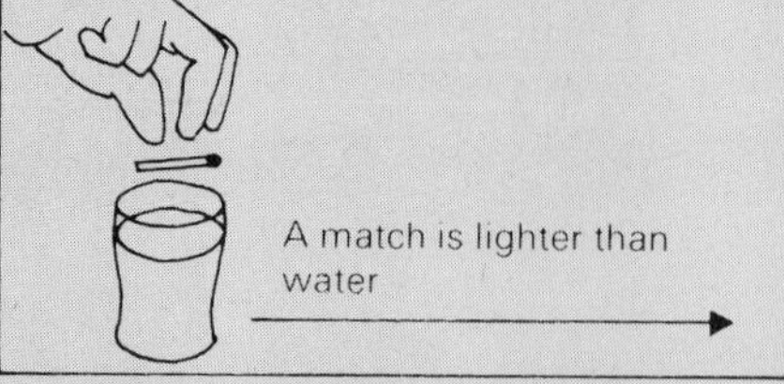

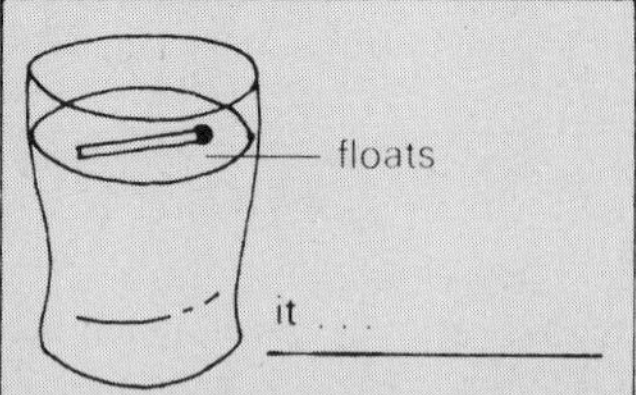

2. Look at this example:

(b)

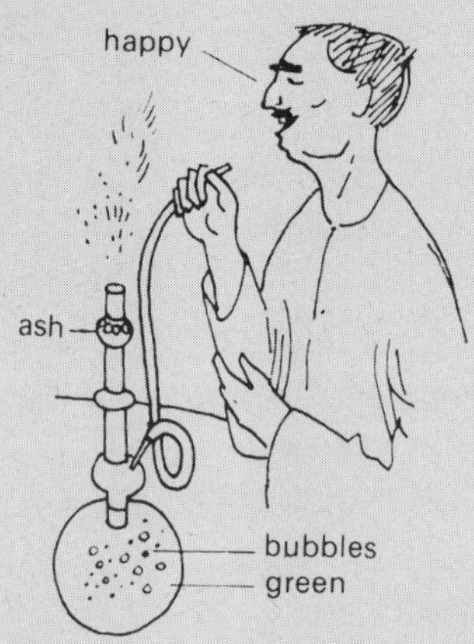

Changes of state

The process of smoking a water-pipe: smoke is sucked down the pipe, and as a result the smoke *changes into* bubbles, the water *turns* green and the smoker *becomes* happy (or ill). *Another result is that* the tobacco *is converted into* ash.

Make statements about the following actions and resulting changes, using *with the result that* or *and as a result*, and the words *become* (+ adjective), *turn* (+ colour), *change into* or *be converted into* (+ noun).

(b) This second activity illustrates the way in which the authors were able to use visuals to generate language. In this respect, *General Science* was far superior to its forerunners and still has not been equalled by more recent textbooks. The instruction is somewhat condensed and it might have been better presented as a diagram.

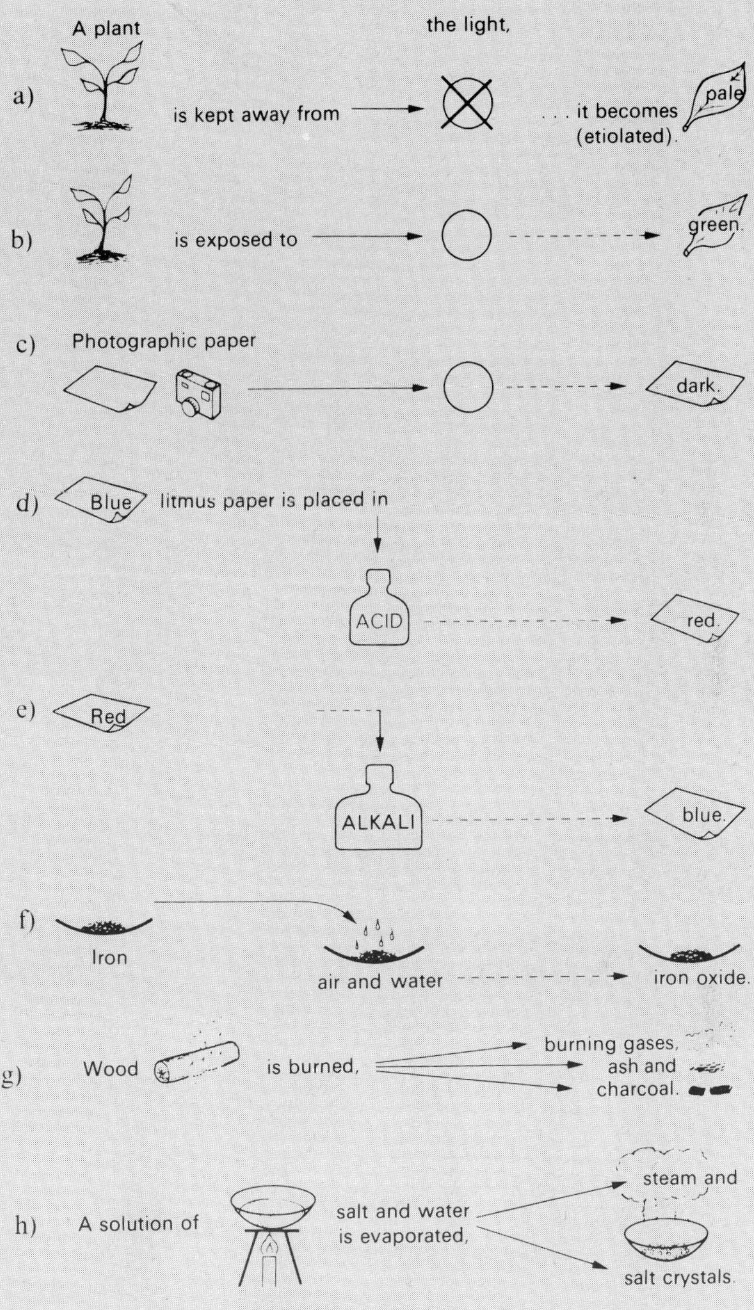

3. Now change the above descriptions of actions and results in the same way as the example:

Example: *If* a plant *is kept* away from the light, it *will become* etiolated.

(c) **4. Now make statements about the following changes of state in the same way as this example:**

Example: If ice is heated to melting point, it will melt, *changing* into water.

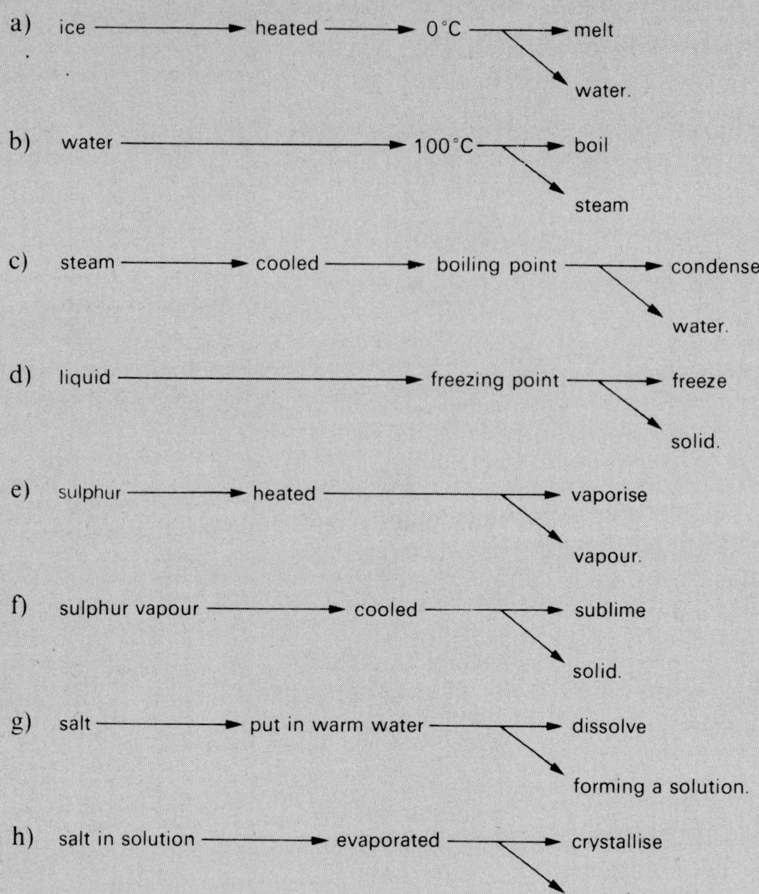

Section 2 Other ways of expressing results

5. Look at this:

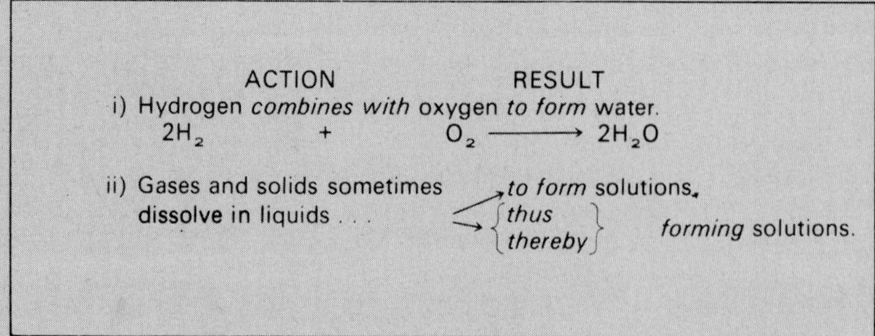

ACTION
RESULT
i) Hydrogen *combines with* oxygen *to form* water.
$2H_2 + O_2 \longrightarrow 2H_2O$
ii) Gases and solids sometimes dissolve in liquids . . .
to form solutions.
{*thus* / *thereby*} *forming* solutions.

(c) Another 'tour de force'. The only minor doubt is with statements (e) and (f) where the morphological relationships between *vaporize/vapour* and *crystallize/crystals* make the final non-finite clause somewhat redundant.

Make sentences describing chemical reactions from this table:

(d)

Potassium Calcium Magnesium Iron Carbon	combines with	hydrogen oxygen chlorine iodine	to form	calcium oxide, CaO. methane, CH_4. potassium iodide, KI. iron (III) oxide, Fe_3O_4. magnesium chloride, $MgCl_2$.

(e) **6. Read these statements about the action of chemical substances and then complete the examples which follow them:**

Example: Elements *combine to make* compounds.
For example, sodium combines with chlorine to form sodium chloride.

a) Many solids burn in gases *to form* different solids.
For instance, calcium . . . oxygen . . . calcium oxide, CaO.

b) Some substances absorb others, *thus producing* other substances.
______, chlorophyll ______ water and carbon dioxide, . . . oxygen and sugars.

c) Gases and solids sometimes dissolve in liquids, *thereby producing* solutions.
Thus, sulphur dioxide ______ in water, . . . sulphurous acid, H_2SO_3.
Another example is hydrogen chloride, which . . . , . . . hydrochloric acid, HCl.

d) Radioactive substances disintegrate *to form* more stable elements.
______, thorium . . . lead 208.
. . . is proactinium, which . . . lead 207.

e) Metals often react with acids *to give* metal salts.
For example, zinc . . . sulphuric acid . . . zinc sulphate, $ZnSO_4$.

f) An acid is neutralised by an alkali *to form* a salt.
______, hydrochloric acid . . . sodium hydroxide solution . . . sodium chloride.

g) Calcium reacts with water, *thereby liberating* hydrogen and *producing* calcium hydroxide.
Similarly, sodium . . . , . . . hydroxide.

h) Calcium carbonate is decomposed by heating *to produce* calcium oxide and carbon dioxide.
(f) ______, potassium chlorate . . . potassium chloride and oxygen.

(d) The table is a 'matching table'; (if necessary, see the Setting to Episode Four).

(e) Not entirely by accident, the extract from *Writing Scientific English* also deals with *result* clauses. The difference between the 'heavy' grammatical treatment in *WSE* and the 'light' treatment in *General Science* is very striking.

(f) The six single-sentence activities have now come to an end. The reader will have noticed an interesting paired development running through these six activities. There has also been a steady increase in the formality of the language used to express result. This is presumably as it should be, but one might have liked some indication of the major factors that influence the choice of one structure rather than another.

7. Read this passage and look at the diagram:

(g) **The carbon cycle**

The life of plants and animals depends on chemical substances containing carbon atoms. Plants obtain carbon from the very small amounts of carbon dioxide in the atmosphere. This atmospheric CO_2 is continually absorbed and given off (released) in the 'carbon cycle'.

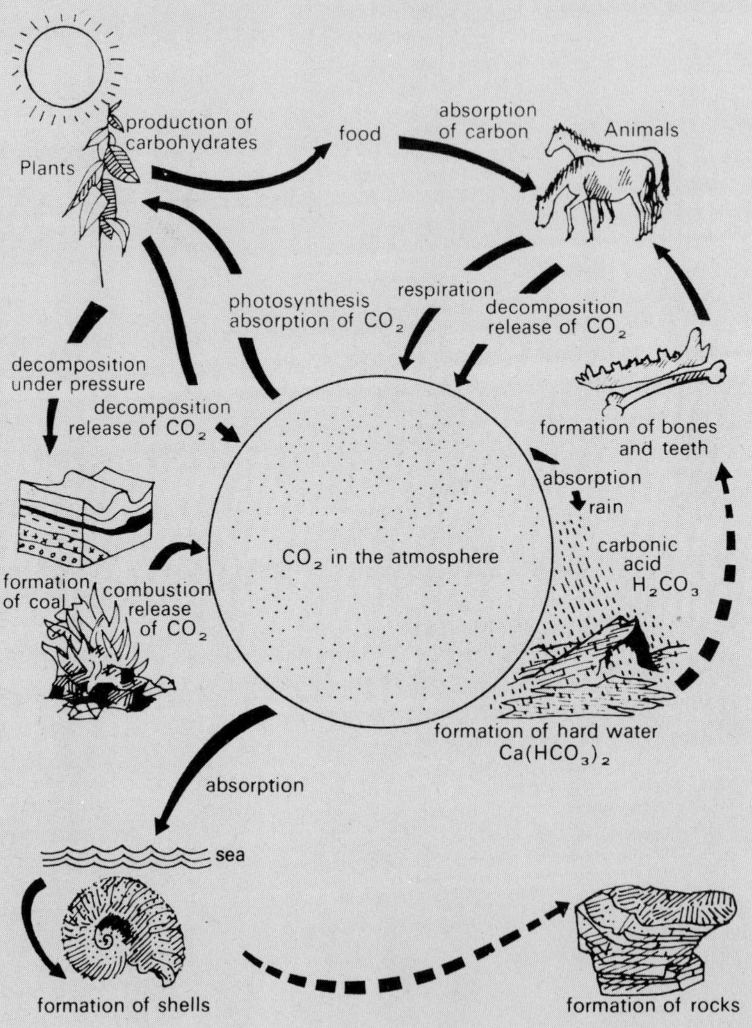

(g) This page nicely illustrates the textbook-writer's dilemma over content. The page may turn out as a dream or as a nightmare depending on the level of background knowledge that the class can bring to the topic. Although in principle the 'carbon cycle' diagram is ideal, because of the large number of result statements required for its verbalization, the very existence of this richness presupposes some familiarity with the subject matter. Unforeseen ignorance would be damaging—as indeed might excessive familiarity.

Look at these:

(A = cause, B = result)

A *results in* B.
B *results from* A.
As a result of A, B occurs.
A *leads to* B (eventually: other events occur between A and B).

(h) Now make ten true sentences from the tables below:

As a result of	eating plants, photosynthesis, combustion of coal, decomposition of dead plants,	carbon dioxide is given off. carbohydrates are produced by plants. animals absorb carbon.

Decomposition of plants under pressure Release of CO_2 into the atmosphere Decomposition of dead animals Formation of hard water Absorption of CO_2 by the sea Production of carbohydrates Formation of carbonic acid Formation of shells	results in results from leads to	respiration. photosynthesis. the formation of teeth and bones in animals. the formation of rocks. the formation of coal. the release of CO_2 into the atmosphere. the formation of shells. the combination of rain and CO_2 in the atmosphere.

(i)

(h) It is interesting to see the way in which Bates and Dudley-Evans handle the difficult problem of article-usage in labelling diagrams and in texts. The carbon-cycle itself has no examples of *the*, and they have tended to carry the absence of *the* across to the sentences to be reconstructed from the tables, especially in subject position. Do they get away with it? Do you accept the following 'true' sentences as being grammatically correct?

(i) As a result of decomposition of dead plants, carbon dioxide is given off.
(ii) Formation of shells leads to the formation of rocks.
(iii) Production of carbohydrates results from photosynthesis.

(i) The remaining two sections deal in similar ways with *causing, allowing, preventing* (Section 3) and explanations involving *because of, owing to*, and *because* (Section 4).

III

ACTIVITIES

(1) This half-Unit presents and practises a number of linguistic structures or devices for expressing *effects* or *results*.

(*a*) Complete the following Table.

Activity Number	*Structure/device*	*Example*
1	so that	burning water is inverted so that the flame becomes bigger
2	with the result that as a result	
3		If a result is kept away from the light, it will become etoliated.
4		
5	to + infinitive of purpose	Hydrogen combines with oxygen to form water.
6		
7		

(*b*) Consider what other structures or devices you might have expected to find.

(*c*) Is Unit 8 properly entitled *Cause and Effect*?

(2) How do the authors use italics? Is their use of italics effective?

(3) How could the carbon cycle diagram be exploited further?

(4) How would you 'repair' the opening activity of this Unit? (When you have done this, you might like to look at the changes introduced in the revised 1982 Edition.)

IV
EVALUATION

(1) Guillielmo Latorre, who wrote *A Basic Course in Scientific English* with Jack Ewer, has described the *Nucleus* volumes as 'brisk and lightweight'. Do you agree? (And does it matter if you do?)

(2) The *Focus* series has happily accommodated volumes in such areas as Education and Social Sciences. *Nucleus – Social Science* was abandoned. Why do you think this was?

(3) Apart from the extract from *Reading and Thinking in English* in *Episode Thirteen*, I have now finished my selections from ESP textbooks as such. From what you have seen, would you prefer to enter a new intermediate-level Scientific English class with *Herbert*, *Swales*, *Allen and Widdowson*, or *Bates and Dudley-Evans*? And what reasons would you have for your preference?

V
RELATED READINGS

The fullest description of 'Nucleus Project' is Martin Bates's 'Writing Nucleus' in *English for Specific Purposes* (see Part V of Episode Four). All the quotations ascribed to Bates in the Setting of this Episode have been taken from this source.

A fascinating early document is:—

M. Bates and A. Dudley-Evans, 'Notes on the Introductory English Courses for Students of Science and Technology at the University of Tabriz, Iran', *ELT Documents* 74/4, The British Council, London.

Much of the interest here lies in the final two pages where we find a 'Provisional Outline of General and Specific Units labelled by Concept, Structure and Topic'. As far as I know this is the only published attempt to chart the Nucleus scheme as a whole.

Shelagh Rixon provides a clear evaluation of her use of *Nucleus General Science* at King Faisal University, Saudi Arabia, in *ESPMENA* (see Episode Ten) 8, 1977/78. It is also well worth mentioning a review of *Nucleus Engineering* by Graham Low in *Working Papers in Language and Language Teaching* (The Language Centre, University of Hong Kong, May 1979). Although the source is rather obscure, Low's review of the *Engineering* volume is one of the very few reports on an ESP textbook that has real substance and quality.

EPISODE NINE 1978

M. K. Phillips and C. C. Shettlesworth: 'How to Arm Your Students: A Consideration of Two Approaches to Providing Materials for ESP', in *ELT Documents: ESP*, The British Council, London 1978.

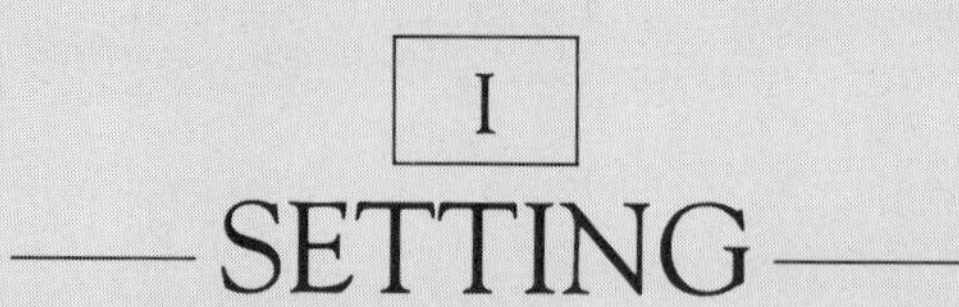

I — SETTING —

By the middle seventies the broad consensus that has been seen in the previous three Episodes was beginning to collapse. Of course there remained a tradition—and it remains to this day—faithful to communicative syllabus design, to specific teaching materials for specific groups, and to the search for utilizable relationships between functions and forms. This tradition has perhaps found its clearest and more overt expression in ESP textbooks for, almost without exception, all the textbooks produced in the last six years or so have been faithful to established approaches to subject matter and to study skills. This phenomenon is in no way surprising if we remember that the textbook is a carefully-assembled *product* designed for an imagined but not directly-experienced market. In addition, a textbook is only produced on the assumption that there are numerous teachers who need help with both the organization and the content of their ESP courses.

If ELT/ESP editors of publishing houses tend towards conservatism, those applied linguists and ESP practitioners of a self-questioning mind tend towards radicalism. Thus it was that by 1975 applied linguists such as Dick Allwright, then at Essex, and Christopher Candlin at Lancaster University were questioning the traditional role of the teacher as 'director of operations'.

The principal early challenge from within the ESP movement to the prevailing orthodoxy came from Martin Phillips and Clarence Shettlesworth. Phillips and Shettlesworth were members of the Department at Tabriz that was to be largely responsible for the *Nucleus* series discussed in the previous Episode. We now meet, therefore, probably the most extraordinary sequence of events in the short history of ESP. From a provincial university in north-west Iran, Bates and Dudley-Evans were to go on to some fame (and conceivably a little fortune) as the Series Editors of *Nucleus*, whereas Phillips and Shettlesworth were to follow distinguished careers based on offering alternatives to most of the *Nucleus* principles.

It came to pass in this way. While at Tabriz University, the two authors of this Episode were recruited by the Tabriz office of the British Council to develop a course for a local machine-tool company. Being of the self-critical cast of mind that I referred to earlier, when they came to evaluate their EOP course they found themselves raising questions about the validity and effectiveness of the techniques they had used and about the solutions they had adopted. A description of their conclusions was presented at the important *Regional English Language Centre* seminar on ESP in Singapore in 1975 and a written version was first published in *ESPMENA Bulletin* (see the next Episode) later that year under the title of 'Problems in Syllabus Design for a Course in Industrial English'. Phillips and Shettlesworth gave a rather more generalized statement of their thinking at the Fourth AILA Congress (also 1975), which was published in

Volume One of the Proceedings. For this Episode I have chosen their revised version of a paper given at a British Council seminar on EAP in London in the spring of 1976, although the paper was not published until 1978. The last of their four joint papers has, for my purposes here, two advantages: it reflects not only the authors' experiences in Iran but also their work at Bletchingdon House, a private language school in England; and it also has much more to say about satisfactory solutions to the difficulties they had encountered.

'How to Arm your Students' is a challenging and wide-ranging paper, so I have offered a fairly extensive commentary. Its main argument runs something like this. Evaluation of ESP materials has largely ignored considering 'the kind and relevance of the language practice they engender in the classroom'. This is particularly unfortunate, because FL classroom discourse has a number of very unusual characteristics and thus there may be a big gulf between classroom discourse and the discourse typical of situations for which the students are learning English. In other words, the area of overlap between the two linguistic worlds may be surprisingly small. Further, because traditional ESP materials (whether textbooks or produced 'in house') are designed as *teaching* materials, they will, by their very nature, tend to encourage communicative acts typical of the classroom. A related distortion brought about by standard ESP materials is that they may well, as we have seen in the last two Episodes, be selective in language and rely on adapted and simplified texts. And, despite all these uncertainties, everybody knows that ESP materials are time-consuming and difficult to write.

As the theoretical and practical problems that arise in writing ESP teaching materials are greater than have been supposed, a case can be made for using ARMS or Authentic Resource Materials. But if ARMS are used there are several consequences. Traditional selection and grading must be replaced by something else, because ways have to be found for coping with 'the unrestricted nature of the linguistic content'. One way is to grade ARMS in terms of their *accessibility* to the learners; another is to pay more attention to *task-difficulty* rather than *text-difficulty*: for example, students may no longer be required to actually 'read' certain texts. The authors then present two methodologies for handling authentic materials, one methodology aiming at language development and the other at communication skills. The adoption of such approaches requires a different classroom environment. The teacher needs to lose his undisputed authority and the student needs to learn to take on greater responsibility. Task-oriented activities emerge, of which group work is an important component. In the end, such changes will allow a closer approximation to the students' real English-using situations than is likely in a traditional ESP classroom provided with fully pre-prepared Units and with a teacher busy organizing his teaching around those materials.

Phillips' and Shettlesworth's thesis is, as we shall see, not without its own difficulties, but for *certain* ESP situations, it has gained a wide measure of acceptance. Indeed, as Episode Fourteen will show, the thesis will undergo considerable and quite startling further modifications.

II

TEXT AND COMMENTARY

How to Arm Your Students: A Consideration of Two Approaches to Providing Materials for ESP

by M. K. Phillips *and* C. C. Shettlesworth
The British Council

Teaching materials and classroom discourse

Criticism of ESP materials is in general restricted to the adequacy with which they meet certain theoretical postulates and to discussion of the postulates themselves. To our knowledge relatively little has been done in the way of surveying the output, so to speak, of the materials, that is, the kind and relevance of the language practice they engender in the classroom. This is
(a) perhaps the more surprising since the ultimate touchstone of any materials must be the pragmatic one of the amount and quality of the learning they stimulate.

The specialized nature of classroom discourse is becoming well-documented[1]. McTear, for example, suggests that language in the EFL classroom operates on three levels: metalinguistically, as the means of instruction; pedagogically, as the content of instruction; communicatively, as a general means of communication[2]. Other observers have made similar distinctions. This implies that the gap between classroom discourse (in any normal classroom) and the target discourse of the learning objective is perhaps surprisingly wide. We confirmed this hypothesis in our own case through a short study based on transcripts of classes in EST and which revealed that not only did the kind of discourse generated bear little obvious relation to communicative uses or language in scientific situations but even arguably differed from the teacher's perceptions
(b) of the kind of discourse that was generated[3]. ESP materials are designed as teaching materials and their centrality in the teaching situation consequently tends to reinforce the peculiarities of classroom discourse.

(c) This is not necessarily an insuperable criticism: it entails the necessity of creating the conditions for activities which encourage the student to transfer the language taught in the classroom to use in communicative situations.

---

[1] For the references numbered 1 to 5 on this and the succeeding pages, see page 114.

(a) There is, of course, a well-established counter-argument to this position and one frequently advanced by advocates of formal grammar teaching. This is that the classroom can never be the real world and should not therefore attempt to be like it; the classroom is an ideal place for learning the linguistic code, which the students then apply in the real world as and when necessary.

(b) Indeed, research does seem to show, and show consistently, that language teachers are poor judges of what is going on interactionally in their own classrooms. Uncomfortable, but true.

(c) Or, as *(a)* above indicates, it entails the necessity of showing that transfer from classroom discourse to target-situation discourse can occur in other ways.

Problems in ESP materials design

The philosophy of materials designed for teaching purposes, however, inhibits the development of such activities. One typical illustration of this is the control of syntax and lexis that is exercised over specially written reading passages. It is difficult any longer to accept such simplification as an adequate basis for control of written discourse; it is only one element and arguably not the most important. The current concern with the rhetoric of written discourse
(d) has clarified linguistic features peculiar to texts such as the devices used to secure cohesion on the one hand and the organization of the information content, the management of coherence, on the other. Unless these aspects of text are accorded at least equal attention in the process of writing teaching texts to that given to the traditional criteria, the information structure of the text is correspondingly distorted and thus (i) the adapted texts cannot be viewed as a helpful stage towards dealing with authentic materials and (ii) this distortion renders the adapted text potentially more rather than less difficult to comprehend. It is clear, however, that achieving a simplification procedure which allows for these considerations is less than straightforward as
(e) Mountford[4] has pointed out.

A further problematic area is whether the material provided by the course can be exploited in the way a specialist would use authentic materials; whether, for example, the operations performed by the student on text and diagrams correspond to the use a scientist would make of them. This is one aspect of the wider problem of providing students with an adequate introduction to the language skills involved in studying in English. It has become clear that in the teaching of language for academic purposes, it is insufficient to develop materials which aim to introduce the student only to the linguistic features which are salient in a particular field of discourse without paying attention to the strategies required by the student which justify the study of those features in the first place. It has rarely been the case hitherto that teaching
(f) materials attach sufficient importance to the behavioural aspect of specialist language.

Related to this point is the disparity that can arise in ESP between the demands of materials designed with a pedagogic objective and the requirements of the subject matter. The original purpose of the materials, which is to equip the students to deal with authentic examples of specialist discourse, can be negated if, in the process, fidelity to the subject matter is not maintained. The result of such inaccuracy or over-simplification is often highly counter-productive; the credibility gap yawns.

(d) *Cohesion* is usually taken to refer to overt structural links between sentences, such as the use of pronouns or sentence connectors; *coherence* as the links between the communicative acts that sentences are used to perform, such as the ways in which a discourse handles 'given' and 'new' information.

(e) The argument in this paragraph is well taken. In the distinction made by Mountford and Widdowson, the re-writing of text according to traditional linguistic criteria will produce *simplified versions*; the incorporation of a full range of discoursal and contextual features will produce *simple accounts*, which may well be longer and (conceivably) more linguistically complex than the originals.

(f) Another powerful paragraph, but it needs a little interpretation if it is to be related to the surrounding literature. Following Widdowson, it has become customary (at least in some quarters) to refer to *authentic* texts (i.e. 'undoctored' ones) as *genuine* texts and reserve 'authenticity' for the *authentic* tasks and activities referred to in the paragraph to which this note relates. A major area of controversy is whether ESP needs both *genuine* and *authentic* material (as Phillips and Shettlesworth are here arguing) and this issue will surface again in Episodes Twelve and Fourteen. It is clear that setting, say, multiple-choice comprehension questions on a science text is asking the science student to do something that he does not do as a student of science rather than of Scientific English. The converse is rather more obscure. Suppose we set a communicative rather than a linguistic task; let us say we ask the class to prepare a memo for their government summarizing the national implications of the scientific breakthrough described in the assigned text. The fact that the task is *communicative* does not necessarily make it *authentic* in the authors' sense of being typical of what scientists do. This type of authenticity can only be established by ESP-related educational research; and I personally believe that many fashionable 'information transfer' exercises are suspect for the very reason that they are rarely replicated in that form in reality.

A final point regarding the use of specially written materials is that of the techniques (g) employed for student assessment. Given the powerful structuring provided by such materials, testing is normally conducted within the terms of the course. Such assessment is thus open to precisely the same criticisms as the course design: it tells us less about the student's communicative ability than about the extent to which the student has assimilated and can reproduce the course content.

Authentic materials

It is with such considerations in mind that we approach the specification of ESP courses at the Centre for English Studies and in particular pre-sessional EAP courses. These generally raise the problem of catering for groups of mixed and very specific interests and varying levels of attainment. Moreover, the time available for finding a solution is more often than not, strictly limited. These factors lead us to question the practicability of preparing specialized teaching material to a high standard when one is dealing with a diversified demand often on a 'one-off' basis at very short notice. In ESP situations where such a solution is attempted experience has shown that either the time and manpower involved can quickly become costly out of all proportion to the economic viability of the course or the quality of the materials suffers. Yet in an effort to avoid the latter, institutions continue to suppose that the first alternative is the only solution[5]. Even were it always possible to adopt this solution, however, and it is of course very unrepresentative of the average ESP situation which is the need to meet an immediate demand with existing resources, it is, as we have seen, questionable whether the expenditure of time, (h) effort and finance is justified by the end product.

We see one possible solution to the problem of providing specialist materials in different disciplines in a manner which is both practical and which avoids most of the theoretical criticisms levelled at specially prepared materials in the exploitation of authentic documents from the student's field of study. The absence of conventional selection and grading naturally entails a fresh look at the ways in which materials and the organization of the classroom are structured. Nevertheless, there are two fairly obvious ways in which a degree of control over the content of authentic materials can be exercised. Firstly they can be graded in terms of *accessibility*. One would want to take into account the absolute length of the passage, the density of new information and the presence of supportive graphic features (see Appendix Ex. (i) 1). In addition it is not difficult to establish a cline of accessibility depending upon the sophistication of the information content, although caution needs to be exercised in accepting

(g) The place of testing is another highly controversial issue in ESP, much of the controversy deriving from a wish to use a test which will at one and the same time measure students' progress, evaluate the programme and offer research data. Clearly ESP programmes need careful evaluation, especially as they tend to be more expensive than the educational arrangements they have replaced, but this is a separate issue. Also any information we can get about the strategies students are using to tackle tests or about the way they organize written descriptions of processes is indeed valuable, but that again is a separate matter. It is less clear whether ESP examinations have any real value except to raise motivation and effort and to satisfy the larger organizations' requirements. After all, if we really are concerned with student performance in 'real' communicative situations, then it follows that our ex-students can only be evaluated by how far they succeed or fail in the real world. It is not clear to me whether Phillips and Shettlesworth take this position, or would look for some form of in-class test based on ARMS.

(h) The authors' arguments make much sense when we restrict their contexts to those that require 'a diversified demand often on a "one-off" basis at very short notice'. However, they probably err when they imply that 'one-off' courses are representative of the average ESP situation; or at least, they may be right in terms of the *number* of ESP situations around the world, but are probably wrong in terms of the *volume* of ESP activity. The 'bread-and-butter' of ESP is providing courses for numbers of repeating groups of students with fairly stable but specialized requirements, and the University of the Andes referred to in Reference 5 at the end of the text is very much in the category of having a stable demand, few 'one-offs', and adequate preparation time.

(i) *Cline* means *scale*, and is something of a buzz-word in ESP—not surprisingly, since few things are black and white.

the relative simplicity of the popularized account, for example, which is frequently achieved at the expense of introducing an unrepresentative register of discourse.

Secondly it is possible to remove the forms of control from the materials themselves to the task complexity demanded of the student and for which the material acts as a stimulus. It does not always follow that because an authentic written text is being exploited that the objective of all lessons is necessarily reading comprehension. Indeed it must be accepted that total comprehension has often to be abandoned as a lesson aim. Moreover, the traditional classroom approach aimed at predicting the language the student needs to learn and allowing him the smallest possible margin of error in its acquisition is unlikely to hold good when using authentic materials, which, for the student, represent very much of a confrontation with the language.
(j) Consequently an approach which accepts the inevitability of error and aims at its progressive elimination as successively more accurate hypotheses are tested out against the evidence of the materials seems to be more appropriate.

Two Methodologies for ARMS (Authentic Resource Materials)

There seem to be two major ways of approaching an authentic text for use in the classroom. On the one hand it can be viewed as a repository of natural language use and on the other it can be seen as the stimulus for a variety of communication skills. The former is concerned with explicating the text, the latter with developing skill transfers of the type involved in, for example, note taking. The former deals with information extraction, the latter with its application; both approaches therefore are relevant.

1 Natural language use

Authentic materials lend themselves admirably to procedures involving the induction of grammatical rules which can be tested against other occurrences in the text and generalized to create new formations. The criterion for selection of the text is thus (a) the relevance of the subject matter and (b) the importance of the language points exemplified and their frequency of occurrence. This is illustrated by example 2 which has been used by us for practice in the interpretation and production of complex noun phrases. The passage serves the usual purpose of
(k) specially constructed texts in that it exemplifies a particular language point with high frequency but has the marked advantage consequent upon its being a sample of discourse in that its authenticity is a considerable motivational factor and the linguistic point occurs in a natural context.

(l) A less rigidly structured approach to the use of authentic materials for the teaching of grammar would be to adopt the cloze technique. There is no reason why the technique should not be applied to authentic discourse, indeed, it is arguably most appropriately applied to natural samples of language use. The rich context that is thereby provided furnishes a maximum of contextual clues to interpretation. Such an approach, illustrated in example 3, has two distinct advantages. Firstly it provides practice in inductive techniques for the interpretation of authentic discourse which are of vital importance for the student to acquire if

(j) The two solutions offered in the closing two paragraphs of the *Authentic Materials* section are most interesting, but of course easier said than done, especially if the authors keep to their earlier pre-condition that the tasks have some semblance to what goes on in practice. Another potential difficulty is student confidence; an unremitting struggle with authentic materials may in the end be somewhat dispiriting for the participants.

(k) The points are well made, but on a practical level most ESP practitioners know that looking for texts that massively exemplify language points can in fact be more time-consuming than adapting texts so that those texts 'foreground' the desired features.

(l) The 'cloze' technique was originally designed to measure readability, but is now more widely used for teaching and testing reading comprehension. Phillips and Shettlesworth adopt a standard approach. There is an unmutilated 'lead-in' and then every seventh word has been omitted, which the students are asked to reconstruct using the range of clues available.

he is to achieve autonomy in handling the language and in his own language learning. Secondly, the representative sample of language points covered by cloze procedure will ensure that problems of real difficulty to the student will be identified; the cloze passage can act diagnostically and provide the input to straightforward language improvement sessions. In effect the student selects his own personalized syllabus, a technique which is virtually impossible when using specially written pedagogic materials since they tend to be based upon a predicted item selection and sequence.

There always remains the possibility, however, that the unrestricted nature of the linguistic content will lead to immediate difficulties in the classroom. There is no reason why this eventuality should prove disruptive; there are several options open to the teacher. The simplest is to ignore the problem accepting, as mentioned earlier, that total comprehension is an unrealistic initial objective. We have found that our students are prepared to accept this limitation provided it is explained to them. The converse is to teach the point in question; although this may have the disadvantage of deviating from the teacher's preconceptions regarding his lesson, it is acceptable in an approach based upon the progressive elimination of error through a syllabus determined by the student himself. Finally, the difficulty can be positively exploited as an exercise in linguistic problem solving.

There is a more serious difficulty, however, to be faced. The adoption of a grammatical focus in this manner, whilst it is significantly different in technique from traditional approaches, has no implications for the authenticity of the discourse generated in the classroom. In other words, this use of ARMS may not overcome the problems mentioned at the beginning of this paper as inherent to the discourse generated by materials developed solely for teaching purposes. Authentic materials can only stimulate more realistic classroom discourse if a task-orientated methodology is adopted; this brings us to the second approach to the exploitation of ARMS, their use as a stimulus for the acquisition of language skills.

2 Language skills

It could well prove that the major difference between traditional approaches to language learning and the approach loosely characterized as ESP in so far as the latter does represent an identifiable unified approach, lies less in the attitude to language that the two techniques represent than in the essential difference in methodology characterizable as the predicted language item syllabus—whether this is expressed in structural or notional terms—as opposed to task orientated learning. The former, through having no specified task relevance, has to rely
(m) upon inventing teaching techniques which are extrinsically motivating as a result of the
(n) entertainment value of the devices used. The latter, by definition has no such problem; it is difficult, for example, to conceive of an EAP course which is not centred on study skills in English.

Authentic texts can be used as stimulus for discrete skills of the type involving different modes of information transfer. The information contained in the text as reading or listening passage can be transferred to the written mode as in report-writing or to the oral mode in 'lecturettes' through the mediation of note-taking. In order successfully to stimulate the art of taking notes in the lecture situation it is precisely the redundancy and richness of textual

(m) Many ESP practitioners are likely to think that the authors of this Episode are overstating their case when they claim that a pre-established functional course can have 'no specified task relevance' or intrinsic motivation; although equally many will admit that such task-relevance may be more difficult to achieve in an established framework. Indeed, in the two following Episodes we shall be considering some samples of imaginative work from largely within the traditional approach.

(n) Here the authors may be concentrating on their experiences with undergraduates in the Middle and Far East. It is, of course, possible to conceive of an EAP course with no required study skills component—unless *EAP* is defined as including study skills, in which case the argument is circular. Imagine, if you will, a group of senior Russian scientists taking an EST course. They perhaps have all published articles, participated in seminars, and conducted highly complex library searches in their native language; indeed they are the sort of people who teach study skills rather than need to learn them.

(o) rhetorical clues provided by authentic discourse that is the point of the exercise. One kind of practice material we have devised is illustrated in example 4. It has also proved possible to use authentic texts to provide the content of sessions intended to practise seminar strategies. Obviously the presentation of lecturettes based upon the subject matter of the text will give students the opportunity to practise such techniques as interrupting, time-gaining, floor-keeping, clarifying etc. By dividing the class into groups and giving them different texts or different parts of the same text upon which to work with the instruction that they will have orally to convey the 'gist' of the passage to the other members of the class, a situation is created in which there is a real communicative need for these verbal strategies. Any passage in which the information is itemized can prove suitable for this purpose, each group having to communicate the content of one or more sections to the other members of the class (see example 5). It is also possible to manipulate the access different groups of students have to the information contained in a series of texts in order to set up a problem solving situation based upon the sharing of relevant knowledge.

Such techniques approach a full study skills simulation where students are given either individual research projects or a cooperative case study integrating different disciplines. In either case the full range of study skills will be required. The task of the teacher will be to monitor the efficiency of the skill techniques, to identify language problems as they arise and to prescribe remedial work where necessary. It is difficult to see how such task-orientated activities
(p) could be successfully encouraged by anything other than authentic materials and as a result a greater degree of authenticity in classroom discourse is to be expected.

Classroom organization

It is clear, however, that one consequence of the use of authentic materials in this manner is that the teacher is no longer the undisputed authority on the text and must acknowledge the student's expertise in the subject. As a result, the teacher must adjust his role to meet the changed relations obtaining between teacher, student and text. Even in the case of a lesson orientated towards structural learning and where the teachers' role will most closely resemble the orthodox one, it is quite possible, as mentioned earlier, that it will be the students rather than the teacher who set the objective for the lesson. In classes devoted to a direct attack on the comprehension of a text the responsibility will be more evenly shared between teacher and student; the teacher's role will be an advisory one, that of, in effect, a linguistic consultant called in by the students to elucidate difficult points. We are thus suggesting that the emphasis has to be placed on student-centred situations where the focus is upon *learning* strategies rather than *teaching* technique and ultimately the student is responsible, and rightly so, for his own progress.

The student, for his part, must appreciate that the teacher is dependent upon him for the evaluation of difficulties and must be prepared to participate in a higher level of cooperative activity than is normally the case. Such an acceptance of his own responsibility is essential if he is ever to settle into further study in this country but by no means easy for students whose experience derives from several years of authoritarian classroom methodologies. Indeed one objective of the majority of our EAP courses is to achieve precisely this readjustment. If the
(q) burden of elicitation is thrown upon the students, then one of our tasks is to equip the students with the appropriate strategies to facilitate this role. We have often found that this is most effectively done in the context of fieldwork (see example 6).

(o) Phillips and Shettlesworth are clearly right about the inadequacy of prescripted material—and of the virtual impossibility of taking notes from a single reading aloud of such material. However, the status of the extract in Example 4 is obscure; is it a transcript, or what?

(p) As I have already mentioned, this conclusion will not go unchallenged.

(q) This issue has been most prominently investigated at Lancaster University where Dick Allwright now lectures, but the advantages and disadvantages of 'learner training' cannot be discussed here.

Group work also clearly has an important function. It allows for differential pacing within a class which can be vital when authentic materials are used. It permits the differential handling of language problems; it obliges the students to discuss their problems and then fosters a high level of cooperative activity in their approach to a text: this turns the lack of homogeneity in terms of linguistic level to advantage and permits the integration of students of widely differing achievement. At the same time, grouping within the class allows for different selections of material for different groups both to stimulate communication and to increase the degree of specialization.

(r) A parting shot in the ARM: or Resources for Courses

We have argued that ARMS represent a more practical alternative—certainly they are readily and cheaply available in all subjects at different levels—to the expense and time involved in creating specially written materials which tend to suffer from the defects discussed in the first part of this paper and in any case are an unrealistic solution when faced with an immediate but short-term need. The course materials could then become less an ESP textbook in the accepted sense rather than a set of resource material together with procedural guidelines for their exploitation. These we are building up as a teachers report in note form on the manner in which they have used authentic texts (see example 7)'. Most ESP materials are an attempt to insert a specific subject content into an EFL framework. This attempt, we suggest, has doubtful validity. We attempt to tackle the problem from the opposite viewpoint, that of accepting the subject-matter and the modes of behaviour appropriate to it and adapting or developing our
(s) exploitation or techniques.

APPENDIX

Examples of ARMS exploited for teaching purposes

Example 1

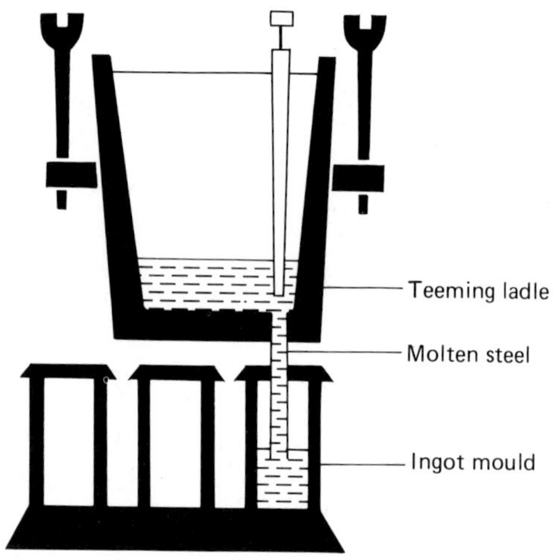

INGOT CASTING

Ingots are a convenient form in which to handle steel, and the molten steel is released through the base of a ladle into moulds. When the metal has solidified, the mould is removed. Each ingot is of carefully pre-arranged dimensions and weights from which articles of required size can be rolled or forged.

(from 'Making Steel', British Steel Corporation)

(r) The play on words is nicely managed.

(s) 'How to Arm Your Students' is a forceful and combative paper, and with its three precursors, caused considerable heart-searching in many ESP Departments around the world. In retrospect, I believe it had the stronger influence on the activities our students undertook both inside and outside the classroom than it did on our sources of materials. In the end, the majority view was that there was a time to stand to ARMS, but also a time to lay them down.

Example 2

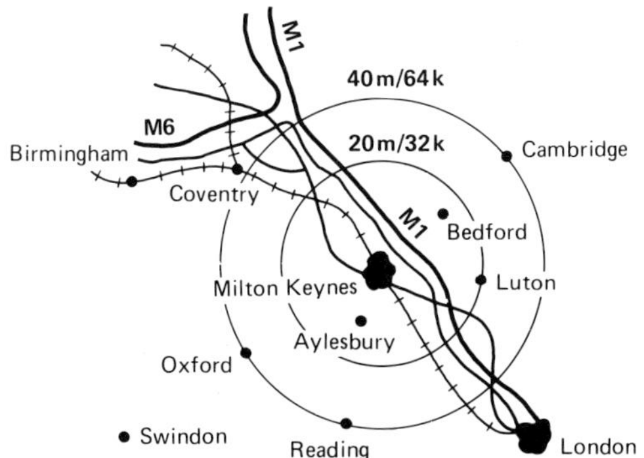

The best way to Milton Keynes is via Heathrow

From November 25th to November 27th, officers of the *Milton Keynes Development Corporation* will be at the Post House Hotel, West Drayton (Heathrow), between 10.30 am and 7.00 pm.

They'll be there to explain the very considerable advantages of moving a business to Milton Keynes.

As the map shows, Milton Keynes is an ideal location for most kinds of *manufacturing industry* and *distributive and service trades.* 60% of the country's population is within a 55 *mile radius* of the city, housing is guaranteed to all *company staff* moving, and *factory sites* and *office space* are available to suit individual needs.

It could be well worth your while to come along to find out why. Especially since you'll be saving yourself a 55 *mile journey* up the M1.

Milton Keynes
The logical place
for your business

(from advertisement in 'The Guardian')

Example 3

In distinguishing its work from that of the trade associations, the CBI describes its work as 'horizontal' rather than 'vertical'. The CBI sees itself as being concerned not only with national questions which concern all or several industrial sectors but also with those which cut across industries and affect groups of firms (or all firms) which have certain interests in common; such as being close companies, overseas investors, ____________ users or taxpayers. The CBI points out ____________ only in matters of detail which are ____________ prime importance to a particular sector can ____________ Trade Association gain the ear of the ____________. Even in such circumstances, the CBI is ____________ to take up the cudgels on behalf ____________ in support of the sector concerned, probably ____________ greater effect than the Association itself can ____________.

(from 'Business' Open University)

Example 4

Transport in Britain

Transport and transport planning are regarded by the British Government as an essential part of the management of the environment how we get to work how we carry our goods and passengers from one part of the country to another in particular, in and out of the conurbations can no longer be regarded as a relatively simple matter of building roads or providing trains transport today is an integral part of land-use planning of local authority finance of pollution and of regional development.

(from 'The Human Environment: The British View' HMSO)

Example 5

Some Basic Guidelines and Rules for Group Operation

When first operating in a group it is important and of real value to set down some of the factors which could cause friction amongst members.

The following Rules and Guidelines should be considered by all groups.

1 How is the purchase price divided? This can be divided by acreage, tonnage, gallonage or hourly use. It is advantageous to make all members of the group liable for the group's debts.

2 How are the running costs and other expenses divided? It is desirable for the group to appoint one member as a secretary who should keep the account books, machine maintenance records and, if necessary, a minute book of all meetings. The group should ensure, if they are borrowing money, that a bank account is opened in the group's name.

3 How is the work pattern organized? This can only be .... etc.

(from Group Operations in Farm Management HMSO)

Example 6 CENTRE FOR ENGLISH STUDIES

Materials Exploitation

Date	Group .... Teacher ....
Skill:	Note-taking/Listening Comprehension
Materials used:	Transport and Road Research Laboratory: tree diagram of organizational structure: TRRL booklet, p.5.
Duration:	25 minutes
Procedure:	1 SS draw tree—lines 2 Teacher 'reads' out information, with *some* redundancy features (recapitulation mainly). 3 Simultaneously SS write information on to the diagram, thus completing it. 4 Vocabulary written up, to avoid spelling mistakes. It is not a spelling exercise. 5 Language used by teacher: *is divided into*; *is organized into*; *to sum up*.

Evaluation: The group were able to write down all information correctly without section headings (see attached sheet) having to be said more than once. The temptation to repeat and repeat has to be avoided.

A useful exercise in highly guided listening for information, and showing comprehension by completing a given frame.

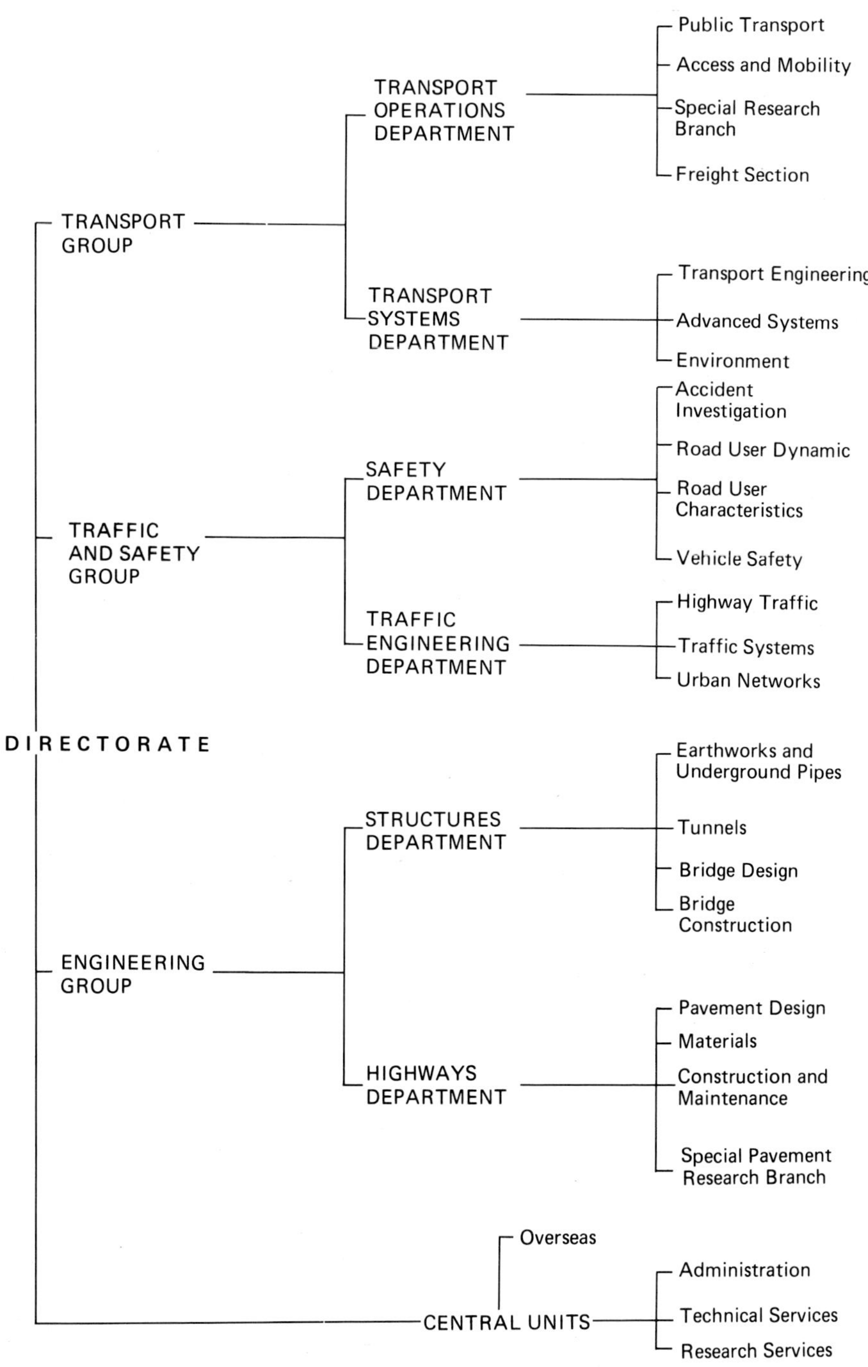

Example 7

PROJECT—Oxford Planning Department

Remember:

Excuse me ....

(Can you tell me ....
(Could you tell me ....

Could you explain ....

(I'd like to know ....
(I've heard about ....

In your talk/lecture/description, you said ....

1 Public participation in planning?
2 Current major planning schemes?
3 Extend pedestrian precincts?
—etc.—

References

1 For example: Long, M. H., 'Group Work and Communicative Competence in the ESOL Classroom' in Burt and Dulay (eds), *On TESOL '75.*

2 McTear, M., 'Potential Sources of Confusion in the Foreign Language Lesson', 4th International Congress of Applied Linguistics, Stuttgart 1975.

3 Phillips, M. K. and Shettlesworth, C. C., 'Questions in the Design and Use of Courses in ESP', Proceedings of the 4th International Congress of Applied Linguistics, Stuttgart 1975.

4 Mountford, A., 'The Notion of Simplification and its relevance to materials preparation for EST' in *Teaching English for Science and Technology: Selected Papers from the RELC Seminar in the Teaching and Learning of English for Scientific and Technological Purposes in SE Asia.* Singapore 21–25 April 1975.

5 See for example Newsletter 1 of Universidad de los Andes, Bogota, Colombia.

III
ACTIVITIES

(1) The authors state that Example 2 'has been used by us for practice in the interpretation and production of complex noun phrases'.

(*a*) How would you exploit the italicized noun phrases?

(*b*) You will have noticed that the ARMS comes from an advertisement. Is complex noun phrase usage in advertisements the same as in descriptive technical texts; and does it matter if it is different?

(2) (*a*) Complete the passage given in Example 3.

(*b*) Do you consider that there is an error (perhaps typographical) with the seventh gap?

(*c*) Produce an alternative version of the cloze test to the one given with the gaps all moved one space back. Give the two versions to two individuals or to two groups with approximately the same command of English. Observe your results. Do these results affect in any way your view of the authors' arguments in the second paragraph of the 'Natural Language Use' section?

(3) Here again is the short 'authentic' passage from Example 1. What language work can you derive from it?

INGOT CASTING

Ingots are a convenient form in which to handle steel, and the molten steel is released through the base of a ladle into moulds. When the metal has solidified, the mould is removed. Each ingot is of carefully pre-arranged dimensions and weights from which articles of required size can be rolled or forged.

(from 'Making Steel', British Steel Corporation)

IV
EVALUATION

(1) 'I have said that an uncritical acceptance of the need to present learners with "authentic data" can lead to an avoidance of pedagogic responsibility', H. G. Widdowson, 'The Authenticity of Language Data' in Fanselow, J. F., & R. H. Crymes (eds.), *On TESOL 76*, Washington DC: TESOL.

Produce evidence *for* and *against* Widdowson's criticism.

(2) Do you think the main argument in this Episode is generally relevant, or is only applicable to local situations—particularly those in which it is easy to obtain quantities of 'authentic' materials?

V

RELATED READINGS

The classic work on classroom language is:—

J. McH. Sinclair and R. M. Coulthard, *Towards an Analysis of Discourse: The English used by teachers and pupils*, OUP 1975.

The two other versions of the paper discussed in this *Episode* are:—

'Problems in Syllabus Design for a course in Industrial English', *ESPMENA* 2, 1975.

'Questions in the Design and Use of Courses in English for Specialized Purposes', *Proceedings of the Fourth International Congress of Applied Linguistics* (edited by Gerhard Nickel), Vol 1, 1976.

EPISODE TEN 1978

Karl Drobnic, James Herbolich, Paul Fanning and Phil Skeldon: 'Teaching and Learning Materials', *ESPMENA Bulletin 10*, University of Khartoum, Sudan, 1978.

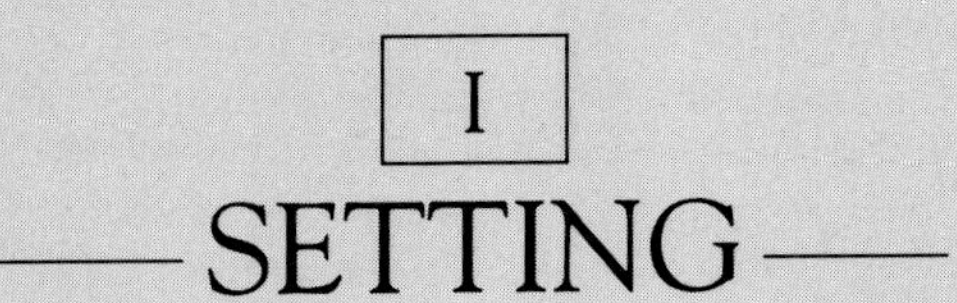

I — SETTING —

The first five years of the seventies saw a considerable increase in the numbers of people working in ESP and by the middle of the decade it was becoming clear that something had to be done about the exchange of information and ideas between the mushrooming ESP groups. Obviously, personal correspondence between a small band of enthusiasts was no longer sufficient. The main concern was about the problems of communication on a regional level, rather than nationally or globally. Although South-East Asia was well served by its Regional English Language Centre, elsewhere the situation was—and to some extent still remains—serious. One factor that has contributed to weaknesses in regional co-operation has been the way in which major International Agencies such as the British Council and USIS/ICA operate 'centre-periphery' communication networks. In the case of the British Council, for instance, the overseas career and contract ELT staff have often proved highly effective at a national level in bringing special-interest groups together, and they also have excellent lines of communication with the London headquarters and its specialized library and information services. However, the system is set up in such a manner that English Language Officers usually know very little about developments taking place in countries in their own region apart from the one to which they have been posted.

Therefore, the mid-seventies also saw the establishment of ESP 'little magazines', partly as a reaction against a feeling of isolation and partly in response to a sense in certain ESP Departments that the experiences gained in the previous years would be worth sharing with others. The contribution to ESP of these departmental journals has not been insignificant and an extract from one of them constitutes this particular *Episode*. Of course, 'little magazines' have fluctuating fortunes. Some proved exceedingly short-lived such as *The Petroleum English Bulletin* from Indonesia and the *ESP Newsletter* from Alexandria; others have proved immune to all the diseases that small departmental journals are prone to, particularly the *EST Newsletter* from University of Oregon (see the next Episode). One of the first of these journals, and one of the few with truly regional ambitions, was *ESPMENA Bulletin*, the somewhat unpronounceable acronym standing for 'English for Specific Purposes in the Middle East and North Africa'. *ESPMENA 1* appeared in 1975 and although the Bulletin failed to appear for a couple of years in the early eighties, it has now recommenced publication.

ESPMENA is produced by the English Language Servicing Unit at the University of Khartoum, the editors of *Bulletin 10* being Tony Bex and James Crofts. The average length of a Bulletin was about 25 heavily-packed pages and, as the following extract demonstrates, the editors consistently abridged longer contributions. The main sections of ESPMENA have changed little over the years: Conferences, Seminars, Workshops; Developments in ESP

Projects and Centres; Teaching and Learning Materials; Reviews and Users' Reports; Interference, Problems, Puzzles; and main Articles. This list of contents indicates the Bulletin's aim to offer and exchange information and useful suggestions. Particular attention was given to serious reviewing and in its earlier years ESPMENA gained some notoriety for its hard-hitting criticisms of ESP textbooks. Certainly its reviewers were no respecters of reputations (see the 'Related Readings' for Episode Seven).

I have chosen the *Teaching and Learning* section for this Episode because it usefully brings us back to the crafts of materials writing and the setting up of purposeful activities within the classroom; and it does so largely independently of the contrasting arguments from principle offered by Allen and Widdowson and Phillips and Shettlesworth, and of the restrictions imposed by a textbook format. In other words, this Episode offers examples of imaginative ESP practice that can best be judged in terms of their own qualities.

There are four items, one from America, one from Kuwait and two from the University of Khartoum itself. The items also cover a rather wider range of subjects than we have seen up until now: physics, engineering, medical technology, and architecture. The first of the four pieces is by Karl Drobnic, who was the founder-editor of the *ESP Newsletter* from the University of Oregon and who also started the excellent Oregon 'Clearing House' for ESP materials and papers. In it, Drobnic applies one of the main concepts of the 'Washington School' (Episode Six), the *conceptual* paragraph, to an actual teaching situation. In the second, James Herbolich identifies *outlining* as a neglected study skill and then describes how he teaches it; third, Paul Fanning offers examples of how to teach conditional sentences in well-contextualized situations; and finally, Phil Skeldon in a shorter piece describes how he successfully adapted well-used arrangements for getting students to give 'lecturettes' to a class of first-year architecture students. Skeldon's encouragement of 'visitors' to his ESP classroom foreshadows attempts in Episodes Eleven and Twelve to end the communicative isolation of ESP work by involving other interested parties in it.

II

TEXT AND COMMENTARY

Teaching and Learning Materials

Teaching Conceptual Paragraphs in EST Courses— A Practical Technique ESPMENA Bulletin 10

by Karl Drobnic, *Oregon State University*

INTRODUCTION

It has been found that a problem common to many students taking courses in English for Science and Technology (EST) who by traditional university standards are proficient in English is that 'they often seem unable to comprehend the total meaning of the EST discourse even when they understand all the words in each sentence and all the sentences that make up the discourse' (Selinker, Trimble & Trimble, 1976). The 'Washington' school of EST, cited above, has made extensive investigations into the rhetoric of EST which have produced results that prescribe the extension of traditional English language reading instruction to include *(a)* rhetorical as well as linguistic competence.

The Washington research contends that 'in EST the conceptual paragraph is the basic unit of discourse' (Lackstrom, Selinker & Trimble, 1973). The somewhat standard practice of teaching that a paragraph is a group of sentences set off by indentation which have a topic sentence and form a complete unity of thought does not always correspond to what the conceptual paragraph is. The Washington research suggests restructuring this view of paragraphing to include the concepts of the *physical* paragraph and the *conceptual* paragraph. In this approach, the physical paragraph is 'a group of sentences marked on a page of text by *(b)* spacing or indentation', while the conceptual paragraph is 'a group of organizationally (rhetorically) related concepts which develop a given generalization in such a way as to form a coherent and complete unit of discourse. It can consist of one or more physical paragraphs' (Konecni & Trimble, 1976).

Central to conceptual paragraphing is the 'core generalization' (Lackstrom, Selinker & Trimble, 1973), a generalization from which the rest of the conceptual paragraph develops. If this core generalization has no logical subdivisions which the writer wishes to develop, he is likely to finish off his paragraph in much the traditional manner of adding supporting information and specific details and then pass on to a new idea in a new paragraph. In such cases, the physical and conceptual paragraphs correspond. However, if the core generalization of the first physical paragraph contains one or more sub-parts that the author wishes to develop, the sub-parts will be developed in separate physical paragraphs, each with a sub-core that relates back to the core generalization of the first physical paragraph. Thus, several physical paragraphs may be related in terms of concept to a particular generalization, and all of these physical paragraphs, in terms of reading strategy, should be treated as one paragraph—a conceptual paragraph.

In line with this, a series of lessons were developed at Oregon State University to introduce a group of Taiwanese nuclear engineering students to selected rhetorical features of EST

(a) Readers of Episode Six will be familiar with this position.

(b) Many discourse analysts have expressed the view that physical paragraph boundaries are not good indicators of text-structure. However, indentation is presumably not an arbitrary matter, and research into why in fact writers begin new paragraphs at certain points would be welcome.

discourse. The lesson described herein is a technique for teaching conceptual paragraphing that makes use of flowcharting. Material for this lesson was selected from a US Government (c) publication entitled *Atomic Fuel* (Hogerton, 1966). The text has not been modified. The Taiwanese engineers had an advanced level of English and were targeted for graduate-level study. The lesson has been revised slightly for this article, but is essentially the same as that presented in the classroom.

Introduction

1. The reading below makes extensive use of *definition* to classify 'atomic fuel'.
2. Remember the formula for definition: 'A is B which C'
3. Remember the information needed to classify:

   (a) a class (b) class members (c) differences

4. The reading below develops one idea in what appears to be three paragraphs. The three paragraphs you see are called *physical* paragraphs. They form one *conceptual* paragraph. The writer uses three physical paragraphs to develop one idea, or one conceptual paragraph.

READ:

'*What Atomic Fuel Is* Atomic fuel consists basically of a mixture of fissionable and fertile materials. The essential ingredient is a fissionable material, a material that readily undergoes nuclear fission when struck by neutrons. The only naturally available fissionable material is uranium-235, an isotope of uranium constituting less than 1% (actually 0.71%) of the element as found in nature.

'Almost all the rest (99.28%) of the natural uranium element is the uranium-238 isotope, which is of interest to us for a different but related reason. For when neutrons strike uranium-238 a fissionable material is generally formed, namely plutonium-239. So, although natural uranium actually contains only a little fissionable matter, almost all of it can be converted to fissionable matter.

'Because it has the property of being convertible to a fissionable material, uranium-238 is called a fertile material. A second substance that has this property is the element thorium. Its fissionable derivative is still another isotope of uranium, uranium-233.'

Discussion and Analysis

1. The purpose of the three paragraphs above is to classify atomic fuel, the first sentence *defines* 'atomic fuel'. The rest of the reading develops classifying information. Identify the following:

(d) (a) term to be classified—(atomic fuel)
(b) class to which it belongs—(fuel)
(c) members of the class—(U-235, U-238, etc.)
(d) differentiating information—(fertile, etc.)

2. The most important unit in writing in scientific English is the conceptual paragraph. Discuss:

(e) (a) core generalization
(b) sub-cores.

(c) The text is, all the same, clearly an introductory one—as we can see from the title, *What Atomic Fuel Is.*

(d) Drobnic has obviously added the answers in brackets.

(e) Getting the students to undertake various kinds of textual analysis is a common enough practice in ESP. Certainly, such cognitive activities are believed to be appropriate to learners of intellectual maturity and with intellectual interests. However, I know of little hard evidence that textual analysis actually leads to improved reading comprehension.

Exercise 1. Using the information in the reading, write out definitions for each of the following terms. Use 'A is *B* which C'.

Physical Paragraph 1

1. Atomic fuel is ______________________________.
2. A fissionable material is ______________________________.
3. U-235 is ______________________________.
   It is also ______________________________.

Physical Paragraph 2

(f) 4. U-238 is ______________________________.
5. Pu-239 is ______________________________.

Physical Paragraph 3

6. U-238 is also defined as ______________________________.
7. A fertile material is ______________________________.

Exercise 2. Construct a flowchart of the information presented in the reading. Use the questions below as a guide.

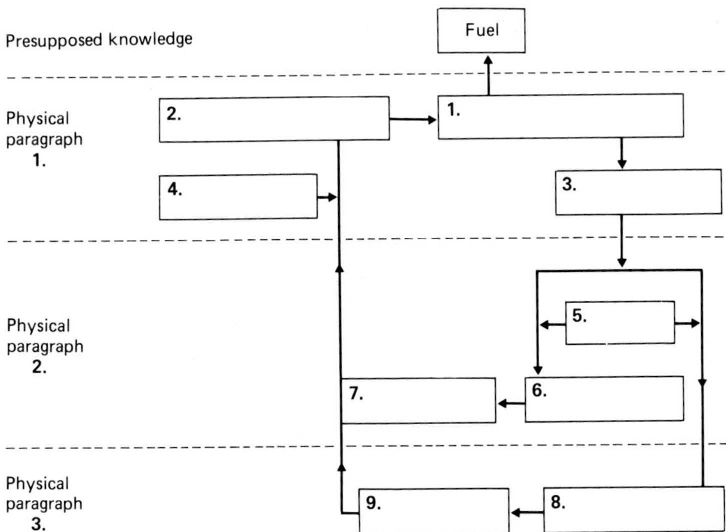

Flowchart Questions

1. What is the term being classified?
2. What is the essential ingredient?
3. What is the other ingredient in the mixture?
4. What is the naturally occurring fissionable material?
5. What must strike fertile material to form fissionable material?
6. What is the majority of the natural uranium?
7. What is the fissionable product of U-238?
8. What is a second fertile material?
9. What is its fissionable product?

End of Lesson ....

* * *

(f) This strikes me as a highly appropriate and useful exercise.

Results Being already practising engineers, the Taiwanese were thoroughly familiar with the idea of flowcharting. Representation of conceptual paragraphing in graphic form employed a
(g) familiar cognitive process. It required the transfer of verbal information to a visual form that the students already knew was used to represent logical inter-relationships. The intent to use the students' cognitive skills from their field of expertise was fulfilled; the students quickly
(h) grasped the conceptual unity of the stretch of text and in subsequent lessons proved to be adept at recognizing conceptual paragraphs.

References

Doherty, Michael P. (1977), 'An Investigation into the Cognitive Variable in EST Programmes'. University of Kuwait, Kuwait.

Hogerton, John. (1966), *Atomic Fuel.* U.S. Government Printing Office, Washington, DC.

Konecni, Evica and Louis Trimble. (1976), 'Scientific and Technical Rhetoric, Glossary of Technical Terms'. Skopje, Yugoslavia, and Seattle, Washington, USA.

Lackstrom, John, Larry Selinker and Louis Trimble. (1973), 'Technical Rhetorical Information and Grammatical Choice', TESOL Q., Washington, DC, Vol 7 No. 2.

Selinker, Larry, R. M. Todd Trimble and Louis Trimble. (1976), 'Presuppositional Rhetorical Information in EST Discourse', TESOL Q., Washington, DC, Vol 10, No. 3.

Trimble, R. Mary Todd. (1976), 'Literary Training and the Teaching of EST to Non-native Speakers'. English Teaching Forum, Washington, D.C.

This contribution has been somewhat condensed to save space.—Ed. ESPMENA

(b) *Teaching Outlining to The ESP Student* James B. Herbolich, Kuwait University

(i) This article is abridged and reprinted by permission from EST Newsletter 9.

Outlining has long been recognized as a skill that university level EFL students should master in order to organize and comprehend information gained through reading textbooks. Indeed, it would be a rare language centre where one did not find a unit of a study skills course devoted to outlining for the EFL student, but, for the most part, outlining as a skill for the engineering
(j) student has largely been ignored in ESP textbooks.[1] This may be the result of ESP textbook writers believing that engineering articles do not lend themselves to the basic outline form. However, in teaching a reading skills class as part of an intensive English course for engineering students at Kuwait University, I have found that engineering articles are 'outlineable' and that teaching students to outline aids them in organizing and comprehending the important facts of a reading.

Yorkey (1970) defines an outline as 'an organized list of related items or ideas'.[2] With this definition in mind, I began teaching topic outlining and the following is a brief discussion of a technique I have found effective with engineering students.

---

[1] The references 1 to 6 on this and succeeding pages refer to the Notes on page 124.

(g) Rather less so with Exercise 2. For one thing, there is a piece of conventional wisdom that *flow-charts* are best used with dynamic and process passages, and that static classificatory passages such as this are better articulated through tables, matrices or tree-diagrams. Secondly, Drobnic's need to add 'Flowchart Questions' is perhaps a sign that he himself recognizes that the flow-chart is rather unwieldy. Doubtless Phillips and Shettlesworth would have set a more open and creative task for the engineers to undertake, and one that would have led to genuine discussion.

(h) Drobnic in this abridged article has shown how the rhetorical approach can be used to considerable effect, particularly, as in this case, when the materials writer finds an excellent passage to work with.

(i) The *EST Newsletter* will be discussed in the next Episode.

(j) My experience is somewhat different. My own guess is that language centres rarely give any serious attention to outlining—which makes Herbolich's discussion all the more valuable.

Phase I: *An explanation of 'What is an outline'* (1 one-hour class)

First, a list is written on the board[3], such as:

HCl	Salt	NaOH	Acids	HNO_3
Bases	NaCl	KOH	H_2SO_4	Alkali

When students are asked about the list, the answers usually given are 'terms from chemistry', or 'formulae' or 'solutions'. The students are then asked for ways to organize the contents of the list. Various suggestions given are alphabetical ordering, numerical arrangement or breaking the list into smaller lists. Using the third suggestion results in:

Acids	Bases	Salt
HCl	NaOH	NaCl
HNO_3	KOH	
H_2SO_4	Alkali	

Before arranging the three above lists into an outline, a skeleton outline is written on the board, as such:

I. ______________________
    A. ______________________
    B. ______________________
    C. ______________________
II. ______________________
    A. ______________________
    B. ______________________
        1. ______________________
III. ______________________
    A. ______________________

(k) Using the skeleton outline, the students are introduced to the terms: 'Main headings', 'Roman numerals', 'Arabic numerals', 'indent', and 'sub-headings'. After discussing the skeleton outline, the students are quite capable of filling in the outline using the three lists.

Phase II: *Examination of a model topic outline* (1 one-hour class)

After reviewing 'what is an outline?', the students are given a short (1 page) reading entitled *The Classification of Compounds*, which discusses in three paragraphs acids, bases and salts. The students are reminded that a paragraph contains one main idea with supporting facts. Using the
(l) suggestions given by Harris (1966) for finding the main idea of a paragraph[4], the students are instructed to read the article and to write the main idea of each paragraph in the margin. After this task is completed, an oral discussion of each paragraph brings out the supporting facts for each main idea: 'an acid is a compound of hydrogen', 'a base turns red litmus blue', etc. The students are then given a model topic outline on the reading[5] and we discuss its organization. The following points are stressed:

1. Each paragraph contains a main idea which becomes a main heading—3 paragraphs = 3 main headings.
2. The supporting facts should be brief and, as much as possible, in the students' 'own words'—not copied word for word from the reading.
3. A good outline will contain all the important supporting facts.

Phase III: Controlled outlining (4 one-hour class periods)

For the next two or three weeks the students, after reading an article and jotting down the main ideas of the paragraphs, are required to complete a partially filled topic outline on the

(k) A nice illustration of getting the simple things right.

(l) I have not been able to find a copy of Harris.

(m) reading. The students are told that if they have culled all the important facts from a reading, then they should be able to answer any question on a reading using solely their outline. If they can answer easily from their outline, then they have produced a 'correct' outline. To emphasize
(n) this point, the students answer multiple-choice or true/false questions on the reading using their outlines.

Phase IV: *Free Outlining* (throughout the course)

To move from controlled outlining to free outlining (i.e. the students produce the outline form and supply all the items to the outline), the students must be convinced that outlining will help them in their future classes. Given the exam-orientation of our students, it is mentioned that throughout the semester, if a student has outlined reading assignments, then, when it is time for an examination, there will be *no need to re-read* all the assignments, but only to go over the outlines for they will contain the essence of the readings.

After doing three or four controlled outlines, the students are quite capable of producing outlines on their own. In fact, students have said that it is easier for them to produce a free
(o) outline than it is to complete my controlled outlines, which indicated to me that outlining is a personal skill—there is no *one* correct outline for a reading.

The free outlining is done as a homework assignment after a discussion of the main points of a reading. At the beginning of class, I quickly check the outlines for (1) correct form; (2) enough supporting facts; and (3) briefness of expression. As in Phase III, the students are required to answer questions using their outlines; however, the questions usually entail writing complete, grammatical sentences as answers—in a sense, recreating parts of the reading from the outline.

By the end of the course, the students, hopefully, are convinced that outlining is a useful skill, not just a skill to learn in order to pass their English course. I have found this technique of teaching outlining effective because the students practise the skill throughout the semester, not as a one-week unit where outlining is forgotten soon after it is mentioned. Initially, outlining for the engineering student is difficult, but eventually the students quite easily recognize the important points of a reading. The resulting ability to pin-point the central points necessary results in a 'reduction of uncertainty' about the contents of a reading[6], which is a step towards
(p) complete reading comprehension.

Notes

1 Of the six ESP textbooks for engineering students listed in the bibliography*, *none* contain a unit on outlining.
2 Richard C. Yorkey, *Study Skills* (New York: McGraw-Hill, Inc. 1970) p. 77.
3 Since the reading skills class begins with readings in chemical engineering, the initial phase of the technique reflects this bias; however, any reading of classification will yield a list with which to begin outlining.
4 David P. Harris, *Reading Improvement Exercises for Students of English as a Second Language* (Englewood Cliffs, New Jersey: Prentice-Hall, Inc., 1966) p. 54.
5 This was suggested by a fellow teacher, Maureen O'Brien.
6 Frank Smith, *Understanding Reading* (New York: Holt, Rinehart and Winston, Inc., 1971) p. 185.

* Omitted here for reasons of space—Ed. ESPMENA

(m) 'culled' = 'extracted' (in this context).

(n) One can easily see the motivational force of this arrangement.

(o) I do not believe that the observation about the students finding it easier to produce a 'free outline' in any way invalidates Herbolich's approach. Indeed, there is much in favour of saying 'Look, this is a standard way of doing things; prove to me you can do it the standard way. When you have done that, you are perfectly free to do it your own way if you find that easier or more comfortable.'

(p) *Teaching Outlining to the ESP Student* describes a thoughtful, patient and well-structured approach to a particular study skills problem and gives some idea of the quality of work being produced in the Middle East at that time.

c) *'If' Sentences in Instructions*

Most textbooks simply treat 'if' sentences as sentences in which a statement of 'a condition' is followed by a statement of 'a result', and learners are asked to produce sentences like

If ice is heated to 0°C, it will turn to water.

or

If a stone is dropped, it falls to the ground.

There seems little attempt to place the different types of conditional in a situational or textual context. In Bulletin 1 we included some material which attempted to show learners
(q) how to use 'if' sentences in giving examples and making definitions and classifications. Recently Paul Fanning has devised the following approach to 'if' sentences as they are used in instructions for laboratory technicians.

First the students read a passage describing a method for testing urine, which includes 'if' sentences to give alternative procedures and explain the conclusions that can be drawn from different results in the test. They are then asked to fill in a flow chart summarizing the procedure.

Then simple flow charts like this

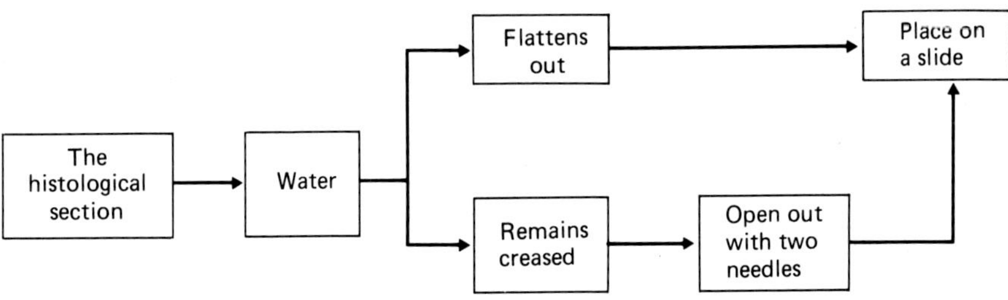

are given to generate 'if' sentences to present alternative strategies, for example,

(r) Place the histological section in water. If it flattens out, place it on a slide. If it remains creased, open it out with two needles and then place it on a slide.

(q) The section in *Bulletin 1* opened with a claim that there were two principal uses of simple conditionals:—

(i) to make general statements;
(ii) to illustrate rather abstract propositions.

Here is an example of the latter:—

Speed is the ratio of the distance travelled by a moving body to the time taken. For instance, if a lorry travels 200 km in 4 hours, it has an average speed of 50 k.p.h.

This second use can be easily practised by getting the students to produce their own illustrations and examples in conditional form. However, the first function is not so easy to generate. *Bulletin 1*, amongst other things, suggested looking at General statements and their potential conditional equivalents:—

A square has four sides

(a) If a figure is a square, it has four sides. TRUE/FALSE WHY?
(b) If a figure has four sides, it is a square. TRUE/FALSE WHY?

This extract concentrates on a third use of conditionals, and one particularly related to the language of instructions and procedures.

(r) Paul Fanning worked for a number of years on developing courses for para-medical students at the University of Khartoum; one tangible result was the textbook, *English in the Medical Laboratory*, written by Paul Fanning and myself (Thomas Nelson, 1980). In terms of the 'conventional wisdom' I referred to in the Commentary on Drobnic, this seems a more successful use of flow-charting.

The other use is generated by using this matrix table

Type of jaundice	Bilirubin	Bile Salts	Urobilin	Urobilinogen
Haemolytic	−	−	+	+
Obstructive	+	+	−	−
Hepatic	+ +	+	+	+

Key: + = is present; − = is absent.

to complete sentences like this:

If the tests for bilirubin, bile salts, urobilin and urobilinogen are all positive, ...

to express conclusions that can be drawn from the test results.

Finally the students write a short paragraph describing another urine test presented in flow chart and diagram.

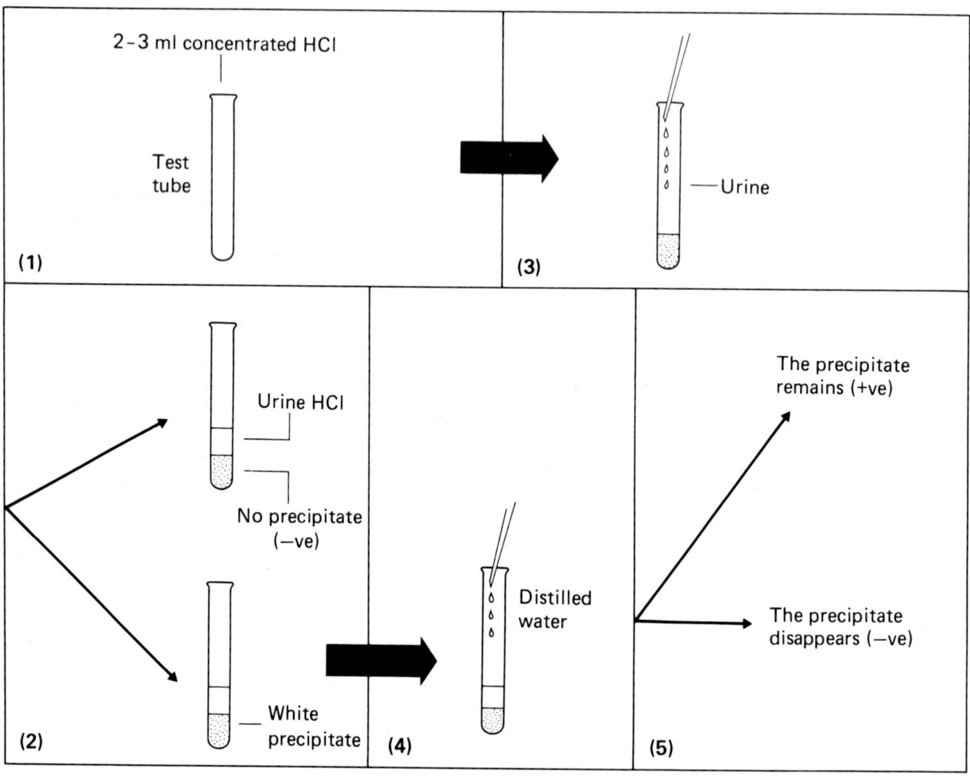

(s) In addition to practising 'if' sentences functionally in a well contextualized situation, the students are given valuable practice in handling two very common methods of presenting summarized information.

Paul Fanning

(s) This extract gives the impression of being well-researched and well-planned. We can also notice that the traditional principles of material design are adopted, even though the content is highly specific and the paramedical context somewhat unusual. Thus, we find *presentation* followed by *practice* followed by *production*. Alternatives to these principles, such as *information search*, *information exchange* and *information synthesis*, have on the whole been slower to emerge in EST than in some other ESP areas such as *English for Business*. I suspect that this is largely due to the fact that academic success is essentially an individual matter, whereas commercial success is essentially co-operative.

d) *Lecturettes*

(t) After reading Patricia Hines' explanation of the use of lecturettes in Bulletin 7, I was interested in introducing the idea into our course for First Year Architecture students at the University of Khartoum. However as more basic work had a greater claim on our limited time, it was not possible to allocate time for each of our fifty or so students to give a lecturette. In an effort to find a solution, it was decided to invite two final-year students to give short talks about (u) their projects. They were eager to do so since oral discussion plays a large part in the assessment of their project. The only preparation involved was to select three or four drawings from each portfolio and suggest that the student 'lecturers' pay attention to topics we had been working on in our English classes with the first-year students: shapes, properties of materials, function and purpose etc. The lecturettes lasted 10–15 minutes with a slightly longer period for a question and answer session. In both cases question-time had to be called to a halt by the teacher and we certainly had the 'excitement of the game' and not the dullness of the practice session. A question sheet was compiled from teachers' notes from the lecturettes to ensure attention was given. It was completed in the next class and the average score was slightly over 70%.

There were favourable conditions for the experiment. The two 'lecturers' were both fluent and confident performers. The drawings had already been made and provided a focus of attention for the listeners and a visual prompt for the speakers. Architecture seems to be a subject where it is not too difficult for the expert or more advanced student to communicate intelligibly with the layman or the beginner.

Nevertheless it was an encouraging success for us and both sets of students. Genuine communication took place: explanations of unknown terms, more detailed explanations and re-explanations of points were sought; misunderstandings occurred and were cleared up; and (v) there was even some mild disagreement. The first-year students, still overawed by their lecturers in ordinary Architecture and English classes, were certainly less inhibited about asking questions. Finally, this sort of activity makes use of intrinsically interesting material for useful language practice instead of being a dull re-run of material already known from subject lectures which many ESP lessons become.

It is hoped to extend this exercise next year to include more final year students giving lecturettes to first- and second-year classes. There also would seem to be scope for exploiting it with, say, post-graduates in botany, zoology, medicine etc. giving talks to their junior (w) colleagues on research projects. It kills two birds with one stone and as a real activity it has more interest than even our most creative efforts at simulating reality.

Phil Skeldon

(t) Patricia Hines was describing the way in which she organized her course on ten-minute oral presentations in the Faculty of Engineering, Kuwait. One of the most interesting aspects of Pat Hines's approach was her system of evaluation. Each speaker had to provide a set of model notes for his talk, and his talk was evaluated by how well his *fellow-students* had managed to note down his main points. Putting the responsibility on the listeners in this way is surely a brilliant improvement on the standard systems of the teacher passing judgment or of class-voting; and, of course, fits in well with the comments on classroom organization by Phillips and Shettlesworth.

(u) Again we can see the importance of motivation and involvement.

(v) A valuable point.

(w) Although Phil Skeldon is describing some very preliminary work, one of the interesting things about the piece is its attack on what might be called the 'four walls problem'. We have seen in this and the three previous Episodes a clear trend towards communicative teaching, but so far efforts have been concentrated on increasing the communicative purposiveness of what goes on *within* the four walls of the ESP classroom. Phil Skeldon's involvement of 'outsiders'—in his case other students—is a first move towards dismantling part of those walls, and we shall see other moves with that objective in the next two Episodes.

III

ACTIVITIES

(1) Construct a modified version of Drobnic's *Exercise 2*.

(2) Produce your own outline of Herbolich's article. Then ask somebody else to produce one, and compare your results. How far do your results support Herbolich's conclusion that 'outlining is a personal skill—there is no *one* correct outline for a reading'.

(3) Take a section from any scientific textbook and:—

  (*a*) note all occurrences of the simple conditional (with the main clause in the Present Simple or with the modal *will*).

  (*b*) classify, if you can, the *functions* of the simple conditionals.

  (*c*) How many of the conditionals fall within the four uses noted in Fanning's piece and in the associated commentary?

  (*d*) If there are some that seem to be fulfilling other functions, how would you characterize those functions?

(4) Have you been in a teaching situation where you could have made use of Skeldon's ideas? If so, what modifications should be made?

IV

EVALUATION

(1) Rank the four extracts in order of interest to you and be prepared to explain why.

(2) Imagine you have been asked to edit a new ESP Journal to be called *The ESP Practitioner*. What kind of contributions would you like to commission? What emphasis would you give to practice and theory? Which of the ten Episodes so far are of the type you would like to encourage? Outline your editorial policy.

V

RELATED READINGS

The most relevant Related Reading for Drobnic is his paper in the volume *English for Specific Purposes: Science and Technology* (see Episode Six) entitled: 'Mistakes and Modification in Course Design: an EST Case History'. The paper deals in an entirely honest way with problems met in planning a course for the same group of students as described in the first item of this Episode.

The Language Centre of the University of Kuwait produces its own Journal called *Al-Manakh*. This can be obtained free of charge by writing to the address below:—

Al-Manakh
Journal of the Language Centre
PO Box 5486
The University
Kuwait

The broader context of the Fanning extract can be seen in:—

John Swales and Paul Fanning, *English in the Medical Laboratory* (Thomas Nelson), 1980.

The reference in the final piece is to:—

Patricia Hines, 'The Lecturette—An Aural/Oral Teaching Technique', ESPMENA 7, 1977.

EPISODE ELEVEN 1979

James B. Herbolich, 'Box Kites', *English for Specific Purposes*, Issue 29, English Language Institute, Oregon State University, Corvallis, Oregon, USA, 1979.

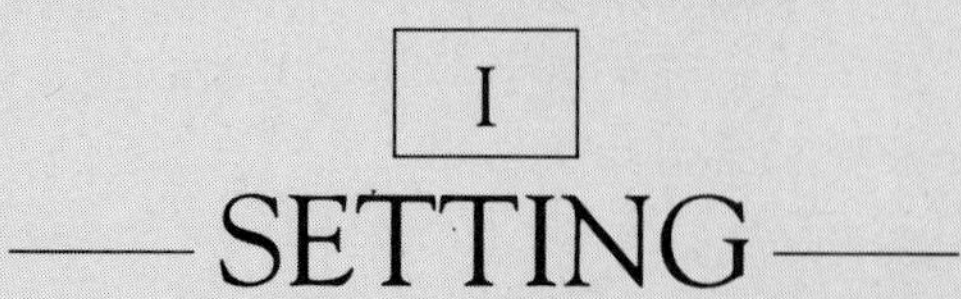

This short Episode is a continuation of the previous one in so far as it offers another example of imaginative ESP work emanating from the Arab world in the late seventies. However, I have set it apart because it illustrates a developing ESP interest in project work.

You may recollect that in their final paragraph Phillips and Shettlesworth conclude that 'the course materials could then become less an ESP textbook in the accepted sense rather than a set of resource material together with procedural guidelines for their exploitation'. Projects are an obvious means of getting away from the textbook. And the resource material will often have to be found and assimilated by the students themselves—with equally obvious advantages for purposeful study skills practice. Further, in English-medium or partly English-medium institutions, an ESP project can (at least in theory) shadow the reality of project work in the students' subject disciplines.

Of course a project is no more a magic solution to underlying ESP dissatisfactions than any other initiative. As always, enthusiasm needs to be moderated by educational realism. A typical project is a major undertaking since it asks the learners to commit to it a considerable amount of both in-class and out-of-class time and it may well require the teacher to spend long hours setting the project(s) up, helping the class to get organized, correcting drafts and marking the final reports. If things go wrong (because of time-pressures, loss of student interest, tasks either too easy or too difficult, incompatibility between individuals, administrative problems and so on) much of this time and effort may be wasted. After all, ESP practitioners rarely have as much contact-time with their classes as they would like. They therefore have a continuing responsibility to weigh high-risk and high-reward activities against other activities that may prove less beneficial but are more certain of *some* productive outcome. An example of such cautious assessment of priorities and possibilities was seen in the final piece of the last Episode. We can also see something of a similar sort in Herbolich's description of the 'Box Kite' project.

James Herbolich was working in the late seventies at the University of Kuwait, more specifically in the English Language Unit for the Faculty of Engineering. This Unit, which was originally headed by David Blackie, was at that time probably the best of its kind in the world. The very fine team also included Maureen O'Brien and Patricia Hines (both mentioned in the previous Episode) and Jonathan Elliman, Bill Robinson, Noel Simon and Bill Starkey. The members of this team have all now moved on, but I think it is relevant to any discussion of 'Box Kites' to bear in mind the high quality of the ESP staff involved.

Like so many of the most interesting short ESP articles to appear in recent years, 'Box Kites' was published by the ELI at the University of Oregon. The ELI's Departmental Journal was originally entitled the *EST Newsletter* and first appeared in 1977; in 1979 its name was changed to *English for Specific Purposes.* A production schedule of ten issues a year has been maintained with awe-inspiring regularity and at the time of writing *English for Specific Purposes* is about to enter its seventh successful year of publication. If I were asked to identify the one activity that has done most to keep the widely-scattered community of ESP practitioners in touch with one another in the last few years—particularly by maintaining contact between the Americas and the rest of the world—it would be the editorial work of Karl Drobnic and latterly Kathryn Michaels at Corvallis, Oregon. I thus feel it fitting that one Episode in this volume will offer some token recognition of their services to the ESP profession.

'Box Kites' is a delightful and heart-warming piece. More than anything else, it demonstrates that a successful project can generate an educationally-valuable sense of personal satisfaction for all parties involved—something that is not so easy to achieve in any other way.

II

TEXT AND COMMENTARY

Box Kites

by James B. Herbolich, *ELU Engineering, University of Kuwait*

(a) *INTRODUCTION* This article concerns itself with one aspect of course 221, manual writing, and will describe the box kite project, which was successfully carried out by the English 221 students.

(b) *PREPARATION* Accepting that, in order to write a manual one must 'understand the mechanism'[1], it was decided the students should actually construct something, which had to be simple because only $2\frac{1}{2}$ weeks were allotted to the Manual component of the course. The 'mechanism' should be: (1) relatively new to the students; (2) related to a field of Engineering; (3) a device which allowed the attainment of new lexis; (4) a device which actually would operate; and (5) enjoyable to construct and test.

It was decided that the English 221 students would construct *box kites*.

PRESENTATION The students were first instructed to read chapter 13, in Pauley. The chapter was discussed in class and a general format for their manuals was decided upon.

The students were then told that their manuals would be entitled 'A Manual for Constructing a Box Kite'. Most of the students were totally unfamiliar with the term 'box kite', so they were given a library research exercise[2] in which they had to find: (1) a definition of the box kite; (2) the inventor of the first box kite; (3) alternative names for the box kite; (4) scientific uses of the box kite; and (5) a labelled illustration of a box kite. In the next class the students presented and discussed their findings on the box kite and were now able to expand (c) their basic outline for writing the manual. The following outline was agreed upon:

A Manual for Constructing a Box Kite

1.0 Title Page
2.0 Table of Contents
3.0 List of Illustrations
4.0 Introduction
  4.1 Purpose
  4.2 Scope
5.0 General Description
  5.1 Kites (in General)
  5.2 Box Kites
    5.2.1 Inventor
    5.2.2 Uses
    5.2.3 Description/Illustration

[1] Pauley, 232. See bibliography of previous article.
[2] Handout 8, Course 221, devised by William Starkey.

(a) 221 was a second-level course in Technical Report Writing, of which manual writing was a component. The Faculty of Engineering at Kuwait University is English-medium.

(b) The reference is to Stephen Pauley's *Technical Report Writing Today* (Houghton Mifflin Co, USA, 1973). The point here is that only by making something yourself is it possible to see what other people need to be told if *they* are going to succeed in making it.

(c) Notice how Herbolich is now able to capitalize on his previous work on outlining. We can also see that the project-designer is maintaining very tight control of developments, a decision which we will look at again later.

6.0 Detailed Description
    6.1 Frame
        6.1.1 Struts
        6.1.2 Braces
    6.2 Cover
    6.3 Bridle
7.0 Assembly
8.0 Testing and Adjustments
9.0 Bibliography

At this time the students were also given two hand-outs which contained various bits of information concerning box kites, since the Engineering Library did not offer an abundance of literature on box kites. They were told that they could work in pairs and should take detailed notes and make drawings while constructing the kites. To further encourage motivation for the project the students were told that the box kites had to fly and that the instructors would be present to witness the 'launchings'.

PROGRESS After a week, the class met again to discuss any problems they were having either with constructing the box kite or writing the manual.

Many students had already obtained the materials and had done further research on box kites. (i.e. they were searching for complete instructions on how to build the box kites.
(d) Fortunately, within the Engineering and Science Libraries, only the barest essentials could be found. A few students did find relevant books in book stores.)

Some students had already constructed their box kites, but they did not fly. This was mainly due to (1) the struts being too heavy; (2) poor supporting braces; (3) incorrect bridle attachment.

During this class, various points in writing the manuals were given to the students:

(1) The detailed description of the box kite parts should give the kind of material used (bamboo, aluminium, balsa wood, plywood); the dimensions of the struts, braces, and cover; the kind of cover material used (nylon, tracing paper, wrapping paper, crepe paper) and the colour of the cover material.
(2) The box kite the instructors would inspect had to correspond exactly with the instructions in the manual.
(e) (3) The assembly instructions had to be written in the active voice, imperative mood.
(4) The testing and adjustment section had to discuss the attempt to fly the box kite and, if the attempt was initially unsuccessful, to state the adjustments which were then made.
(5) The manuals had to contain illustrations, properly labelled, to help clarify written points in the manual.

ROUGH DRAFTS After a week-and-a-half students were required to hand in a complete rough
(f) draft of their manuals. These were corrected for mistakes in format and grammar and returned to the students ungraded[3]. They were told to hand in the final versions of the manuals in the next class.

---

[3] For a discussion of student errors see the section entitled 'Final Copies'.

(d) A problem-solving project of this type does rely on the students being *unable* to find 'short-cut' solutions in books—and it would seem Herbolich has managed to ensure this.

(e) If the students had been asked to produce a technical report rather than a manual, the description of the assembly would presumably have been in the past passive.

(f) As so often in project-work, the objective is to obtain an end-product in which the student can take some pride, even though (as here) the teacher has helped considerably in the creation of the satisfactory end-product.

FINAL COPIES The completed manuals were handed in and graded. In general, the manuals, which ran between 9 and 12 pages, were given grades of A or B, 'very good' to 'excellent'.

Few common grammar mistakes were evident in the manuals; however, two are worth noting. In giving the dimensions of a strut or brace, the students repeatedly confused and mixed nouns and adjectives within a sentence: 'The strut is 50 mm. in length, 5 mm. wide and 5 mm. thickness.' Secondly, most of the students did not know the past tense of 'fly' e.g. 'The box kite *flied* the first time.'

With the illustrations, three problems were noted. Firstly, illustrations were put in the manuals but were not referred to in the text. Secondly, the illustrations were not given titles; a student would label an illustration 'Figure 3' instead of 'Figure 3. Braces.' Thirdly, the arrows going from the label to the illustration often pointed to the label instead of to the part of the box kite.

FLYING THE BOX KITES

(g) On a clear, but windy day, the 50 English 221 students, instructors and on-lookers gathered to fly the 25 completed box kites. All the kites were measured to determine the smallest and largest kites. At the same time, the teachers noted the box kites they considered the 'best looking'. The smallest box kite which flew was 32 × 32 × 65 cm. while the largest flying box kite was 42 × 58 × 120 cm. The 'best looking' box kite was made of bamboo painted black with copper strips glued to the struts to reflect the sunlight when flying. The best performing box kite, which was the only one to have the cover sewn to the frame, was chosen because of its stability when flying and because of the height it flew. (It would have kept on going but they ran out of string.)

All the students then tested their box kites at the same time. The box kites were launched! Some did not move. Some took off, but crashed. Most of them, to the satisfaction of the students and teachers, 'flied' and 'flied'.

Bibliography

(h) The following bibliography lists articles on kites/box kites which should help ESP teachers in duplicating the box kite project.

Fowler, H. A *Practical Guide to Kite Making and Flying.* New York: McGraw-Hill, 1979.
Hunt, Leslie. *24 Kites that Fly.* London, Selpress, 1979.
'Kite' Britannica Junior Encyclopaedia. Vol. 9, 1977, p. 30.
'Kite' Compton's Picture Encyclopaedia. Vol. 8, 1962, p. 62.
'Kite' Encyclopaedia Britannica. Vol. 5, 1974, p. 842.
'Kite' The Encyclopaedia Americana. Vol. 16, 1962, p. 466.
'Kite' The New Caxton Encyclopaedia. Vol. 11, 1977, p. 351.
'Kite' The World Book Encyclopaedia. Vol. 10, 1962, p. 263.
'Kite' Compton's Encyclopaedia. Vol. 14, 1978, p. 62.
Pelham, David. *The Penguin Book of Kites.* England: Penguin Books, 1976.
The Reader's Digest Family Book of Things to Make and Do. New York: The Reader's Digest Association, 1977.

(g) It will have been noticed that the Engineering staff were not involved in this project. This weakness in the scheme of work—if it be such—was put right in future projects which were assessed by a 'panel' of ESP and Engineering staff members.

(h) I originally considered omitting the Bibliography on 'Box Kites', but a little thought showed that such a move would be offensive to the splendidly helpful spirit in which Herbolich had provided it.

III — ACTIVITIES —

(1) In paragraph two Herbolich gives these five requirements for the subject of a manual report:—

1. It should be relatively new to the students.
2. It should be related to a field of Engineering.
3. It should be a device which will cause some new vocabulary to be learnt.
4. The device should actually work.
5. It should be enjoyable to construct and test.

Which of these attributes do you consider essential and which only advantageous?

(2) Like Herbolich, many ESP practitioners have found that expressing dimensions is particularly liable to confusion.

(a) What are the major ways in which dimensions can be expressed in English?

(b) Why do you think it such a grammatical problem for so many students? In particular, is there evidence for this being an instance of teacher- and textbook-created confusion?

IV — EVALUATION —

(1) 'Box Kites' was obviously a highly 'controlled' project.

(a) Which of the following features do you think Herbolich took into account when deciding on a high degree of *control*:—
(i) the size of the class (50 students);
(ii) their educational level (largely second-year undergraduates);
(iii) their level of English (intermediate/upper intermediate);
(iv) the amount of time available for the project as a whole;
(v) the time available for writing—as opposed to obtaining materials, making drawings and constructing the mechanism;
(vi) the fact that *Technical Writing* courses (for NS and NNS) tend to be highly prescriptive anyway.

(b) Are there other relevant factors?

(2) Imagine that it has been decided that the 'box kite' class are to have another component on *manual writing* the following year. What will you suggest?

V

RELATED READINGS

A simple introduction to the background situation out of which projects such as 'Box Kites' emerged is:—

D. J. J. S. Blackie, 'Service English for Students of Science and Technology', *English Teaching Forum*, Vol XIV, No 2 (1976).

EPISODE TWELVE 1980

T. F. Johns and A. Dudley-Evans, 'An Experiment in Team-teaching of Overseas Postgraduate Students of Transportation and Plant Biology', *ELT Documents 106: Team Teaching in ESP*, The British Council, ETIC, London, 1980.

I — SETTING —

The previous four Episodes have all reflected—at least in part—Middle East experience. As I have already said, the Middle East in the seventies offered excellent opportunities for developmental ESP work. There were (and still are) probably more ESP practitioners employed in the Arab World than in any other comparable area and in many cases, especially at undergraduate level, Special English programmes had an established, regularized and recognized place in degree courses. This situation contrasts strongly with that in British universities. In Britain the total number of people employed full-time on an annual basis for 'Service English' work with overseas students has never exceeded thirty. Although this group is small—indeed smaller than quite a number of single ESP Departments around the world—it has been innovative and productive both in papers about ESP work and in teaching materials and in textbooks.

In a broader sense, therefore, Episode Twelve must serve as an example of the work of the small *Association of Lecturers and Tutors in English for Overseas Students*. More particularly, however, it takes up a number of the issues of the last three Episodes and offers a very different type of resolution to them. Johns and Dudley-Evans review the 'authenticity debate' that has already figured predominantly in Episodes Seven and Nine and conclude that authenticity is neither a linguistic property of texts nor a characteristic of the relationship between text and reader, but rather something that belongs to the *role* of a text in a wider *organizational* setting. They take up Skeldon's concern with the comprehension of lectures and Herbolich's interest in developing writing but place their involvement with such matters in the students' 'real world' of their subject courses and written assignments. But before we consider Tim Johns' and Tony Dudley-Evans' 'Experiment in Team-teaching' in any detail, we need first to say something of the background situation out of which their imaginative work has developed, especially as this Episode is yet another illustration in ESP of necessity being 'the mother of invention'.

The authors of this Episode have worked since the mid-seventies at Birmingham University and, by and large, their teaching situation is typical of their colleagues in those other British universities which employ lecturers and tutors to look after the English language needs of overseas students. The first priority must be students on one-year Master's courses, for undergraduates or research students have a longer 'lead-in' time to adapt culturally and educationally to their environment and to develop the linguistic and study skills they may need. However, MA and MSc students have less time than the other groups to take advantage of the language and language-related services offered to them; further, and even more paradoxically, those Master's students with the least proficiency in English (and so in greatest need of help) have least time available because their Departmental work is taking them so much longer.

The programme of 'in-sessional' courses the authors refer to briefly in their introduction is broadly similar to that offered by other UK institutions; more or less voluntary classes in report writing etc., offered outside the main University timetable. The fact that such provision is both necessary and yet insufficient is widely accepted, the real question being what to do in addition. One obvious (perhaps over-obvious) line of approach is to encourage students to attend pre-sessional courses before their Master's year begins; other 'extra-timetable' schemes that have been tried are mid-year vacation courses, week-end working parties, and the opening of self-access centres. However, as all practitioners concerned with English for Academic Purposes will know, an early priority must be to see what collaboration is possible with the relevant subject departments. For many years prior to the publication of the Birmingham work, such explorations had been taking place in many different countries, and reports of various types of co-operation can be found in the ESP literature, particularly in the 'little magazines'; reports of ESP staff 'sitting in' on lectures, of joint-preparation of assignments, of subject work going through various types of 'English filter', of co-marking of examination scripts, of the interweaving of English and subject syllabuses, of the ESP tutor acting as 'language assistant' in subject classes and so on. Episode Twelve is therefore more of a culmination of an ESP tradition rather than a new departure. However, it is brilliantly and successfully original in at least one way. In all the previous efforts at collaboration between ESP and subject staff the question of the relationships between the parties involved was never satisfactorily resolved—and we need to remember that there are now three, which can be expressed in a schematic triangle:—

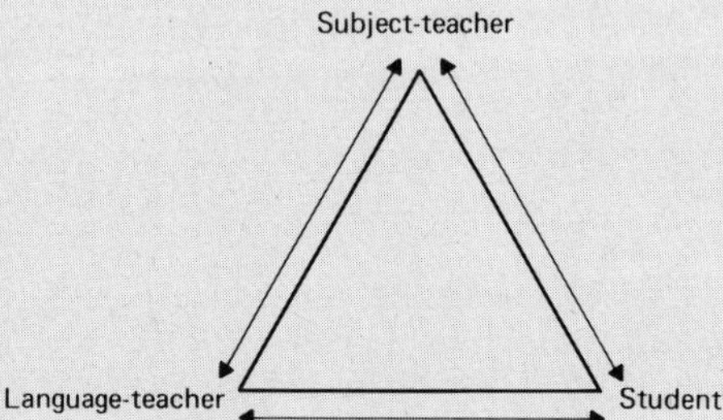

The methodology that Johns and Dudley-Evans have devised to reduce the tensions of such triangular situations is most ingenious.

Despite a somewhat forbidding and restrictive-sounding title, the paper that follows is an extremely valuable one in a number of other ways. First, it represents, at a highly sophisticated level, the ESP practitioner's growing concern with the total educational environment of the student. Here I will only single out two aspects of this concern: a recognition that non-native speakers of English have been insufficiently prepared in most ESP courses for coping with written examinations; and a recognition that the language teacher 'needs to be able to grasp the conceptual structure of a subject his students are studying if he is to understand fully how language is used to represent that structure'. Secondly, the authors demonstrate that close collaboration between language and subject teachers *can* be made to work and that this is yet another way of bringing relevance and communicative reality to ESP activities.

However, the general value and wider applicability of particular team-teaching schemes is very hard to evaluate. So much seems to depend on the personalities involved, on whether there is mutual educational and intellectual respect, and on circumstances that may encourage or discourage the maintenance of a team-teaching initiative. In addition, we would do well to bear in mind, as we did in the previous Episode, that approaches such as that reported in this Episode achieve their considerable and impressive purposes only by considerable and impressive expenditure of time and effort on behalf of restricted numbers of students.

I should like to make a further acknowledgment here, especially as in the opening remarks to the two previous Episodes I have referred to the contribution of Departmental Journals to the development of ESP. This Episode as well as Episode Nine was published by the British Council in their *ELT Documents Series.* About half of the volumes of 'ELT Docs' (as they are affectionately known) have been devoted to English for Specific Purposes, and many of the most useful articles to appear in the last ten years can be found within their covers. Further, the volumes have often had a 'thematic' approach, such as Number 106 with its eleven articles on team-teaching (including, incidentally, no less than three from the University of Birmingham) and the proceedings of the two-yearly conferences of the Association of Lecturers and Tutors in English for Overseas Students (also known as SELMOUS).

Episode Twelve is the last of five episodes (the others being Three, Five, Nine and Eleven) that describe ESP responses to particular learner situations. It demonstrates, I believe, how far ESP has progressed towards maturity in the twenty years or so covered by this anthology. But it also demonstrates something else. It shows the wide range of skills required of the ESP teacher aspiring to offer the kind of service provided by Johns and Dudley-Evans. He does not need, of course, to acquire the sum of human knowledge like some grand Renaissance figure, but he does need wide-ranging insights into educational processes and interactions.

II

TEXT AND COMMENTARY

An Experiment in Team-teaching of Overseas Postgraduate Students of Transportation and Plant Biology[1]

by T. F. Johns *and*
A. Dudley-Evans,
English for Overseas Students' Unit, University of Birmingham

Since 1971, the English for Overseas Students' Unit at Birmingham University has concentrated in its in-session teaching on the 'common-core' language problems of students across as wide a range of subject-areas as possible. Within the overall programme these problems are identified both from the stand-point of the form of the target language, and from the stand-point of the functions to which the language will be put in the overseas student's life in a British industrial city, and—more particularly—his work in a British university department. Courses defined formally include Remedial Grammar, Vocabulary Studies, and Pronunciation, while those defined functionally (Johns, 1975) include Academic Writing, Scientific Report Writing, Structured Dialogues, Listening Comprehension, and Note-taking and Reconstitution. The programme is elective in that, with the advice of the Unit, students
(a) select that course or combination of courses which is most likely to meet their particular needs or learning-styles.

The experience of the past seven years has confirmed that the 'common-core' approach has both theoretical validity, and—particularly in the training of the productive skills—practical applicability. Not only are most of the formal features of the language, and areas of potential difficulty with form, consistent across different subject areas, but the communicative uses to which English is put also have more points of similarity than of difference. In all subjects, for example, the language is used to describe structure and process; to give precise expression to
(b) spatial, temporal, and cause-and-effect relationships; to identify, define, compare, and hypothesize; to refer to and evaluate previous academic research and debate, and set the writer's own work and ideas against that background; and so forth. Inevitably, however, a common-core programme of this sort entails a degree of 'abstraction' from the actual situation of the

---

[1] This paper is a revised version of Johns and Dudley-Evans (1978); our thanks are due to our colleagues in the subject departments who helped us to avoid inaccuracies in the earlier version, and to Roz Ivanic whose perceptive comments on that version prompted the revision. Any remaining errors and obscurities are our responsibility.

(a) The advice deriving in part from an English language test administered at the beginning of the year and in some cases from performance on a pre-sessional course.

(b) Although it may well be true that 'in all subjects, the language is used to describe structure and process', it remains very uncertain whether it is the *same* language being used, for example, in botany and geology. Further, it would appear that (rhetorical) activities such as *identifying* and *defining* may have an importance that varies considerably from one subject to another. Clearly more research is needed; research that may underpin or may undermine the validity of the 'common core'.

student battling with his particular problems in his department. In order to ensure that the generalizations on which the programme is based and the priorities it embodies correspond to the reality of that situation, it became increasingly evident that it needed to be supplemented by some sort of 'involvement' at the cutting-edge in departments, both in order to help students more directly, and as a form of 'on-the-ground' research. For administrative and pedagogical reasons, that involvement has taken the form of an experiment in team-teaching in certain departments between subject teachers and language teachers.

The main administrative problems which prompted the experiment were those of the timetabling and information. With some MSc courses involving over 25 hours of subject tuition a week, it is difficult for the students attending them to find the time—or the energy—to attend all the classes they may need in the Unit. In addition, with students from over twenty departments in all Faculties attending classes in the Unit, it is impossible to find times for classes which can be attended by all the students who may need them. Partial solutions to these (c) problems have been found by holding classes in the lunch break (1300–1400) and in the late afternoon (1700–1800); by some departments writing certain classes from the common-core programme into their own timetables; and by attempting to design teaching materials in such a way that they can be used on an access basis by students who are unable to attend classes. Despite these measures, the timetabling problem remains. The problem of information derives from the difficulty of keeping track of the progress of each of the 180 or so students attending classes in the Unit. It has not proved possible to keep all departments informed on a regular basis as to the progress of each of their students: conversely, the Unit often does not hear until too late of a student who is falling behind in his work because of language difficulties. We are aware that our administrative procedures in this area could be tightened up: nevertheless, it would be over-optimistic to expect that administrative procedures alone could overcome the problem. What is needed is that there should be as much personal contact as possible on a regular basis to ensure that difficulties are discussed as they arise, and that assessment is made from both sides as to diagnosis and whatever remedial action may be necessary.

The pedagogical problems arise from the perception, reinforced by discussion with subject teachers and with students (particularly in the one-to-one consultations which form an essential component of the Unit's work) that an overseas student's failure to keep pace with his course or with his research is rarely attributable to 'knowledge of the subject' or 'knowledge of the language' alone: most often, these factors are inextricably intertwined. If their work is separate, it is difficult for the subject teacher, and even more so for the language teacher, to take account of that intertwining. In the triangle of which the three angles are the student, the subject teacher, and the language teacher, each needs a certain type of assistance and feedback from the other two. The student needs to know how his performance is measuring up to the expectations of his teachers, and to have immediate assistance with his difficulties as they arise: a type of monitoring and assistance that may not be available from the subject teacher or the language-teacher working in isolation. The subject teacher needs to have a clearer idea of how (d) effectively he is communicating with his students, and how that communication might be improved. Since learning a subject in any case centrally involves learning how that subject is talked about (at the simplest level, for example, how entities and relationships are named), his teaching inevitably incorporates an element of language teaching, and there is at least a *prima facie* case that that side of his work may be assisted by a language teacher.

The language teacher, we believe, needs to be able to grasp the conceptual structure of a subject his students are studying if he is to understand fully how language is used to represent

(c) Somebody once described ESP as the 'lunch-time profession', and here we can begin to see why.

(d) The authors will make further reference to the advantages for the subject teacher of such collaboration—especially advantages in terms of the subject-teacher improving his or her own teaching.

(e) that structure; to know how the range of different subjects are taught during the course; and to
observe where and how difficulties arise in order that he can attempt to help both student and
subject teacher to overcome them. Only within such a framework can he hope to solve the
problem of 'authenticity' which looms so large when language teaching is divorced from subject
teaching. Much has been written in recent years about the desirability of using written and
spoken texts for subject-specific language classes which are 'genuine': that is to say, which have
not been simplified or in other ways doctored by the teacher. However, genuineness does not
guarantee relevance, for understanding a text must include understanding the significance of
the text within the overall learning/teaching process. How does the information in the text
(f) relate in terms of what is 'given' and 'new' to information already acquired? How far does it
confirm or supplement the student's conceptual framework, or modify that framework? What
use will the student be expected to make of the information or ideas? The language teacher is
unable to answer questions such as these without reference to the subject teacher: in the
absence of the answers, the teaching of comprehension can easily become an arid affair,
divorced from the contextual factors which are always present when 'real' comprehension takes
place.

The problem of authenticity is not limited to comprehension, but extends also to the
productive skills. Here, the assistance of the subject teacher is particularly important when it
comes to the teaching of writing. Most overseas students are given far too little instruction or
practice in the task by which their success will mainly be judged, namely the writing of
examination answers under time pressure. If the language teacher is to offer training in this
(g) skill, he needs to know exactly what the subject teacher intends by the questions he sets; what
sort of structuring is expected in the answers; and what sort of performance is accepted as
adequate. Feedback on the last of these is vital to ensure that the language teacher's priorities in
the teaching of effective communication (for example, the significance accorded to 'mechanical' errors in the assessment of written work) reflect those of the subject teacher.

The departments where we have, in recent years, introduced experiments in team-teaching in an attempt to overcome the problems and meet the needs outlined above are the Development Administration Group of the Institute of Local Government Studies, the Department of Transportation and Environmental Planning, and the Department of Plant Biology. This paper concentrates on the last two of these.[2] The main characteristics of the work of these departments may be worth noting. Both teach one-year MSc-courses comprising course work and project work: in Plant Biology the course is on the Conservation of Plant Genetic Resources, while in Transportation we are concerned with two courses with a considerable degree of overlap, the one being on Highway and Traffic Engineering, and the other being on

[2] For an account of the first term's work in the Development Administration Group, see Johns (forthcoming), which touches on and elaborates some of the points raised in the present paper. The second term's work in DAG closely resembles that in Transportation and Plant Biology; it has given rise to some ongoing research in the Unit on the linguistic and communicative features of examination questions in Development Studies courses at a number of British universities.

(e) Notice Johns' and Dudley-Evans' careful position here. They are not claiming that the language teacher needs to understand fully the subject-matter itself, but rather *its conceptual structure*; that is to understand the *rationale* behind devising particular teaching programmes in certain ways. It is my belief that the authors have identified the correct line to take in a matter that continues to cause anxiety for many ESP teachers; and it follows that coming to terms with the conceptual structure requires in the first instance open-minded educational initiative rather than skill in linguistic analysis.

(f) The question of how the ESP practitioner should react to information that can be taken as either 'given' or 'new' for his or her students is discussed in Episode Fourteen.

(g) For many years the ESP profession has been too concerned with performance on English exams rather than in subject exams (where set in English); the authors demonstrate clearly that if the ESP teacher is (belatedly) going to assume responsibility in this area the language teacher has himself or herself to behave with great responsibility. Thus, the previous neglect is understandable if not entirely excusable.

Highway Engineering for Developing Countries. In both departments the work is highly specialized, and is not replicated exactly elsewhere in the United Kingdom. As a result of this specialization, and the world-wide applicability of the training given, a high proportion of the students are from overseas (9 out of 10 on the Transportation courses, and 3 out of 4 on the Plant Biology course). Most of them are in their late twenties and in their thirties, having had some years' working experience in their profession. They are faced by the problems of returning to academic life; of adjusting to the special conventions of study in a British university; and, often, of having to tackle unfamiliar subjects (for example, economics and sociology in Transportation). Finally, there was before the experiments started, an awareness in both
(h) departments of underachievement among some of their overseas students as a result of problems with English: both responded readily to the idea of collaboration, and members of staff were willing to give time and trouble, and to tolerate a degree of intrusion on their teaching, to help make the experiments a success. Work got under way in the 1977/8 session in Transportation and Environmental Planning, and in 1978/9 in Plant Biology.

In order that individual attention can be given to each student, and that all students should have an opportunity to participate, team-taught groups are restricted to 10–12 students. Since there may be more than that number of potential participants in a department, some form of selection is necessary. At the moment this is done mainly on the basis of the Assessment and Diagnostic Test taken by all overseas students on arrival at the University, preference being given to students with lower scores on the test. Each class meets once a week; in theory the session should last an hour and a quarter, but such is the heat of the discussion generated on all sides, that in practice it may last two hours or more. For each term a programme is worked out with the department so that subject teachers take part on a rota basis, each contributing one or two sessions a term, while the language teachers alternate week by week in the two departments.

It was decided, after discussion with the departments and with the students that the work in the first term should concentrate on comprehension, with an emphasis on comprehension of lectures; and in the second term on production, and in particular the writing of examination answers under time pressure. In the first term, one of the subject teacher's lectures is recorded during the week before the session on a small cassette recorder with a built-in microphone. The language teacher is not present during the recording: we have found that this arrangement causes the least alarm to the lecturers, who soon forget that they are being recorded, and who tell us that their recorded lectures are fairly typical. The language teacher listens to and
(i) analyses the lecture in preparation for the team-teaching session—the recording is never used in the session itself. In most cases he has the lecturer's own notes or handout to guide him through the material, and subject teachers have been generous of their time in explaining the more obscure topics and their significance in relation to the course as a whole. For about half the number of sessions, we prepare—in some haste—an 'ephemeral' handout as a starting-point for the session's activities. We regard the job of preparing a handout as most valuable in concentrating the language teacher's mind on the task in hand, and in providing a general framework for the session: the materials, being ephemeral, cannot become an end in themselves.

(h) I think we can detect here the concern about language common in internationally-minded departments. In contrast, Departments that accept only an occasional overseas student may be tempted to take a 'sink or swim' attitude.

(i) Tim Johns has on several occasions stressed the dangers of using actual recordings. A replayed audio recording is almost always humiliating for the speaker, however articulate. Of course, as the rest of the paragraph goes on to show, this crucial consideration for the speaker exacts a price—the price of preparing a handout on an individual lecture that will be used only once (hence 'ephemeral' or lasting only one day).

The general pattern of activities within each session in the first term's work is as follows:[3]

Global Understanding

Questions are asked to check whether the students have understood the main points of the lecture. These questions are usually answered without reference to the students' notes. Activities include:

(a) Re-arranging a randomized list of the points made by the lecturer into the order of presentation in the lecture. The following example is taken from a session in plant Biology on 'Classification'.

1 Phylogenetic Systems of Classification
2 Difference between 'Character' and 'Character State'
3 The Controversy over Phylogenetic Systems
4 Natural Systems of Classification
5 General Aims of Taxonomy
6 The Various Forms of Expression of 'Character'
7 Artificial Systems of Classification
8 Definition of 'Character'
9 Definition of 'Unit Character'

(b) Showing that the overall argument of the lecture has been grasped by completing a representation of it in non-linear form (eg a matrix, a tree diagram, or a flow diagram). For example, students were asked to complete a simple 2 × 2 matrix to show that they could distinguish between 'Technological' and 'Pecuniary' cost benefits, one of the key points in a lecture on Cost Benefit Analysis in Transport Economics:

3 Difference between technological costs and benefits and pecuniary costs and benefits

	Definition	Example
Technological Costs and Benefits		
Pecuniary Costs and Benefits		

(j) In the following example students were asked to use a tree-diagram to classify the various kinds of molecules described in a lecture on 'Biochemical Systematics':

[3] The traditions within which we are working in our teaching will be apparent to our fellow practitioners. We would particularly wish to draw attention to the parallelism/indebtedness of our approach to the ideas of Professor Henry Widdowson, in particular the concept of 'information transfer': see, for example Widdowson (1973).

(j) The well-established techniques of 'information transfer' and of 'jumbling' or 'scrambling' items are clearly appropriate to the rapid production of 'ephemeral' handouts. We can, I think, get an idea from this section of the skills of the authors in selecting the right technique for a particular type of content.

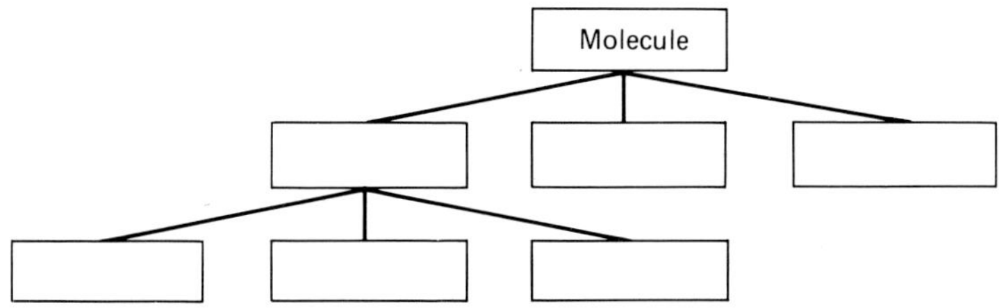

Understanding of Detail

Students answer questions on some of the subsidiary points in the lecture, including some of the lecturer's examples and 'asides'. In this case they are allowed to consult their notes. The purpose of this phase of the session is to discover how accurately students understand and record detailed information and, more importantly, whether they understand its relevance to the main argument. As in the work on global understanding, considerable use is made of diagramming techniques to represent information and argument. This example is taken from a session in (k) Plant Biology following up a lecture on 'Cucurbitaceae':

The work on global understanding and understanding of detail gives the subject teacher an opportunity to check possible gaps in background understanding, and on occasion to see how modifications in his presentation might improve communication; allows students to catch up on points missed, or not completely understood, and, through the techniques used for testing comprehension, enables him to understand and take notes from future lectures with a greater awareness of the lecturer's intentions; and allows the language teacher to note the questions that arise that he had not foreseen, and to assess the role played in them by the relationship between comprehension of the subject-matter and comprehension of the language. This observation has proved invaluable in analysing material and planning activities for future sessions. The general pattern of group interaction in this part of the session is that the language teacher starts by questioning the students with the subject teacher acting as 'consultant'; passes the students to the subject teacher on points of explanation, clarification and application, the language teacher acting as 'monitor' and occasionally as 'mediator'; and often ends with the subject and language teacher jointly summarizing the main points that have arisen. We have found it important that the subject teacher and the language teacher should sit fairly close together in the group so that students do not suffer from the 'Wimbledon effect' as the lead passes from one to the other.

Nomenclature		Characters						
Botanical Name	Common Names	Leaf	Flower	fruit				
				Shape	Size	Skin	Flesh	Seeds
Citrullus vulgaris								
Cucumis sativus								
Cucumis anguria								
Cucumis melo								
Luffa cylindrica								
Lagenaria siceraria								

(k) *Cucurbitaceae* are, loosely, a plant family that includes cucumbers and gourds.

Vocabulary

The overseas student often identifies his difficulties with English as 'not knowing enough words'. In the past language teachers have tended to give a low priority to the learning of (l) vocabulary, and to concentrate instead on structure. The work on comprehension has pointed up the very real difficulties students do have in this area; a subject-specific team-taught class offers an opportunity to 'point students in the right direction' in order to overcome those difficulties, and we try to devote part of each session to vocabulary difficulties. The recording of the lecture is analysed with reference to the following main areas, one or more of which may form the focus of the work done in the session.

1 Technical Vocabulary

Subject-lecturers often assume that technical terms are familiar to students; much of the time this assumption is justified, but checking students' comprehension does occasionally reveal terms or groups of terms which are not fully understood, particularly where these derive from subject areas 'on the fringe' of their academic knowledge. The main problems seem to be:

(a) Sound-spelling correspondences. Many technical terms are international, and may be used in the student's first language in the same way as they are used in English. However, the familiar term, while presenting no difficulty on the printed page, may be difficult to recognize when spoken—for example because of different rules of stress-placement in English polysyllabic words such as 'phylogeny', 'phylogenesis', 'phylogenetic'. We attempt to give guidance where necessary not only on the sound-spelling correspondences of individual words, but also on some of the underlying principles—eg the effect on stress-placement and thereby on vowel reduction, of 'strong' suffixes (Guierre, 1975).

(b) Problems in understanding the 'meaning' of technical terms may be divided between those which relate to the denotation of the term (ie the relationship between the term and the entity, state, or process in the 'real world' to which it refers) and those which relate to the sense-relations between a term and a set of other terms (eg the relations of 'synonomy', 'antonomy', 'inclusion' and 'converseness').[4] Establishing the denotation of a term in the sciences is complicated by the considerable degree of abstraction in the 'real world' as the scientist describes it—and indeed the coining of technical terms is an essential step in that process of abstraction. However, we have found that fairly simple concrete denotations, of the sort which can be established by a 'diagram-labelling' exercise, may not be fully grasped by many students. This was the case when we asked students to indicate their understanding (m) of three crucial terms during a session in Transportation on 'Gap Acceptance':

[4] The distinction between 'denotation' and 'sense', and the framework of sense-relations, is drawn from the work of Professor John Lyons: most recently, Lyons (1977).

(l) This observation is particularly true of ESP, and the matter of vocabulary will be taken up again in the Prospect at the end of this book.

(m) The diagram may not be self-evident. 'Gap acceptance' is the term for deciding that there is a sufficient space between two vehicles to enter a stream of traffic. On a more general level, the distinction between *denotation* and *sense* is not always very workable, especially in disciplines with elaborate technical vocabulary. Although *gap*, *lag* and *lead* refer to different perceptions of drivers, they are also obviously interrelated. The work in the (b) part of this section perhaps again suggests that technical vocabulary is an obvious area for subject-teacher involvement.

1 Define the terms gap, lag, and lead

(a) by labelling the following diagram:

(b) in words:

gap is ....

lag is ....

lead is ....

We regularly set short exercises on sense-relations where these appear to be important and where they may present difficulties in the technical vocabulary of a subject area. Here is an extract from an exercise on antonyms for a session in Transportation on Statistics:

1 A histogram may be symmetrical or ....

2 A variable may be continuous or ....

3 A population may be real or ....

2 Semi-technical Vocabulary

Here the emphasis is on terms drawn from the 'common core' of English which take on a special significance in a number of different subjects, either in description or as a result of the nature of the teaching/learning interaction. An example of the first is provided by the transitive verbs of process, which we have found to cause difficulties (eg 'affect', 'effect', 'yield', 'deplete', 'withstand'). An example of the second is the importance in many of the lectures we have (n) recorded of the linguistic signals—for example the 'implicative verbs' (Karttunen, 1971)—by which the lecturer mediates the work and ideas of other people: that is to say, the way in which he indicates his assessment of their validity. The following is an extract from an exercise set for

(n) Karttunen is a theoretical linguist who has been concerned with the presuppositions attached to 'reporting' verbs, particularly between those that are *factive* and those that are *non-factive*. A *factive* verb implies that the writer accepts what other people have done, a *non-factive* has no such implication. Compare:—

Johns and Dudley-Evans have demonstrated that team-teaching can work. (*factive*)
Johns and Dudley-Evans have claimed that team-teaching can work. (*non-factive*)

a session in Plant Biology on 'Cassava and Sweet Potato': what was valuable was the opportunity both language teacher and students had to check with the lecturer (in this case, the head of the department) their interpretations of the linguistic signals.

2 What do the underlined phrases tell you about whether an idea is generally accepted or about the lecturer's own attitude to the idea?

(a) From the work of Abraham *et al.* reported in the Indian Journal of Botany it looks as though Manihot esculenta can be considered a tetraploid already.

(b) One explanation is that man got to know several varieties of Manihot esculenta and he gradually tried the more bitter varieties until he found methods to deal with the most dangerous. One very different hypothesis is that the bitter varieties were originally used as fish poisons.

(c) Most authorities have considered that Manihot esculenta is American in origin.

(d) Rogers even goes so far as to say that many of the wild species are nothing more than escaped esculenta.

(e) From one point of view one might think that there were two centres of origin of the sweet varieties of cassava from the diversity seen. Others have said the centre of origin might be the eastern foothills of the Andes. Rogers even suggested cassava might be domesticated on the west coast of Mexico.

(f) It has been pointed out by Yen that secondary association cannot indicate hybrid origin. He points out that Ipomoea rarely reproduces . . .

3 Colloquial Vocabulary

An overseas student may have acquired in his own country a fair command of the written language of his subject, but still be puzzled by the colloquial words and phrases used by a lecturer when he talks about that subject. A few examples drawn at random from our recordings:

'This is **pretty** difficult'
'We'll need to **jack up** the figures'
'Well, **you pays your money and you takes your choice'**

Here the work concentrates on developing the student's ability to guess the meaning of colloquialisms and to find equivalents in formal written English. Part of an exercise from a session in Plant Biology on 'Storage of Seeds':

Colloquial Words and Expressions

Explain the words or phrases underlined. What equivalents would you use in formal written English?

(a) The viability of the seed has a lot to do with the rate of cooling and the rate of thawing.

(b) Storage in air is somewhat better than storage in pure oxygen.

(c) There is little evidence as to how much oxygen is needed to keep a seed ticking over.

This part of the session requires a degree of tact on the part of the language teacher, and of self-awareness on the part of the subject teacher, most of whom do not realize how many colloquialisms they use. The majority react to the realization by attempting to control the type and density of colloquial expressions in their lectures; on the other hand, one lecturer in Transportation appears to have increased his use of sporting metaphors, perhaps with the (o) intention of putting the language teachers on their mettle:

'Are you trying to **hedge your bets**?'
'What are you going to put in the surface? **Mouldy old jockstraps**?'

Follow-up Work

Both subject teachers and language teachers are concerned to drive home the point that understanding a lecture is not simply a matter of knowing the information it contains, but also—and crucially—of being able to evaluate and use that information. Follow-up activities are usually agreed on in advance by the subject teacher and the language teacher, and have included the following:

1 Application of the general principles explained in the lecture to a practical task. These have ranged from describing the characters of flowers in Plant Biology to designing a road in Transportation.

2 Reading a short text related to the lecture, and assessing how far the information in the text supplements or modifies the information in the lecture.

3 Use of the underlying 'conceptual structure' as exposed by diagramming in the work on comprehension as a way of developing 'creative thinking' in the subject. The following example is taken from a session in Plant Biology on Adaptation, in which students are led to form their own hypotheses and to decide how they would test them.

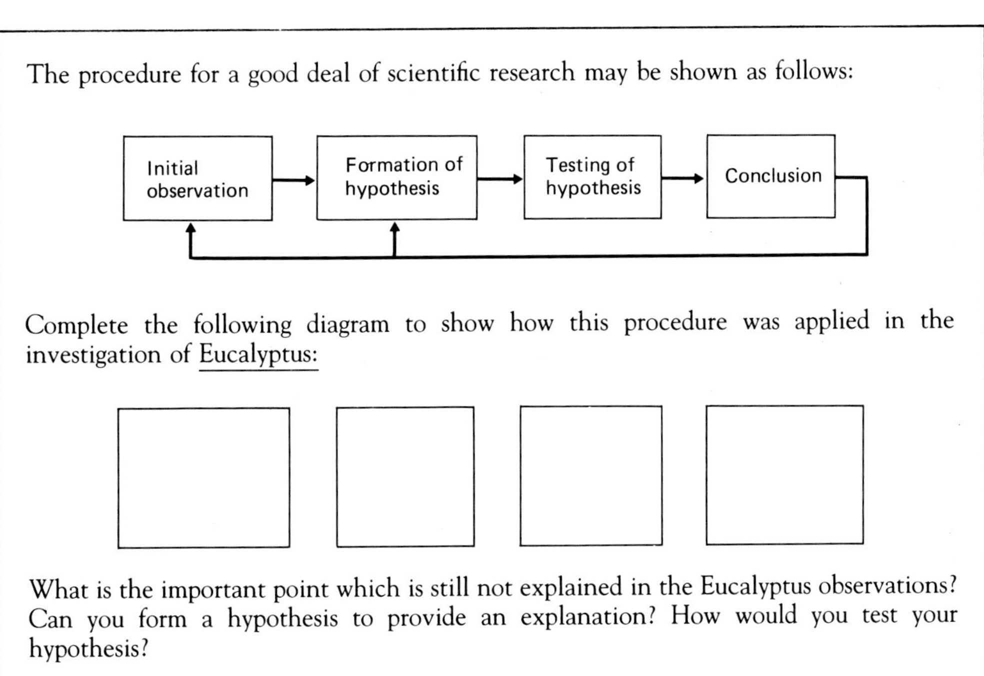

The procedure for a good deal of scientific research may be shown as follows:
Initial observation
Formation of hypothesis
Testing of hypothesis
Conclusion
Complete the following diagram to show how this procedure was applied in the investigation of Eucalyptus:
What is the important point which is still not explained in the Eucalyptus observations? Can you form a hypothesis to provide an explanation? How would you test your hypothesis?

(o) The use of metaphors in lectures is an interesting one, and it may well be that different disciplines have different preferences. Certainly management seems prone to military analogies.

4 As preparation for the work in the second term, use of the students' notes as input to limited writing tasks:

(a) Construction of sentence-long statements (eg definitions, explanations) according to a model.

(b) Completion of a longer clozed written passage based on the lecture. An example taken from the session on 'Adaptation':

> (a) Complete the following written description of Clausen's experiments on *Potentilla glandulosa*:
>
> Clausen collected samples of *Potentilla glandulosa* .... a wide range of ...., distances, and habitats, and .... that his samples differed .... many characters. These variations .... geographically patterned in that .... races growing at high .... were quite different from .... growing at low altitude.
>
> (b) Rewrite the passage, using the passive to describe what Clausen did (eg 'Samples of *Potentilla glandulosa* were collected . . .').

(c) Conversion of section of notes to paragraph (model notes and paragraph given).

As has been mentioned, the second term's work in the two departments concentrates on production, with the major emphasis on the writing of examination answers.

Examination Questions and Answers

Each session is taught with the subject teacher responsible for setting the question studied, and has three principal components:

1 Understanding the question

It is necessary for both students and teachers to realize that the language of examination questions is highly conventionalized (eg 'How far . . .', 'Discuss critically . . .', 'Compare and contrast . . .', '. . . with reference to . . .'), and that by the time the student reaches the examination-hall it is too late for him to start to learn those conventions. As a basic functional distinction for questions set in these subject-areas, it has been found necessary to divide questions—and sub-parts of questions—according to whether they ask for **definition**, **description**, **explanation**, **discussion**, or **calculation**: in the team-taught sessions we concentrate on the first three of these. The skills we attempt to develop in the students are: (p)

(a) Understanding of form-function correspondences in examination questions: for example, the different ways the 'same' question can be phrased (for **definition**, 'Define . . .', 'Give a definition of . . .', 'What do you understand by . . .', etc).

(b) Assessment of the examiner's intentions and expectations. For example, in a **definition, a description** or an **explanation**, what needs to be included, and what can be 'taken as given'; and which of the various interpretations of 'Discuss . . .' is most appropriate in the context of a particular question.

(p) This pioneering work on examination questions preceded the contemporary upsurge of interest in this topic.

2 Planning the answer

This is usually done through group discussion, and involves:

(a) Structuring of information and argument. In addition to basic 'linear' methods such as listing points to be made, we encourage students to organize information and to think through arguments in a 'non-linear' way by using diagramming methods, the work on production thus being linked to that on comprehension in the first term.

(b) Discussion of the relevance of students' own points in relation to the overall framework.

(c) Initial decisions as to the presentation of the answer: eg ordering of points, paragraphing.

3 Writing up the answer

Students individually write up a section of the planned answer under time pressure: the section (one or two paragraphs in length) may be selected by one of the teachers, or by the students themselves. In doing the writing-up students are able to obtain immediate assistance on any point of difficulty either with the subject or with the language. Where possible, completed work is checked by both subject teacher and language teacher.

Oral Presentation

The ability of students to communicate orally on their subject is considered important by both departments. In our second-term work in Transportation we have had two sessions which attempted to develop students' fluency and self-confidence in this area. In the first of these, students were asked to prepare and give a short talk to the rest of the group, presentations being commented on for content and language. In the second, students were asked to prepare a course of action for a particular road-engineering problem, and to present it to the imaginary works committee of a local authority, the committee consisting of two language teachers who attempted to simulate the sort of cross-examination to which an engineer might be put in the real situation. Students then had to write up a short description and justification of their proposals. The sessions, both of which were prepared by the subject teacher concerned (the second session being organized by the head of the department) were very successful, and have shown us a further possible development of team-teaching for the future.

Project Work

In both Transportation and Plant Biology, students have to carry out and write up a project after the examinations. Towards the end of the second term they are required to present a research proposal for approval by the department. In Plant Biology the preparation of the proposals was made the focus for two consecutive sessions. In the first, students were asked to present their proposals orally, the subject teacher commenting on the feasibility of the project, while the language teacher, with the help of the subject teacher, commented on problems that might arise in organizing the proposal, and in handling the language. During the following week, students prepared the first drafts of their proposals: in the second session the subject teacher and the language teacher together discussed the drafts with each student individually.

We believe it is still too early to make any definite evaluation of the work described in this paper: however, some general and largely subjective observations may be found useful by teachers considering the possibility of introducing a similar programme, where resources do not permit the 'ideal' of full-time collaboration between subject teacher and language teacher at all
(q) stages of the teaching process (Skehan & Henderson 1979). In general, we feel that the approach we have adopted has gone a long way to filling the need for three-way feedback described above. Attendance and interest on the part of the students has, on the whole, been

(q) Skehan and Henderson describe a rather different team-teaching operation (but also at Birmingham) in which the collaboration took place outside the classroom and 'the teachers were never in the classroom at the same time'.

excellent. Lecturers in the departments have told us that they have observed improvements in the students' English, or in their command of the subject, or both. Such evidence, while encouraging, cannot be regarded as conclusive in view of the small numbers of students involved and the variations which can take place between one year's intake and the next, irrespective of the teaching they are given. It may also be worth noting that there has been a
(r) total absence of that suspicion and even hostility which language teachers often report encountering when attempting to set up some sort of cooperation with subject teachers. We
(s) believe that our good fortune in this respect is not simply a matter of luck or of personal compatibility, but that it may be related to certain aspects of the approach adopted. Firstly, a clear framework was agreed in advance for the pattern of activities, and the responsibilities of each side were defined. Secondly, we attempted to reduce intrusion on the subject teachers to a minimum, while exploiting the help they could give us to the maximum. In doing this, we hope we avoided the hubris which can too easily afflict the EAP teacher when, with a smattering of knowledge in the subject area, and a view of himself as an expert on communication, he comes to regard himself as an expert—or the expert—on how the subject ought to be taught, and even on what the subject ought to be. For our part, we attempted to engage with the subject areas on their own terms, and to understand as best we could what was being taught and what was being done. Where in an operation of this kind subject and language are so enmeshed, finding out what the language teacher has learnt of the subject may be as reliable a way of estimating its success as measuring the improvement in the students' English. On this criterion we could certainly not claim to be entirely successful, but we enjoyed the effort at understanding, even where we know that our understanding is still incomplete.

Experience over the last couple of years has shown that one of the most important conditions for the success of this work is group homogeneity. In the best-organized departments there may turn up from time to time a student who seems to be 'ineducable', no matter how he is taught: the presence of one such can hold up both teachers and other students. Conversely, if—as in one department in 1978/9—the numbers of overseas students are such that they can all be admitted to the team-taught sessions without reference to initial language competence, the danger is that the linguistically more able (who tend also to be the more able from the point of view of the subject) do not, as a result, get the level of teaching or the amount of individual attention they require. In the department in question it was the impression of both subject teachers and language teachers (an impression borne out by the examination results) that while there was some improvement attributable to the team-taught sessions for all students, that improvement was far greater with the stronger students than with the weaker: that is to say, they achieved the reverse effect to that intended.

The unresolved problems with this approach have in large part been a product of its success. Students may have been led to concentrate, inappropriately, on those topics covered in the team-taught sessions, to the exclusion of others: in one department, they asked for similar follow-up sessions to all lectures—a request that had to be turned down. Some subject teachers remain concerned that we may be giving an 'unfair advantage' to the students given this additional help: should it not be available to all students in the department, including native speakers? The language teachers are also conscious of a degree of discrimination in that the limited resources of the Unit make it impossible to offer this sort of help to all the students who may need it. Clearly it is better that some students should be helped in this way than none, and we hope that it will be possible over the next two or three years to set up team-teaching cooperation in at least one new department a year: nevertheless, for the foreseeable future it will be only a minority of overseas postgraduate students who will benefit.

(r) Many ESP practitioners have indeed experienced such suspicions, particularly a communicated feeling that they are 'interfering' and that their motives for wishing to understand what happens in a subject department are suspect.

(s) In their closing paragraphs, the authors evaluate their experiment with a most attractive combination of modesty, honesty and insight.

Bibliography

Guiere, L., *'Drills in English Stress-Patterns'*, Armand Colin–Longman, Paris, 1975.

Johns, T. F., *'The Communicative Approach to Language Teaching in the Framework of a Programme of English for Academic Purposes'*, in Roulet, E. and Holec, H. (eds), *'L'enseignement de la Competence de Communication en Langues Secondes'*, CILA, Neuchatel, 1975.

Johns, T. F. (forthcoming), *'The Text and its Message: an Approach to the Teaching of Reading Strategies for Students of Development Administration'*.

Johns, T. F. and Dudley-Evans, A., *'Team-teaching of Subject-specific English to Overseas Postgraduate Students'*, Birmingham University Teaching News 5, 1978.

Karttunen, L., *'Implicative Verbs'*, Language 47, 340–58, 1971.

Lyons, J., *'Semantics I'*, Cambridge University Press, London, 1977.

Skehan, P. and Henderson, W., *'The Team Teaching of Introductory Economics to Overseas Students'* (this volume), 1979.

Widdowson, H. G., *'Directions in the Teaching of Discourse'* in Corder, S. P. and Roulet, E. (eds), 'Theoretical Linguistic Models in Applied Linguistics', AIMAV, Brussels and Didier, Paris, 1973.

III ACTIVITIES

(1) In the first part of the *vocabulary* section the authors refer to their work on sound-spelling correspondences. Can you produce stress-rules for verbs ending in *-ate*, *-ize* and *-ify* and their corresponding nouns? Here are some examples:—

(a)	calculate	—	calculation
	demonstrate	—	demonstration
	operate	—	operation
(b)	realize	—	realization
	magnetize	—	magnetization
(c)	identify	—	identification
	modify	—	modification
	magnify	—	magnification

(2) How do you interpret the underlined phrases in the semi-technical vocabulary box? Why do you interpret them in this way?

(3) Take a set of a few examination question papers from any area and attempt a functional classification of the questions. Are there any interesting 'form-function correspondences'?

IV EVALUATION

(1) The authors are cautious about the wider applicability of their 'experiment'. What is your view?

(2) Let us accept that one of the main permanent benefits of a team-teaching operation such as that initiated by Johns and Dudley-Evans is the greater communicative sensitivity of subject-teachers. We might then conclude that once this communicative sensitivity has been encouraged, there is little further need for a team-teaching operation. Is this argument reasonable?

V
RELATED READINGS

The key volume is:—

ELT Documents 106 – Team Teaching in ESP (The British Council 1980).

Later papers in this area are:—

A. Dudley-Evans and T. F. Johns, 'A Team-Teaching Approach to listening comprehension for overseas students', *ELT Documents Special – The Teaching of Listening Comprehension*, The British Council 1981, and three items from *Common Ground: Shared Interests in ESP and Communication Studies*, edited by Williams, Kirkman and Swales, Pergamon, Oxford (forthcoming).

Smiljka Gee, Michael Huxley and Duska Johnson, 'Teaching Communication Skills and English for Academic Purposes'.
Tony Dudley-Evans, 'The Team-Teaching of Writing Skills'.
Blanca de Escorcia, 'Team-Teaching for Students of Economics: a Colombian Experience'.
The question of subject-specific functional roles is discussed in:—

John Swales, 'Definitions in Science and Law – Evidence of Subject-Specific Course Components', *Fachsprache* 3 3/4, 1981 (Vienna).

EPISODE THIRTEEN 1980

John Moore *et al.*, *Reading and Thinking in English – Discourse in Action* (Teachers' Edition, pp. 1–12), Oxford University Press, Oxford, 1980.

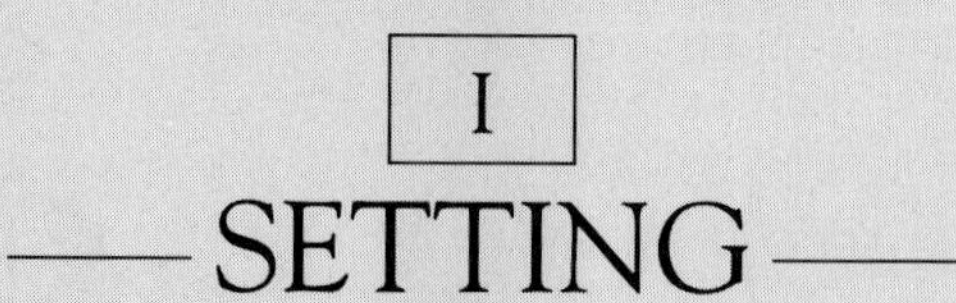

The final Episode illustrating the development of ESP Textbooks is an example of the 'new' Reading and Study Skills materials that have been appearing in the last few years. The *Reading and Thinking in English* series (henceforth RTE) consists of four books and how the four books relate one to the other is clearly described in the introductory matter to *Discourse in Action*:—

> *Concepts in Use* extends students' basic knowledge of grammar and vocabulary and how they are used to express fundamental concepts. It also develops their awareness of how passages are built on combinations of these concepts. *Exploring Functions* deals with the use of concepts in the communicative functions of academic writing. *Discovering Discourse* develops students' awareness of how the devices of language are used to express communicative function. It also shows how passages are built in combinations of simple functions. *Discourse in Action* extends students' knowledge of the functional organization of written English and develops their ability to handle information found in varied types of real academic discourse.

As we can see, this impressive scheme is firmly premised on the notional–functional approach to communicative language teaching that we saw being developed in Episodes Six to Eight—indeed Henry Widdowson acted as Associate Editor to the series. The overall design of RTE can be summarized in a 'Chinese-box' diagram:—

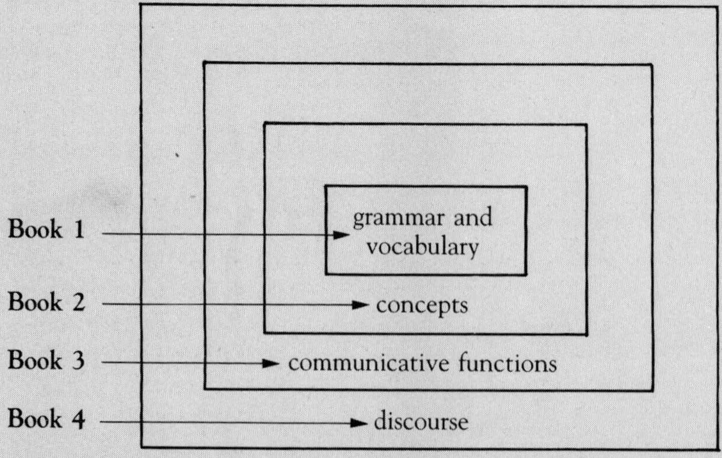

RTE is the second Episode to be based on Latin American experience, the other being the two-part paper by Ewer and Hughes-Davies found in Episode Five. RTE originated in a major materials writing project centred on the University of the Andes, Bogotá, Colombia, and supported by the British Council. The Director of the project was John Moore and the members of the University who participated in writing the Colombian materials that underlie RTE were Dora Bennet de Salgrado, Luisa Fernanda de Knight, Anita Escobar de Tamayo and Teresa Munevar. The pattern established by *Writing Scientific English* and *Nucleus* is therefore continued; modified versions of interesting local materials find their way on to the international market via the major ELT publishers.

The previous three textbook extracts have all been targeted on intermediate-level students; for this *Episode* I have therefore selected some of the more advanced material from the RTE series. In fact, I have chosen the first half of Unit 1 of the final volume in the series, *Discourse in Action. Discourse in Action* falls into two clear halves. Phase One (as it is called) begins with an introductory Unit 'which focuses the student's attention on the way specific features of discourse and reading skills are practised in the context of communicative activities'. The remaining three Units in the first phase each deal with a particular type of discourse; Unit 2 deals with *Exposition*, Unit 3 deals with *Enquiry* (or discourses dealing with formulating hypotheses and testing them) and Unit 4 focuses on *Argument.* The three Units in Phase 2 tackle the more general skills required for using a textbook, for using a source book (such as an edited collection of extracts from different sources) and finally for using a range of sources. The way in which the actual extract is organized I will leave until the following section.

So far I have said something about the source of RTE and about its design principles. This sketch has, I hope, established that the grand design is structured through a scheme of concepts about discourse structure that owes much to previous workers, especially Henry Widdowson. Therefore, as yet we have not seen what is new or what is important about the RTE series; and for that we need to consider the approach to subject-matter and, more particularly, the approach to reading.

RTE is designed for a wide range of students in the general 'English for Academic Purposes' area, some of whom may well be students of science, engineering and technology, but equally some of whom will be students in other Faculties. Thus, RTE is not subject-specific and so contrasts strongly with the earlier *Nucleus* and *Focus* series. In a paper on the pre-publication Colombian materials given at the Paipa ESP International Seminar in 1977, John Moore characterizes the approach as follows:—

> We have attempted to make texts and exercises interesting and relevant by choosing inter-disciplinary topics or themes of general academic interest and to include study skills useful in a variety of disciplines. The criteria for the selection of texts has not been topic but style (the way a text is structured to reflect the methodology of academic disciplines), exemplificatory adequacy and 'exploitability'.

Although the first sentence in the quotation is worth considerable comment, it is the second that is more crucial and controversial and so I shall restrict my observations to it alone. We can take the three criteria for text selection in reverse order: 'Exploitability' we can understand as finding texts that offer the desired range of student activities, and 'exemplificatory adequacy' is the Widdowsonian concept of a text that clearly illustrates the concepts and functions and their exponents which the materials writer is looking for. So far so good. However, the matter of 'style' is more open to doubt, and we can notice that the authors of RTE have *assumed* that there is a generalizable 'methodology of academic disciplines' which will impose (or at least predispose) certain patterns of academic text structuring—perhaps patterns of Exposition (Unit 2), Enquiry (Unit 3) and Argument (Unit 4). To what extent they are correct in this assumption is a question that we have already considered and one that we will have to return to, but here we can notice that the authors of RTE are making a double appeal: that a *range* of topics is in fact motivating, and that a range of topics will share many common features of academic discourse as such. Notice that Moore *et al.* are not claiming that attempting a spread of subject-specific courses is an impractical proposition, or that it will lead to student boredom or teacher reluctance. Rather they are implying that discipline-specific features are essentially superficial ones.

The other major reason for devoting an Episode to RTE is its highly sophisticated approach to the reading process. In the Paipa paper John Moore acknowledges a debt to the British Open University's pioneering courses in this area and describes a model of reading comprehension which involves 'the reader's *purpose*, his *strategies*, his use of *tactics* of recognition, prediction and deduction, and the internal or external *outcome* which are a result of his reading experience'. It is not, therefore, surprising that the approach to study-reading will make use of many features of this model and will give particular emphasis to pre-reading activities of many kinds, or, more exactly perhaps, to preparatory reading activities prior to the main reading assignment.

This approach to reading also is related by the authors to their decision to produce 'broad-angle' EAP courses. In Book 3, for instance, they state:—

> The authors have found that students can best be prepared to use textbooks in particular subjects by being guided to acquire general strategies for reading and thinking, which they can then transfer to more specialized material.

In Book 4, which is the particular subject of this Episode, only authentic materials are used and often authentic materials of a challenging kind. As the Teacher's Guide says:—

> One of the keys to successful reading at an advanced level is to be able to judge the writer's position in relation to the information he is presenting. This involves recognizing whether the writer is presenting information in the form of established facts, whether he is presenting hypotheses, asking questions, considering possible answers, making tentative statements, whether he is supporting or attacking particular points of view or positions. In advanced academic writing, writers are more often questioning and discussing than merely stating facts and this is why *Discourse in Action* introduces the particular features found in these types of discourse.

Discourse in Action thus offers an advanced approach to the teaching of advanced reading and all the volumes of the series have enjoyed a considerable measure of critical and educational success. However, two difficulties seem to recur fairly regularly. The first is that homogeneous groups of fairly narrowly defined students such as economists or chemical engineers soon develop some resistance to the 'inter-disciplinary topics or themes of general academic interest' and request more specific materials of higher 'face-validity'. To be fair, the authors have recognized this potential problem and indeed advocate that teachers develop supplementary specialized materials where necessary. The second difficulty arises because of the fact that RTE offers only very limited assistance with vocabulary. The lack of attention to vocabulary in the original Colombian context may well have been justified by the high percentage of cognate technical and semi-technical vocabulary between Spanish and English. However, this circumstance does not so obviously justify the continued neglect of vocabulary in the International Edition. After all, most teachers find that it is counter-productive to attempt to develop advanced reading skills that contain even a single-figure percentage of words that are not known by the readers.

As I said at the outset of this Setting, this Episode is given over to 'new' Reading Materials. I chose to exemplify such materials from *Reading and Thinking in English.* I could equally well have chosen an extract from *Skills for Learning.* The *Skills for Learning* volumes are the international version published by Nelson of EAP courses developed at the University of Malaya under the project leadership of Malcolm Cooper and with John Sinclair acting as consultant. Although there are differences, the two series have much in common and I would like to end this Introduction by trying to relate these two extensive bodies of work. The main principles supporting *Skills for Learning* include the following:—

(a) There is a core of academic language, such as certain structures of argument and forms of presentation, common to most disciplines;

(b) It is more cost-effective to teach this core than to prepare subject-specific materials;
(c) Reading is a purposive activity and these purposes must be established prior to processing the text;
(d) The reading process involves a dialogue between the reader and writer and therefore an interactive approach based on group and pair work is adopted, although individual self-help is also central to the methodology;
(e) Reading and discussing that reading are closely related academic activities, so spoken communication is a feature of all lessons;
(f) In order to implement these principles, attention needs to be given to the learning setting: classroom layout, the role for the teacher and group dynamics are all important considerations.

As we can see from (a) and (b), *Skills for Learning* takes a rather more cautious and pragmatic attitude to the issue of generality versus specificity. The approach to the reading process as summarized in (c) and (d) is essentially that of RTE. As far as the methodology is concerned, *Skills for Learning* is rather more explicit about the organization of spoken interaction and thus presumably reflects John Sinclair's interest in language in the classroom.

II

TEXT AND COMMENTARY

Reading and Thinking in English – Discourse in Action

by John Moore *et al.*

Phase one

(a)

Unit 1 Introductory unit

This unit introduces the ways in which reading skills are developed in **Discourse in action.** It draws attention to three aspects of reading:

why we read
what we read
how we read

1 Why we read
Reading is necessary in a wide range of real life activities. **Discourse in Action** practises reading for different purposes and relates reading to a variety of realistic tasks.

2 What we read
Reading skills are developed in relation to three types of discourse: exposition, enquiry and argument.

3 How we read
Reading skills are developed as a part of an active process of interpretation involving an interchange between the writer and the reader.

The main reading passage in this unit is about noise pollution and involves these three aspects of reading.

(a) This Unit has five parts. It opens with a full summary of the contents, which is designed to put the student in the class fully in the picture and also to make it easier to use *Discourse in Action* on a self-study basis. It is worth noting that no previous Episode has given much importance to such matters. The second part is *preparation* which occupies 11 of the 21 pages of the Unit and forms Episode Thirteen. *Preparation* is designed to draw attention to various aspects of reading. The remaining three parts are an *abstract* on noise pollution plus associated activities, a *transitional section* on logic and inference, and finally the *main reading assignment* which we do not reach until page 16. We can thus see the emphasis in RTE on orientation and mental preparation prior to an exercise in reading rather than on comprehension work after it.

(b)

Contents

(b) The inclusion of page numbers might have been useful.

Preparation — **Reading with a purpose (why we read)**

Introductory activity

The illustrations on pages 4–9 show examples of the type of material we commonly read in everyday life. Make a list of things you read in any language yesterday:

a as part of your studies or occupation,
b for a particular purpose in your daily activities,
c for pleasure.

Activities involving reading

Write down the kinds of reading material which the following activities probably involve. For example:

a mechanic repairing a car *repair manual, labels, parts list*

(c)

a a businessman selecting and placing an order for a piece of equipment
b a student preparing a report on nuclear energy
c a student revising for an examination
d a postgraduate student deciding on a research topic
e a committee deciding where a new airport should be located

Giving and seeking information

The following advertisement appeared in a professional journal.

1 You have a friend who would be qualified to take up the post advertised. Read the advertisement and extract the most important information for him.

2 You are assessing the suitability of some of the candidates who have applied. Read their details and decide which candidate is most likely to be suitable.
   a Miss A. 25 years old. PhD from the University of Illinois. 1 year's experience as research assistant in a laboratory.
   b Mr B. 40 years old. MSc from the University of Cambridge. 5 years' experience as manager of a small department of drug metabolism.
   c Mr C. 29 years old. PhD from the University of Hawaii. 3 years' experience in a laboratory developing drugs for veterinary use.

3 You are dealing with enquiries from some candidates who have not seen the advertisement. Answer as many as possible of their

(c) These opening activities illustrate the ability of the authors to set activities within functional contexts. However, the second activity also illustrates the vocabulary problem. In order to 'write down the kinds of reading material' the student needs to have a good knowledge of the relevant lexical field. For instance, the *Key* for (a) gives 'Equipment catalogues or lists, manufacturers' specifications, advertisements, technical reports, correspondence' to which one could add 'quotations, tenders, etc.'.

questions using information given in the advertisement.

a How many people would I be responsible for and who would be my superior?

b What experimental approach is pursued?

c Would I be able to develop my own research interests?

d Would I receive allowances for removal, transportation and housing?

e When would I be required to start?

f Are there opportunities for contact with other areas of drug safety work?

(d) g What salary is offered?

Ph.D. DRUG METABOLISM

We need an additional PhD, to lead a small group of research assistants involved with ADME studies. He/she will join our Department of Drug Metabolism, reporting to the department's manager, and will participate in multi-disciplinary project management groups which are concerned with drugs for human and veterinary use.

The successful applicant, who will probably be in his/her late twenties, will have already gained several years' experience of drug metabolism and pharmacokinetic work related to the development and registration of new drugs. He/she will be keen to build upon this knowledge in the wider aspects of Drug Safety Evaluation.

Our Department of Drug Metabolism, which is part of the Drug Safety Evaluation Group, is housed in the recently opened £2·6 million extension to our Research Block. The laboratories are well equipped and allow the pursuit of a wide variety of experimental approaches, and these are augmented by the collaborative work which is undertaken with other departments.

Conditions of employment include flexible working hours, four weeks' holiday, pension and death benefit schemes, bonus, etc. Financial assistance with relocation expenses is given where appropriate.

Applications giving brief details of age, qualifications and experience should be addressed to:—

R. F. Taylor, Personnel Manager, Pharmalab, Central Research, Milton Road, Reading, Berkshire RG5 6DP

(d) A case could be made for reversing the order of 3 and 2, in the sense that 3 requires details whereas 2 involves a broader judgment of the advertisement.

(e) 4 What questions would you want to ask the applicant who wrote the following letter?

Dear Sir,

I am writing to apply for the post advertised in the Science Journal for a research assistant in your Department of Drug Metabolism.

I am a graduate in biology from the University of North Wales and am currently undertaking research work. I have extensive experience of laboratory work and am keen to participate in multi-disciplinary projects as I already have managerial experience.

I am available for interview when required and look forward to receiving a favourable reply.

Yours faithfully,

G R Davies

G R Davies

Reading and discourse (what we read)

Discourse in action deals with three types of discourse: exposition, enquiry and argument.

Exposition is the presentation of knowledge.
Enquiry is the search for knowledge.
Argument is the evaluation of knowledge.

(e) My own feeling is that 4 is unnecessary. I would think that the points had already been well made; and I would expect some class impatience with 'drug metabolism' especially if the students had no involvement with the pharmacy or medical fields.

(f) RTE is an ESP textbook and not a treatise on discourse analysis—so the statements about discourse need to be evaluated in terms of whether or not they are pedagogically-helpful generalizations. At the beginning of the section the authors define *Exposition* as the presentation of knowledge, whereas now they describe it as the presentation of knowledge already acquired. The latter (and the following description of its main features) clearly fits subject textbooks, but does it fit the presentation of 'new knowledge'?

(f) Exposition presents knowledge already acquired. It presents theories, laws, general principles and specific instances. It uses different means of organizing information such as definition, classification, description, explanation and comparison.

Enquiry presents investigations rather than established knowledge. It involves asking questions, suggesting possible answers, putting forward and verifying hypotheses.

Argument presents points of view rather than established knowledge. It involves defending and attacking points of view, persuading and recommending solutions.

Exposition

The article below describes a new device for a particular medical use. Make a summary of the information in it by noting:

a the nature of the device,
b its significance,
c how and why it has been modified during its development,
d whether it has been tried sufficiently to be introduced into hospitals.

Does the passage give sufficient information to enable you to draw a diagram of the valve? If not, what further information is needed?

A new twist to heart valves

(g) A Scottish chemical engineer has developed an artificial heart valve which should cost about one-third as much as the valves in use today. The valve, now undergoing tests in calves, is also potentially safer than current models because it causes no turbulent blood flow and so reduces the risk of blood clotting, and the need for continual anti-coagulant treatment with its associated risks.

(h) Dr Norman Macleod, head of the chemical engineering department of Edinburgh University, has designed the valve which consists of a hollow graphite cylinder about 2 cm in diameter and 1 cm long, with a narrowing cone-shaped hole conducting blood through the middle. The valve opens and shuts by means of an oval plate, which swings to lie across the hole in the valve to block flow, or to lie parallel to the flow of blood to open the valve. There is no collar or any other projection at all inside the valve to cause turbulence. The valve is coated inside with pyrolytic carbon, made by vaporizing carbon and then allowing it to settle on the inner valve surface. Pyrolytic carbon provokes no immune reaction, does not stimulate clotting, is not corroded by blood chemicals, and allows smooth flow over its surface.

The first, short-term trials in dogs to test the effectiveness of the valve's action, gave encouraging results. Now second stage trials, in which valves have been fitted in calves for several months, are well advanced.

Macleod is now at work on an improved valve in which the inside channel is

(g) The question raised in the previous note can now be advanced in the negative. It seems clear that a typical piece of scientific journalism—or the presentation of new information—involves a rather different range of communicative functions. Right since Episode One ESP practitioners have insisted on clearly differentiating study-science materials and popular science. In my view RTE's attempt to place both types of writing within a single category of *exposition* is unfortunate.

(h) It is interesting to note that the passage assumes a fair amount of background knowledge in that there is no reference to the purpose or use of artificial heart valves. Given the anticipated range of students working through RTE, its authors might well have provided information on this point or asked the students to take the matter up. Also the title is obscure.

trumpet-shaped and flared rather than cone-shaped. This gives better blood flow and enables the walls of the valve to be thinner with a larger channel. He has also found a way of making the valve not, as in the first prototypes, from expensive graphite but from cheap plastic moulded to shape and then heated to convert it into hard carbon, with the properties of pyrolysed carbon. Valves made in this way could cost only about £100 instead of the £300 typical today.

This first appeared in *New Scientist*, London, the weekly review of science and technology.

Enquiry

Read the following proposal to set up an experiment and note:

a the phenomenon to be investigated,
b the particular purpose of the investigation,
c how the experiment will be undertaken.

Suggest possible conclusions.

Experience suggests that a common error in processing visual sequence is inversion or transposition of two or more adjacent items. This phenomenon suggests that information concerning the identity of items and their positions may be partially separable. We propose to undertake a perception experiment using a tachiscope with exposures of 5-, 6- and 7-digit sequences. The purpose of the study will be to demonstrate that the phenomenon of transposition can be observed under laboratory conditions and to describe its probable occurrence in a given sequence.

Argument

(i) Read the following letter to a university newspaper and note the views to which the writer is opposed. Write a reply with a similar structure from the head of one of the departments mentioned in the final sentence.

Sir,

I fully understand the opposition expressed by my colleagues to the reduction in the university budget. Nevertheless one is forced to recognize that in times of financial difficulty the university has a duty to decide where savings can be made. I believe however that it would be misguided for the university to make the same cuts in all departments without considering national priorities. May I suggest that there are some departments which must continue to be financed at existing levels if these are to produce the fully trained professionals which the country needs. Surely it is a national priority to train competent scientists, engineers and practitioners of medicine and veterinary medicine. If there have to be cuts they should be shared between departments which cannot claim to be absolutely essential to the needs of the country, such as economics, psychology or modern languages.

James Young
Head of Department of Veterinary Medicine.

(i) In contrast to *Exposition*, *Enquiry* and *Argument* seem very neatly illustrated, even though both make very considerable demands on those undertaking the activities.

Units 2, 3 and 4 each concentrate on one of the three types of discourse. Units 5, 6 and 7 each include passages containing more than one type of discourse.

Reading as a process (how we read)

Reading is an active process, not a passive process. It involves interpreting passages, not just receiving a message. A reader interprets a passage by:

understanding a writer's implications,
making inferences,
realizing not only what information is given but also what information is not given,
evaluating the passage.

Putting a passage in its context

The ways in which we interpret passages can be practised by trying to discover the context in which a passage was written. This involves considering such aspects as: the intended reader, the writer, the purpose of the passage, the type of writing. Read the following two extracts and answer these questions about the context of each one.

1 Was the passage intended for:
  - a specialists,
  - b students,
  - c general readers,
  - d academics and others with an interest in science,
  - e schoolchildren?

2 Is the purpose of the extract:
  - a to teach a subject,
  - b to interest people in a new subject,
  - c to provide new information,
  - d to persuade people to adopt a particular point of view,
  - e to tell people how to do something?

3 Does the extract assume that the reader:
  - a has a scientific background,
  - b is familiar with the nature and use of microprocessors,
  - c already knows about calculators and robots,
  - d has a specialist knowledge of the devices used to store data?

(j)

Passage A

Everyone accepts that the microprocessor will eventually permeate into every kind of equipment and be used by all industries. But even these powerful calculating devices depend on other components. Behind every microprocessor must be a store to hold the results of its calculations and the instructions which control them. The most versatile way of doing this is to hold them in a programmable read-only-memory or PROM. This differs from the random access memory or RAM, by providing long term, instead of short term data storage.

By 1971 semiconductor makers were ready to exploit a very old principle for the memory technology business—the use of miniature fuses which could be selectively blown to change conductor patterns. This is the origin of the modern programmable read-only-memory, or PROM.

(k)

Passage B

THE ROBOT AGE has begun—thanks to the silicon chip which can do the work of a massive computer bank. Already the cheap brain-power of these quarter-inch chips—called micro-processors—has put a calculator in almost everyone's pocket and created a £25 million industry for TV games.

Just press a button and Micro Mum will wake you up, make the tea, read the news, pay the bills and cook the bacon just the way you like it . . .

IMAGINE your home being run by an electronic Micro Mother.

A push-button brain that organizes the shopping and the cooking, pays the bills, and even remembers your birthday!

And imagine all the household chores being handled by a robot Mrs Mop that washes the floor, cleans the carpet and even mows the lawn!

No, it's not just a futuristic dream—tomorrow's world is already here . . .

Micro Mum and Mrs Mop are the forerunners of the first generation of computerized home robots created by the silicon chip.

(j) This is RTE at its best. The introduction to *Reading as a Process* is persuasive and the pre-reading set-up excellently managed. The activity is ideal for pair or group discussion as the answers to the questions are obviously debatable (and so much the better). In the Key we find the following: 1d; 2b and c; 3a, b and c. We may not agree.

(k) Passage B does not work so well, partly because the typography makes it self-evidently from a popular newspaper and partly because 'Daily Mirror' style (Mrs Mop, etc.) is both extremely difficult for non-native speakers and little to the purpose of the intended usership of RTE.

(l) Now answer these questions about the extracts.

4 Write some questions about microprocessors that are not answered in the extracts. Does either passage indicate the dangers or disadvantages of microprocessors?

5 What disadvantages of microprocessors can you think of?

6 Would you wish your home to be run as in Passage B?

7 Predict how each passage will probably continue.
a By giving details of the construction of devices.
b By giving examples of industrial uses of microprocessors.
c By describing how microprocessors are used in supermarkets.
d By giving the history of the devices.

(m) **Prediction**

An important aspect of interpreting passages is predicting what is going to come next. This skill enables the reader to be aware not only of what information is given but also of what information is not given in a passage.

The following sentences form a paragraph on microprocessors. After each sentence there are four questions. These suggest ways in which the passage might continue. Look at each sentence and mark the preceding question (a, b, c or d) which it answers. For example:

Computers were initially used to store, manipulate, retrieve and organize vast quantities of statistical information.
a Why were they used for these purposes?
(b) How are they used in the present?
c What kinds of information were stored?
d What other purposes were they used for?
→1 But now they are increasingly used in control, monitoring, regulation and automation.

a Why has this change occurred?
b How will they be used in the future?
c When did this change take place?
d How has this change affected computer design?
2 Their changing role has been made possible by technological advances which have increased the speed, reliability and power of computers.

(l) It seems to me that Questions 4, 5 and 6 cause some loss of momentum and some loss of focus on the main point. Question 7 is useful because it nicely leads the way to the next section.

(m) I personally find this instruction difficult to process. The exercise-type itself has become quite widely used in recent years.

a What kind of technological advances?
b How has speed been increased?
c What are the effects of this change?
d What else has been made possible by these technological advances?

3 In addition there has been a dramatic reduction in their cost and size.

a How will these changes affect society?
b What other invention is even more important?
c Which of these changes is most important?
d How has size been reduced?

4 Yet it is the invention of microprocessors which will have the most profound effects in the last quarter of this century.

a When will these effects be noticed?
b What kind of effects?
c Why were they not invented earlier?
d What will be of less importance than this invention?

5 The development of microprocessors enables a limited task to be carried out very quickly, accurately and cheaply.

a What is the consequence of this?
b What kind of tasks?
c What about tasks which are not limited?
d How cheaply?

6 They are now being introduced into a wide range of industries and services.

a What role do they have in industry?
b What kinds of industries and services?
c What problems is this causing?
d In what other areas are they being introduced?

7 The speed, reliability and power of microprocessors have vastly increased the potential for automation.

Now look at these single sentences. Write two questions for each one which might be answered in a subsequent sentence.

8 The speed, reliability and power of microprocessors have vastly increased the potential for automation.

9 As the cheap microprocessor penetrates more and more sectors of the economy, it will have increasingly wide-ranging effects.

10 In the 1950s and 60s it was only possible to automate for one specific task.

11 Microprocessors are beginning to have dramatic effects on secretarial work.

(n) Each of the following sentences follows on from one of the sentences in 8–11. Decide where each sentence should go, and notice whether it answers one of the questions you wrote.

12 Now automated robots can be reprogrammed for a variety of tasks.

13 Word processing systems enable a large variety of standardized letters and other documents to be automatically typed.

14 They are already in use in the control of power stations, textile mills, telephone switching systems, welding and fault-finding in the car industry.

(o) 15 This will enable automation to be introduced on a far larger scale than previously possible.

Abstract

In each of the units in Phase One there is an abstract, which consists of a summary of the main passage. It illustrates points introduced in the preparation and helps students to read the main passage more easily.

1 Read the abstract of the main passage and choose which of the following statements best summarizes it.
   a People are apathetic towards noise.
   b Noise pollution is worse in industrialized societies than in non-industrialized societies.
   c Noise pollution is a serious environmental concern.
   d Noise can have harmful physiological and psychological effects.

NOISE POLLUTION

A well-documented body of information exists showing that noise can adversely affect humans in both physiological and psychological ways. Hearing losses in particular occupations such as boiler-making and construction work are well known. In fact, however, we all find hearing more difficult as we age. Young ears can distinguish a wide range of sounds from low to very high frequencies, while older ears lose the ability to distinguish high-pitched sounds. A comparison of

(n) The original feature (notice whether it answers one of the questions you wrote) is a good example of the careful and clever linking together of separate activities.

(o) At this point the *Preparation* part comes to an end. There follows an abstract which consists of a summary of the main passage.

III

ACTIVITIES

(1) Look again at Passage A (the first of the two passages about microprocessors). Imagine that your class is not familiar with the following words:—

eventually, permeate, versatile, random, exploit, miniature, fuse, blow.

What (if anything) will you do about it? In particular, how will you make sure that the primary objective of assisting the learners to put passages in their contexts is not compromised by vocabulary problems?

(2) Reconsider this paragraph from the pharmaceutical PhD advertisement:—

The successful applicant, who will probably be in his/her late twenties, will have gained several years' experience of drug metabolism and pharmacokinetic work related to the development and registration of new drugs. He/she will be keen to build upon this knowledge in the wider aspects of Drug Safety Evaluation.

(a) Comment on how information about the appointment and the qualifications required is communicated. (Consider, for instance, the use of *will*.)

(b) Rewrite the paragraph so that it would be more typical of an advertisement for a University research assistant.

(c) Do you think there is a 'job-advertisement' discourse sub-type?

(3) The *preparation* part of Unit 1 of *Discourse in Action* takes up 11 pages. You have been asked to reduce it to 5 pages. What do you propose?

IV

EVALUATION

(1) In a review article of the first three volumes (*The ESP Journal*, 1, 1, 1980), David Wyatt observes that the RTE approach seems to imply that *either* the most important features of special registers in such areas as science and technology 'are also present in the general academic register, *or* the features peculiar to special registers do not present as much of a learning problem as was previously anticipated'.

Which of the alternatives do you prefer? And what is your evidence? Or do you reject both? And for what reasons?

(2) The more recent textbooks on study-reading have been influenced by first-language work on research into reading and the teaching of reading. Could Episode Thirteen be used with native speakers? Would any changes need to be made?

V
RELATED READINGS

There are two particularly useful background papers:—

J. D. Moore, 'The preparation of rhetorically-focused materials for Colombian University Students' in *English for Specific Purposes: An International Seminar*, The British Council, 1977.

Clara Helena de Saba and Claudía Lucia Ordóñez, 'Procedures and Problems in introducing *Reading and Thinking in English*' in the proceedings of the British Council Regional Conference on ESP, Mexico, 1979.

And two reviews:—

Lewis Kerr, Review of *Discourse in Action* in ELT Journal Volume 36/1, 1981.

David H. Wyatt, 'Reading and Thinking in English – A Review Article', the *ESP Journal*, Vol. 1, No. 1, Fall 1980, The American University, Washington, DC.

The first on *Discourse in Action* is highly complimentary; the second by Wyatt has already been referred to.

EPISODE FOURTEEN 1980

Tom Hutchinson and Alan Waters, 'ESP at the Crossroads', *English for Specific Purposes* 36, Oregon State University, 1980.

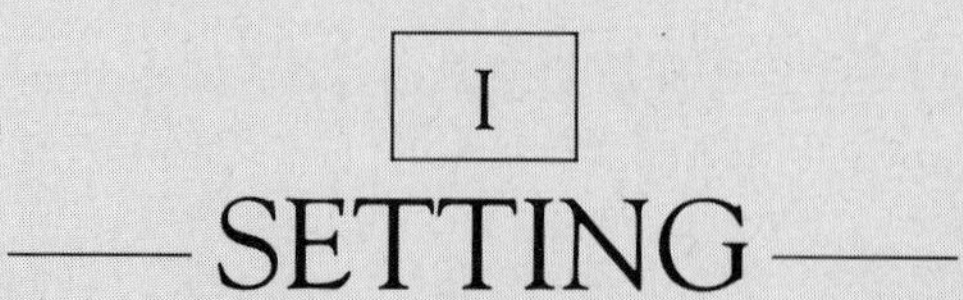

In the introduction to Episode Nine I observed that by the middle seventies the broad agreement that had been built up over the previous ten years was beginning to break down; and we have seen in Episodes Ten through Thirteen some of the different ways in which ESP practitioners have responded to new insights and opportunities and to new objections and criticisms. For Phillips and Shettlesworth the points of departure were, on the one hand, their recognition that the language classroom was, in communicative terms, a decidedly unusual sort of place, and on the other, their realization that the writing of traditional ESP materials was a more fallible activity than had been supposed. For Herbolich in Episodes Ten and Eleven (and for many others not represented in this volume) the answer lay in educationally imaginative responses to the students' learning situation; in developing new exercise-based activities and in offering integrative schemes such as projects. Johns and Dudley-Evans particularized the learning situation of certain groups of students, and their search for the 'real' characteristics of learning situations had led them first to discussion and then to collaboration with colleagues from other departments. Meanwhile, in the closing years of the seventies, major materials writing projects had continued—in Thailand, in Malaysia, in Saudi Arabia, in Colombia and elsewhere. The material results of two of these projects are now commercially available and both are significant for their utilization of what is known about the reading process, for their insistence on developing general strategies for approaching any kind of academic text, and for their belief in the value of student discussion.

Despite superficial differences between these various approaches to ESP, some of the motivations are shared. For one thing, there was agreement that the ESP classroom should offer more than linguistic face-validity. I mean by this that the ESP practitioner should attempt to do more than simply import into the ESP classroom examples and practice work that reflected the grammatical, lexical, rhetorical and textual features of the particular subject he and his class were interested in. The EST teacher needed to do more than to reveal the truth about the language of science; his or her class should no longer be seen as a class in applied or practical stylistics. Indeed, it was beginning to be thought close attention to subject-specific language might well produce an unhealthy narrowness of focus and create in the participants a dangerous and false sense of security. Rather the ESP classroom should lead its occupants towards useful principles which would allow them to cope better with their learning environments, to develop utilizable study habits, to comprehend the processes of academic reading and to discover methods of handling authentic materials. A generally accepted consequence of this type of thinking was a need to restructure the role of the teacher. The teacher was no longer going to reveal the truth about a particular content, but to fulfil two other types of role. On the one hand, he or she was going to replicate the communicative reality of the wider environment for which he or she was providing an English Language Service, and this was to be done by simulations, by *realia*, by projects, etc. On the other, the ESP teacher was going to ask his students to reflect upon and then discuss with fellow students their mental and psychological processes and the conclusions those processes had led them to. If the teacher was no longer going to be creator and controller of input and output, then he or she should withdraw from centre stage and offer prompts, counsel and commentary on the workshop performances that were being generated. And a third common motivation was the ESP practitioner's deep-felt need to be innovative. My own experience suggests to me that ESP differs from ELT in this respect, at least in degree if not in kind. The way the ESP profession is structured, the way reputations are made and advancement is secured, reflects a premium on originality. The ESP teacher gets more credit for doing something *new* rather than for doing something *well*.

In the previous two paragraphs I have tried to describe some of the reassessments taking place on the pioneering frontiers of ESP at the end of the seventies. However, even this type of thinking did not fully prepare the profession for the spanner thrown in the ESP works by Hutchinson and Waters. But before we consider Hutchinson and Waters' arguments it is first necessary to set 'ESP at the Crossroads' against its background, both bibliographical and educational. As far as I know, there are four published versions of their views:—

(1) 'An English Language Curriculum for Technical Students' (with Michael Breen as third author), *Practical Papers in English Language Education*, Vol. 2, University of Lancaster, 1979.
(2) 'Communication in the Technical Classroom', *ELT Documents Special – Projects in Materials Design*, The British Council, 1980.
(3) 'ESP at the Crossroads', *English for Specific Purposes* 36, OSU, 1980.
(4) 'Performance and Competence in English for Specific Purposes', *Applied Linguistics* 2, 1, 1981.

Although there are interesting differences between the four papers, they are not as great as the titles might suggest. I have chosen 'ESP at the Crossroads' for this Episode principally because it is the shortest.

The educational background is most clearly described in the second paper and the following edited extract will serve:—

> In 1977 we were considering what teaching materials to use for a group of Iranian students who were coming to the Institute for English Language Education in Lancaster, prior to commencing their studies at various technical colleges in Britain . . . We got in touch with Lancaster and Morecambe College of Further Education and set up a liaison scheme which enabled us to observe and record a variety of lectures, examine syllabi and course materials and talk with staff and students about their work. In addition, we studied the information put out by the Technician Education Council (TEC), the supervisory body for technical education in Britain. Although we had originally gone to the College because of a concern about the level of teaching, what we learnt there led us to seriously question the whole basis of current ideas and materials in ESP.

Hutchinson and Waters first question the need for subject-specific materials. This sort of question has already been raised and, although their reasons for casting doubt on both the necessity and appropriacy of subject-specific materials are not exactly the same as those of Phillips and Shettlesworth, or Moore and Widdowson, or Cooper and Sinclair, their line of reasoning is within a developing tradition. It is their second question that challenges a 'much more fundamental presupposition inherent in the concept of ESP'. As they say, 'the question is not whether the content of Mechanical Engineering is different from that of Telecommunications, but whether the study of Mechanical Engineering texts is the best way of preparing a student for a course in Mechanical Engineering'.

In essence, their argument takes the following form. It is right that we should investigate the situations in which and for which our students will require English. Hence the contemporary emphasis on needs analysis is justified. Such an analysis will produce information about linguistic and other features of the target situation; this we can call the 'Target Performance Repertoire'. Traditionally such a repertoire has formed the basis of the ESP syllabus and an example of this approach is precisely asking mechanical engineering students to study mechanical engineering texts. However, this is mistaken because it confuses *what the students are expected to cope with* (the actual language) with *what the students require in order to cope* (background knowledge or 'underlying competence'). It is not so much what is in the textbook, the lecture or the demonstration, but what is *not* there because the communicator presumes that it is unnecessary to mention it. After all, we need to remember that the educational process is a continuing and dynamic one and that the technical instructor—if he is any good—will be providing explanations of new information as he goes along. The ESP teacher should therefore supply the *underlying competence* which the overseas student must have as a prerequisite for learning if he is to engage successfully in this educational process, rather than, as it were, 'rehearse' superficial aspects of what will actually happen in that educational setting.

The attack that Hutchinson and Waters make on many of the assumptions implicit in previous Episodes is both important and very persuasively argued for the technical student situation the two authors investigated. 'ESP at the Crossroads' (and its varieties) has led to a good deal of controversy, especially in the United States where, for instance, the issues raised have been publicly debated at TESOL. In addition, Episode Fourteen well illustrates the kind of radical re-thinking associated with the Department/Institute at Lancaster headed by Professor Christopher Candlin and must, in that sense, serve as the chapter in this story that represents 'Lancaster radicalism'.

The issue turns, however, on the wider applicability of the Hutchinson–Waters thesis, for there is little except admiration for what they did for revising our thinking about how we should prepare overseas Technical students for entry to British Technical Colleges. Hutchinson and Waters have been insistent that their arguments are relevant to other situations. For example, in a footnote to their fourth and most polished statement of their case they observe:—

> We concentrate on our recent experience in an area of ESP commonly known as EST (English for Science and Technology) and, in particular, in the preparation of overseas students for study in British Technical Colleges. However, although our examples are drawn from this specific area, we believe that our theoretical conclusions and practical procedures are of relevance and importance to the whole of ESP.

How far they are justified in this claim is something to be borne in mind as the remainder of this Episode unfolds.

II

TEXT AND COMMENTARY

'ESP at the Crossroads'

by Tom Hutchinson *and* Alan Waters
University of Lancaster Institute for English Language Education

In guest-editing this issue of *ESP Newsletter* our aim is to review the present state of ESP, to raise certain questions and, where appropriate, to suggest alternative procedures in the light of our work in ESP course design at the Institute for English Language Education, University of Lancaster, U.K.

1. *Needs Analysis*

1.1 A beneficial aspect of the growing body of ESP dogma is the increasing emphasis given to target situation analysis as a curriculum design prerequisite.* There are, however, a number of *(a)* problems associated with how it is managed, what it should identify, and how the data obtained influences teaching–learning decisions.

1.2 First, 'management' problems. There is a disquieting trend towards isolating needs analysis from other aspects of teaching and learning. The application of elaborate analysis *(b)* models (e.g. Munby, 1978) demands a curriculum 'expert', a creature apart from the teachers and learners (on whose crumbs they nevertheless depend). The whole central business of why teachers and learners are taking part in an English language curriculum in the first place is thus put at one remove: the inevitable 'paper reality' takes its place—static, stereotyped, compartmentalized.

Logistical constraints very often force curriculum designers to evolve a more convivial approach than this (Drobnic, 1978). We need to recognize, however, that making needs *(c)* analysis a central part of the curriculum activities which teachers and learners share in, has a logic of its own.

* Nevertheless it is a simple fact that most published ESP course books, despite the claims implicit in such titles as 'Technical English', are not supported by the thorough examination of the communicative realities of their 'specialism' that is necessary.

(a) The footnote raises an important issue about the evaluation of ESP course books. Can a published course book hope to reflect the 'communicative realities' of its specialism? Are there such general 'communicative realities' or are 'communicative realities' very much the products of particular situations? If the latter is the case, then we might look to the published work for an adequate description of the *linguistic* reality, and leave the communicative aspects to the initiatives of the ESP staff involved at the local level. But even so, Hutchinson and Waters' criticisms about the lack of 'thorough examination' are well taken.

(b) The trend towards isolating needs analysis from other aspects of teaching and learning is one of the reasons why I have not taken needs analysis as central to this volume.

(c) The concept of *ESP practitioner* itself implies a person who teaches, designs curricula, prepares materials and carries out various kinds of investigation, some of which certainly deserving the name of 'research'. The involvement of the *learners* in curriculum design is quite another matter and perhaps reflects the interest at Lancaster in encouraging and training learners to take on greater responsibility for the shaping of their educational experience. It is this type of co-operation which gives rise to the concept of a 'negotiated syllabus'.

1.3 Second, and more fundamental, are the problems associated with the nature of the data identified by needs analysis. The aspects of the target situation which are usually given greatest prominence tend to be merely 'surface' or 'performance' features. A glance at a mechanical engineering class in a Technical College, for example, will reveal that the topic is concerned with mechanical engineering, that there are texts about mechanical engineering and so on; but *what the students are expected to cope with* should not be confused with *what the students require in order to cope.* A distinction needs to be drawn between *the end*—in this example, understanding a lesson on a mechanical engineering topic—and *the means.* It is necessary to examine the *underlying competence* which the learner must bring to the mechanical engineering classroom, or to the study of any specialized subject.

To illustrate the distinction we are making, consider the example of the native speaker student entering a British technical college to study, say, Electrical Engineering. He will have had no previous experience of studying the subject, since it is not part of an English school curriculum, and cannot be assumed to have any knowledge of either the subject itself, or the specific terms associated with it. Yet, assuming he is reasonably intelligent and attentive, he will be able to cope adequately with the flow of new information. It would also be reasonable to assume that if he had enrolled instead for a different subject—technical or otherwise—he would also have been able to cope: students from the same educational background manage to,
(d) at least.

How is this possible, unless there is a basic Underlying Competence that, largely irrespective of subject, enables the student to interpret the flow of new knowledge?

In fact, this Competence is fundamental to the whole teaching–learning process, because it is the starting point for the interaction of teacher and student in the transfer of knowledge.
(e) Before he can start to teach a group of students, the teacher must first make an analysis of what the students already know (cf. Schegloff, 1979). On the principle of working from the known to the unknown the teacher will take the result of his analysis as the basis on which to construct the new complex of knowledge. He will use what the students already know in order to explain, exemplify, and contextualize the new information that he has to convey.

It is the possession of the knowledge and abilities the teacher assumes he has that enables the student to understand and remember the new information that is given on the basis of that assumption. Thus if we are to prepare the overseas student adequately for, say, technical
(f) instruction, what he needs to acquire is this assumed competence.

Clearly, it is not possible to make the overseas student into a native speaker, nor even if it were possible, would this be necessary. Not every aspect of the native speaker's competence will be exploited in the technical classroom, and the foreign student will already possess many of the features in his mother tongue. We need to look at what the native speaker student brings to

(d) The distinction seems to me to be extremely well illustrated; and the logic of the rhetorical question that follows hard to refute.

(e) We need to note at this point that Hutchinson and Waters are concerned with institutions in which *teaching* rather than *studying* is the principal mode for transmitting knowledge in English. Their interest in class lectures and demonstrations is therefore quite different to the interest in book-handling and library-skills we saw in the previous Episode.

(f) The argument is presumably not as generally applicable as the authors imply. They are talking about individual overseas students (or, at most, twos or threes) feeding into technical classes being run for native speakers of English; classes in which the non-native speakers are such a small minority that no special considerations can be realistically made for them. Hutchinson and Waters cannot have it both ways. Doubtless they are right in claiming that 'the teacher must first make an analysis of what the students already know' before he can begin teaching them. Therefore, if the teacher recognizes that (say) half his class are overseas students and with a limited competence in English, then presumably he will need to take these sociocultural and linguistic facts into account. Indeed, in Episode Twelve we saw just such a process at work (see commentary-note *(h)*); and we also saw how ESP practitioners like Tim Johns and Tony Dudley-Evans are able to play a valuable role in that sort of re-adjustment.

the target situation in terms of his Total Competence and then consider this in the light of what happens in the technical classroom in order to discover what elements of the Total (g) Competence are exploited and activated in the target situation.

In Figure 1 then, we need to consider both the Underlying Competence and the Target Performance Repertoire to establish the vital link between them, shown in the diagram by the shaded area. This overlap represents the essence of the knowledge and abilities that are assumed and exploited in the target situation and therefore represents the Competence that the prospective 'specialist' student must develop through the ESP curriculum.

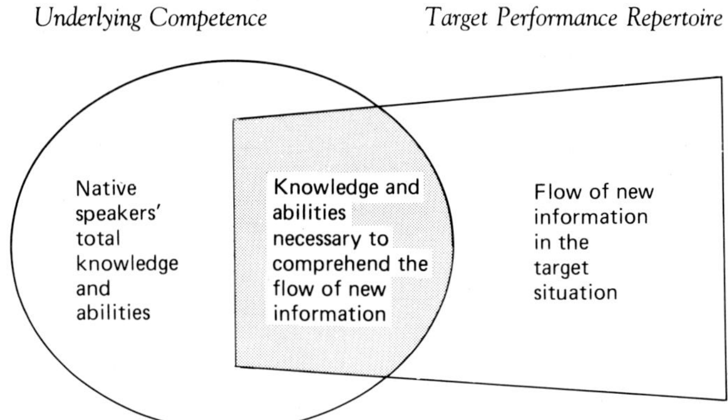

Figure 1: The Basis of the ESP Curriculum

1.4 The third 'problem area' identified above concerns the relationship between the findings of needs analysis and the content of the curriculum. The tendency has been for the performance repertoire—real or imagined—to form the basis of texts in the teaching programme. The points we have already made about the primacy of the target competence, and its relation to the curriculum, should have already clarified our disagreement with this widespread practice. It can be objected to on other grounds, too.

Input material taken unadulterated (or nearly so) from the target context presents difficulties (h) over content. Firstly, a test does not exist *in vacuo* but has a position within a body of knowledge. The specialist teacher does not suddenly produce a text on, say, transistors; this text will form part of a lesson (usually, involving an initial demonstration), which will form part of a series of lessons on the basics of radio communication, which in turn will form part of a technical curriculum. In the 'authentic' situation, therefore, much of the work of understanding the new text will be achieved by reference to other parts of the lesson to previous work in the series and to frames of reference which the learners have derived from other experiences and knowledge. Coming to it 'cold' in the ESP classroom, the student is denied these contextual clues. Comprehension is, therefore, more difficult, and what is of greater long-term importance, the student is less likely to develop the strategies that will enable him to exploit such clues.

Secondly, if language use in the classroom is to in any way simulate real communication there must be discussion of the subject matter, and this will inevitably stray beyond the actual

(g) This is clearly of great importance, especially within the terms of reference I tried to establish in the previous commentary-note. But equally clearly it is a task of considerable complexity. In fact, the most impressive work I know of in this area is Tom Hutchinson's 'The Practical Demonstration' referred to in the bibliography at the end of this article.

(h) Compare Johns' and Dudley-Evans' similar view: 'understanding a text must include understanding the significance of the text within the overall learning/teaching process'. How does the information in the text relate in terms of what is "given" and "new" to information already acquired?'.

text being studied. Yet the ESP teacher often does not know enough about the subject-matter

(i) to be able to handle this sort of situation; nor can the ESP institution generally provide the technical back-up needed to do so. Thus, the specialist knowledge becomes de-contextualized; classroom work gets bogged down in matters that neither teacher nor student fully understands; time is wasted in trying to explain specific vocabulary without the visual aids and expertise that

(j) the target situation can produce. As a result, there is little hope of any lasting language assimilation.

If instead there is an attempt to bypass the problems of content contextualization and shared knowledge by a treatment of the texts which focuses only on their linguistic properties, there will obviously be no 'real' communication. The development and refinement of linguistic resources is of prime importance in language learning, but it is unlikely to occur in isolation from other, more fundamental, knowledge and interests. Put another way, if you are an expert on fluid mechanics, you will probably be able to interpret the gist of a discussion on fluid mechanics in language X, of which you may know next to nothing; on the other hand, you will

(k) probably be unable to make any sense of a mother-tongue discussion about, say microbiology, if you know next to nothing about microbiology.

All three problems tend to produce texts and exercises which contain very few or no opportunities for the learner to grapple with new information, or with new slants on familiar information. Such materials become just a package of exercises in linguistic analysis (Coulthard, 77, Ch. 7) for which the average ESP student, in our experience, has little interest.

2. *Target Competence: an example*

To exemplify a number of the points made so far, we will draw on our recent investigation of communication in the British technical college.

The Competence required of the technical student is, of course, very complex, but for the purposes of this paper we can consider three aspects: mode, language and knowledge of the world.

(l) 2.1 *Mode:* Technical communication is predominantly visual and oral, with the visual being

(m) the most important element. The typical lesson centres around a practical demonstration, i.e. a presentation using a visual display of some kind—an actual machine or apparatus, a model, diagram, chart, graph, etc. Language is used in close co-ordination with paralinguistic features such as gesture and gaze direction, to comment upon, highlight or explain features of the visual display. The technical student must, therefore, be able to cope with the standard visual modes of representation and should be able to interpret information, both as receiver *and* producer, through integrated combinations of the visual, oral and written media.

(i) It is sometimes suggested that the ESP teacher can hand over at this stage to 'subject experts' among his students. However, this idea usually does not work out too well in practice. For instance, it can cause a lot of confusion about perceived roles and be traumatic for the teacher. It *can* work with mature and professional students but in terms of technical students in their late teens Hutchinson and Waters are probably wise not to consider it.

(j) The counterproductiveness of attempting to handle technical vocabulary in the ESP class is at least one thing nearly all authors of Episodes agree on!

(k) There is a fair amount of circumstantial evidence to suggest that this is in fact the case.

(l) Again we need to remember the context—technical communication in the classroom in a British technical college. Technical communication itself is a much wider area and we need only to consider how it is likely to be carried out in manufacturing companies, between ships at sea and in research institutes to realize the merits of being cautious about generalizations.

(m) One of Hutchinson's most interesting findings is that the particular *object* being demonstrated (such as a machine) itself determines the structure of the discourse. After all, it makes no sense to begin a demonstration of a cassette-recorder with the rewind mechanism.

(n) 2.2 *Language:* The language used in technical education is not, except for a few examples of terminology, subject-specific nor even specific to technical communication. Everyday language is used.

We can highlight four reasons for this. Firstly, since the language is predominantly visual-related, the need for specific terms and expressions is lower because the visual display gives precise meaning to objects and actions. Secondly, the teacher cannot assume any knowledge of specialized terms on the part of the students, because the subject is new to them. But he can make use of the very wide technical and semi-technical vocabulary that a native speaker, by virtue of living in a technological society, would possess: terms such as fuse, friction, trigger, screw, tube, valve, etc. Everyday English has a very wide range of such terms. And any subject-specific terms that do occur will normally be explained using this everyday knowledge. Thirdly, technical English is only an adaptation of the existing resources of the English language. Many expressions with a technical sense, therefore, are easily understood and memorized by the native speaker because he is simply extending the use of a known concept: e.g. grip, saddle, play, drag, drum, sleeve, head, chip, etc. Lastly, the socially interactive nature of the practical demonstration (Hutchinson, 78) will compound this tendency to use conversational language.

2.3 *Knowledge of the World:* Understanding discourse is not just a question of knowing the language. Use is also made of conceptual and factual knowledge. Teachers exploit such knowledge to illustrate, exemplify and explain the new information they have to convey; again as with the language, it is general technical knowledge that is used—layman's technology, e.g. the workings of a car, the use of electricity and water in the home, domestic appliances, etc.—and a school level knowledge of general science.*

2.4 Thus the Underlying Competence required of the technical student is that required for any effective use of language, viz. an ability to receive and transmit information effectively through integrated combinations of visual, oral and written media. The linguistic and factual resources that the student requires are those of the technically-minded layman not the specialist or academic.

2.5 *Implications for ELT:* It must be obvious from this brief sketch that there is no justification for subject-specific ESP materials. The Competence we have discussed is transferable to almost any technical subject, because it operates from the basis of the student's knowledge and abilities
(o) on entering technical education—a point at which no specialized knowledge can be assumed by the teacher and therefore will not be exploited.

* (It should be noted that, in the British Technical College, the knowledge exploited is not only technical or scientific knowledge; a large amount of socio-cultural information is also used, but how far this is applicable to situations outside Britain we cannot say.)

(n) Although the authors may be generally right about this, other observers have noted marked differences in the level of *formality* of technical instructors.

(o) It is not clear whether the authors are claiming that there is no justification for subject-specific ESP materials at all, or whether they are claiming that there is no justification in the situation they have just sketched out. If the latter, then perhaps there is little need to make a comment. But if they are advancing the larger claim then the issue is obviously controversial. One way of seeing this is to deny their assumption that 'no specialized knowledge can be assumed by the teacher and therefore will not be exploited'. In 1979 we had at Aston a group of Algerian postgraduate mathematicians and physicists who came to us for an intensive English course before going on to take PhD research degrees in various institutions around Britain. Their specialized knowledge was such that they found the content of the final year BSc maths and physics courses into which we steered them altogether too elementary. They wanted in effect a target situation repertoire; they wanted the English equivalents of the specialized knowledge they had already acquired through the medium of French. The situation I have just described may have been an extreme one, but it does show that each ESP situation is best examined in its own terms.

Furthermore, the use of self-sufficient written texts to exemplify technical discourse is misplaced since the precise forms and language use of this medium are not representative of the greater part of technical communication.

Does this argument, then, mean that ESP should be abandoned altogether? We think not. The basic orientation of teaching materials still needs to be towards a technical content, firstly because the prime interest of technical students in technical knowledge is assumed in the target situation by the teachers. The need is for a shift of focus from the surface structures of technical discourse to the underlying interpretive strategies required to cope with such discourse, and from the specific language and content of the 'academic' text to the more generative knowledge (p) and language of popular technology in whatever form it may be expressed.

3. *Materials and Methodology*

3.1 *Organization:* The materials we have devised in the light of our research are organized into fourteen Units each based on a general topic, e.g. Metals, Sound, Electricity, Light, Chemistry, Pumps, Meteorology, etc. The topic basis simulates the way in which a body of knowledge is built up. It makes it possible to have tasks of greater complexity, since each lesson is not weighed down with new content, and it enables the student to develop and refine his ability to exploit his existing knowledge in interpreting the flow of new information. As the topics are concerned with popular technology and general science, no specialized knowledge is required on the part of the students or of the teacher.

Each Unit is divided into five or six Sections of two hours' teaching each. The Sections are sequentially linked both in terms of Content and of the development of the student's communicative competence (see below: 'Tasks').

(q) 3.2 *Input:* Input material is drawn from a variety of sources *regardless of the language in which it is expressed*—school-level science, consumer information, do-it-yourself manuals, publicity and information from manufacturers, etc. The media are also varied and the tasks which the students perform require an integrated use of the different media.

3.3 *Tasks:* The essential concept underlying the design of the materials is that the students should be presented with simple technical problems which they must solve by using English, rather than tasks about the use of English.

As they proceed through each Section and through the Unit as a whole, the tasks the students have to do become increasingly more complex, building up a body of knowledge and abilities and culminating in the final Section which requires them to make a full-scale presentation to the class, drawing upon his body of knowledge and abilities in order to, e.g., describe a process, report on an experiment, explain a flow-chart, etc.

3.4 *Methodology:* Pair and group work is used extensively in order to create opportunities for communication about the topic. In essence what the students are required to do is to draw information from one or more sources and transmit the information in a relevant form and context to their peers.

(p) Certainly the 'academic' context has received more than its fair share of attention—as indeed this volume as a whole demonstrates.

(q) In the second of the Activities suggested for the last Episode I raised the question of different 'forms' of job advertisement. Widdowson's charge of irresponsibility still has some force; a compromise position would be to accept a wide variety of sources but at the same time to try and ensure that texts taken from those sources are discoursally and linguistically fairly typical of many others. The matter is taken up in the final Episode and in the Prospect.

3.5 *Sample materials:* See the following.

STUDENT WORKSHEET

Unit: Pumps

Section E: Group Work – Pump Mechanisms

Work in groups of 3 or 4.

Step 1: Each member of the group has a picture of a certain type of pump. Study your picture carefully.

Step 2: In your group, discuss:

—what components the pump consists of
—how it works
—what advantages and disadvantages it has
—what sort of jobs it might be used for

Step 3: Draw a large-scale diagram of the pump. Label it and use arrows to show the flow of the fluid and the direction of the moving parts.

Step 4: Prepare a report, describing the pump. Consider all the points you discussed in Step 2 and put this information in your report.

(r) Step 5: Using the diagram you have prepared, present your report to the class.

NOTE: Each group receives a diagram of a different kind of pump. This is just one example.

4. *Some further considerations*

Our argument also raises further questions which strike at the heart of many other current practices and beliefs in ESP, which space unfortunately prevents us from more than merely adumbrating here.

4.1 *Is ESP for 'beginners'?* The answer would generally appear to be: No. However, if what we are seeking to do is to activate the learner's 'process competence' (Breen and Candlin, forthcoming)—to refine and develop his existing knowledge and abilities towards the desired

(r) The series of steps is beautifully constructed and clearly reflects the authors' talents as materials designers.

target competence—rather than merely attempt to teach a specific repertoire of language forms—the whole enterprise is put on a different footing. Learning is no longer dependent solely on the student's knowledge of the target language; and those other aspects of his competence—his previous mother-tongue language learning experience, his knowledge of the subject-matter and other kinds of knowledge in which his expertise may vary, but in no sense is
(s) he a 'beginner'—can be exploited as means to achieving the desired goal.

4.2 *Should the ESP teacher involve himself in the subject-matter?* His students are certainly likely to see learning English as a means, rather than an end in itself, and there is justification, on this ground alone, for the teacher to share their concern. In practice, however, this has traditionally created problems for the non-specialist teacher, asked to provide an authentic
(t) response to areas of knowledge in which he has little or no expertise (cf 1.4 above). Our concentration on the underlying competence—and on materials and methodology which ask learners to consider familiar information in a novel, problem-solving way—puts the teacher on much safer ground. His concern is to facilitate communication on topics (and slants on topics) of concern to and within the grasp of the intelligent layman. The background knowledge this calls upon is surely something we can assume most ESP teachers will have by virtue of their own secondary schooling and their upbringing in a consumer-oriented, technologically-developed society. Communication can thus centre squarely on *doing things with language*, rather than merely *commenting upon it*.

4.3 *What about teacher-training?* It seems to be generally believed that the ESP teacher is a creature apart, a specialist whose training and expertise set him above the rest of the EFL profession. We hope the emphasis we have given in this issue to the large area of common ground between the ESP curriculum and 'General English' shows this belief to be erroneous. ESP has acquired this unjustified aura of separateness largely because its curricula—alone in EFL—are based on needs analyses. But does it really make sense to enter into any teaching–learning contract which does not have the needs of the learner as its prime concern? Keeping in mind what we have said about the use of needs analysis (1), surely the ESP formula should be the rule not the exception. Thus the ESP teacher is first and foremost a teacher, and the 'specialist' nature of his job in fact relates to that sensitivity to the needs of his students that every teacher must have.

4.4 *Is ESP primarily concerned with writing and reading skills?* Our analysis of the communicative realities of technical instruction show such an emphasis to be misguided. More fundamentally, however, ESP has perhaps, suffered from the interest in 'surface' skill practice so prevalent in mainstream ELT. Written and spoken English are the realizations of deeper communicative
(u) processes—the dynamic organization of information according to the varying needs of the audience, the speaker/writer's knowledge of the subject, the linguistic and other resources available, and so on—and, although competent skill-use will not necessarily follow automatically from success at this deeper level it is certainly a necessary prerequisite, and one which has been given far less attention in ESP than it deserves. Perhaps the pedagogic model of discourse analysis applied to so many ESP programmes is due for critical scrutiny, or, at the very least, a reassessment of its traditionally central role.

(s) A most interesting point. In an ESP course a person with no English does not necessarily come 'naked into the classroom', although that person may well do so if he joins a General English class.

4.5 *Do distinctions such as EST, EOP, EAP, etc., make any sense?* ELT as a whole is riddled with distinctions that appear to serve the needs of academic or bureaucratic analysis more than they honour the gestalt of the human learning experience, e.g. EFL, ESL, mother-tongue teaching, the 'four skills', and so on. Most of all, it is doubtful whether the learner sees any significance or (v) attaches any importance to such divisions. The concomitant notion that each of these 'so- (w) called' specialisms calls for widely differing approaches and resources is perhaps the most dangerous result of such labelling. Language teaching can perhaps be looked at more productively as a unity, of which an ESP-type curriculum is the desirable goal of all.

5. *Conclusion*

The problems which many teachers are currently experiencing in the ESP classroom derive directly, in our opinion, from the erroneous assumptions and practices we have noted. It is to be hoped that our own emphasis on the underlying competence required by the learner, the materials and methods we have devised to teach it, and our outline of possible alternatives will relieve many of these problems, and will make the teaching–learning process in ESP not only more effective, but more enjoyable, too.

Bibliography

Breen, M. and Candlin, C. (*forthcoming*), *The Communicative Curriculum in Language Teaching*, London, Longman.

Coulthard, M. (*1978*), *An Introduction to Discourse Analysis*, London, Longman.

Drobnic, K. (*1978*), 'Mistakes and Modification in Course Design: an EST Case History' in *English for Specific Purposes: Science and Technology*, Oregon State University.

Hutchinson, T. (*1978*), 'The Practical Demonstration' in *Practical Papers in English Language Education*, Vol. 1, No. 1, Institute for English Language Education, University of Lancaster.

Munby, J. (*1978*), *Communicative Syllabus Design*, London, Cambridge University Press.

Schegloff, E. (*1971*), 'Notes on a Conversation Practice: Formulating Place' in *Language and Social Context* (ed. Gigliolo), London, Penguin.

Widdowson, H. (ed.) (*1979*), 'Reading and Thinking in English', *Discovering Discourse*, London, Oxford University Press.

(t) As I have already said, Johns' and Dudley-Evans' view (a knowledge of the conceptual structure of the subject) may well offer a manageable intermediate position.

(u) The last few Episodes have in fact been making their own contributions to our appreciation of these 'deeper communicative processes'.

(v) Equally, it is doubtful if the learners really need to be exposed to such questions as whether they are taking an EOP or EAP course in the first place.

(w) The whole of 4.5 is contentious, and it may be significant that no reference is made to its arguments in the Applied Linguistics paper. Distinctions such as EOP and EAP have arisen out of experience of different ESP situations. The acronymic labels are merely indicative but useful nevertheless. In this context, Hutchinson and Waters offer the following condemnation: 'The concomitant notion that each of these "so-called" specialisms calls for widely differing approaches and resources is perhaps the most dangerous result of such labelling.' In my view this is plainly wrong. Worse, it does a grave injustice both to their own work and to that of those they have been criticizing. For me, Hutchinson and Waters have established in a totally professional way that *their* situation is indeed different to John Moore's in Colombia or Tim Johns' and Tony Dudley-Evans' in Birmingham and have brilliantly demonstrated that their EOP situation does indeed call for a widely differing approach and a rather different set of resources. What they have not demonstrated is that *their* 'ESP-type curriculum is a desirable goal for all'.

III

ACTIVITIES

(1) In section 2.2 we find the following:—

> Thirdly, technical English is only an adaptation of the existing resources of the English language. Many expressions with a technical sense, therefore, are easily understood and memorized by the native speaker because he is simply extending the use of a known concept, e.g. grip, saddle, plug, drag, drum, sleeve, head, chip, etc.

(a) What are the technical meanings of these eight words? (Use a dictionary if necessary.)

(b) Show how the technical meanings are related to their everyday meanings.

(c) What conclusions would you draw for 'teaching' such items to non-native speakers?

(2) Look again at the Pump Exercise, particularly at Step 4. What difference does it make if the report is prepared orally or in written form? If you think there will be or should be linguistic differences between the two forms, how will you cope with any problems that arise? Can you see ways of exploiting any such differences?

IV

EVALUATION

(1) What would the authors of this Episode say about the Exam Preparation work in *Episode Twelve?*

(2) How much say should the students have in the kind of ESP course they get?

(3) I have been arguing in my interpretation of this Episode that the degree of difference between an *underlying competence syllabus* and a *target performance syllabus* should be variable because it will depend on certain characteristics of the particular ESP situation. The degree of difference can be expressed in a diagram such as this:—

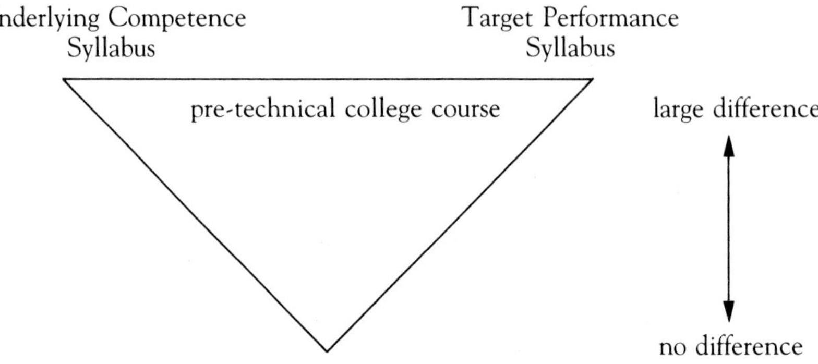

Where do you think the most appropriate syllabuses for the following should be placed on the diagram?

(a) the Algerians in commentary-note *(o)*;

(b) an English course for experienced airline cabin staff;

(c) an English course as part of basic training for airline cabin staff;

(d) a course for the architecture students described by Skeldon in Episode Ten;

(e) an overseas engineer wanting help with the delivery of a scientific paper in English;

(f) a course for radar technicians in Saudi Arabia;

(g) the students taking course 221 in Kuwait (Episode Eleven);

(h) Phillips' and Shettlesworth's students at Bletchingdon House (Episode Nine).

V

—RELATED READINGS—

The relevant readings have already been referred to in the body of this *Episode*. I repeat them here for convenience:—

T. Hutchinson (1978), 'The Practical Demonstration' in *Practical Papers in English Language Education*, Vol. 1, IELE, University of Lancaster.

T. Hutchinson, A. Waters and M. P. Breen (1979), 'An English Language Curriculum for Technical Students', *Practical Papers*, Vol. 2, IELE, University of Lancaster.

T. Hutchinson and A. Waters (1980), 'Communication in the technical classroom: you just shove this little chappie in here like that' in *ELT Documents Special – Projects in Materials Design*, The British Council.

T. Hutchinson and A. Waters (1981), 'Performance and Competence in English for Specific Purposes', *Applied Linguistics* II, 1.

For a more general discussion of some of the issues raised in and by 'ESP at the Crossroads' see:—

M. P. Breen and C. N. Candlin (1980), 'The Essentials of a Communicative Curriculum in Language Teaching', *Applied Linguistics* 1, 2.

EPISODE FIFTEEN 1981

Elaine Tarone, Sharon Dwyer, Susan Gillette and Vincent Icke, 'On the Use of the Passive in Two Astrophysics Journal Papers', *The ESP Journal* 1, 2, 1981.

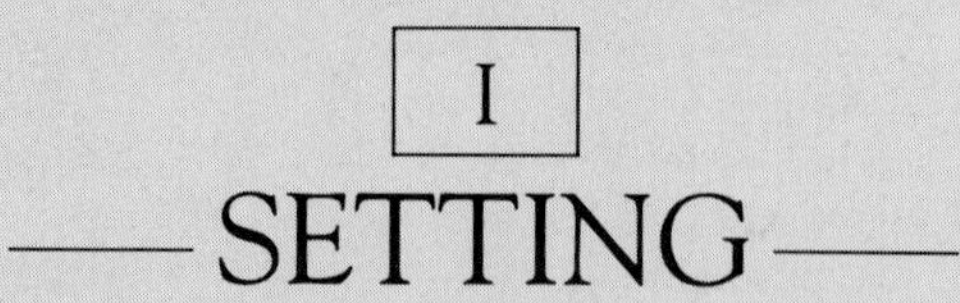

SETTING

The latter Episodes have been principally concerned with approaches to selecting materials for ESP classes and with the roles of those materials in the development of communicative and educational competence. These accounts have, I trust, given some idea of the change and controversy that surrounded ESP principle in the last years of the nineteen-seventies and first years of the eighties. In fact, controversy had arisen from the best of motives. The varied, imaginative and novel answers that we have seen proposed in Episodes Nine to Fourteen are all essentially answers to the same question: How best can the ESP practitioner serve his students? And putting the underlying motivation in this form points to at least one admirable characteristic of most ESP work in the period covered by this volume—its educational responsibility. I do not want, by claiming a tradition of educational responsibility for ESP, to imply in any way that ESP practitioners are 'superior' in this respect to their colleagues in other branches of the foreign-language teaching profession. If those of us in ESP have thought long and hard about how best to serve our students' interests, it is simply because circumstances have tended to make us do so. In circumstances of restricted educational opportunity we have been forced to search out ways of providing maximum educational value.

Those ways have all been responses to particular and often localized experiences, and perhaps we can now see that the recommendations made in previous Episodes have often been overgeneralized. Although the dust has not yet settled, I suspect that old educational truths are beginning to re-emerge. One such truth is that there is nothing so dangerous as a little educational success. A fair proportion of curriculum development work around the world in different subjects and at different educational levels has suffered from a line of reasoning which goes 'This worked in situation *x*, so let's hope it will work in situations *y* and *z*'. In fact, what worked in situation *x* does not often work in situation *y* or situation *z*. There are rarely global solutions to local problems.

As for ESP itself, we are beginning to see that the types of work illustrated in the last six Episodes have greatly extended our options rather than required us to choose between these options. Thus, there is a place for authentic materials but not often a permanent place. There are several different types of team-teaching or collaborative arrangement and which, if any, is to be preferred depends on local factors. Truly *preparatory* materials (as opposed to *rehearsals*) have a real role to play but only in certain educational contexts. And so on. However, there are two other dimensions of ESP classroom practice that have not been fully brought out in previous Episodes, and for that reason they ought to be mentioned here: the human and the social aspects. The 1978–82 period also saw the rise and fall of the approach to Needs Analysis most prominently represented by John Munby's *Communicative Syllabus Design*. In this approach all the preliminary work is devoted to specifying the particular communicative needs the learner will require if he or she is to perform in the particular target situation. Doubtless Munby's 'Communicative Needs Processor' was applied in ways he would not have approved of, but it did give rise to the view that ESP teaching should be completely instrumental; the learners were apprentices to their needs-driven syllabuses and were to be chained to their benches until they had acquired the necessary skills. Of course, many ESP teachers continued to recognize that their learners were human beings who had wishes and expectations as well as externally-defined needs, but the charge levelled against ESP in the immediate past that it was 'anti-humanistic' or even 'inhumane' had a certain force and has done something to isolate ESP from the rest of ELT (which in that very period was taking a greater interest in humanistic approaches). The second dimension is social and applies particularly to programmes for overseas students going to or already in English-speaking countries. The crude separation of 'social survival' elements (General English) and 'educational survival' elements (ESP/Study Skills) came to be seen as unhelpful and unworkable, and one reason for this was a growing realization that in many cases linguistic, educational and social difficulty were all inter-related. Indeed, it has been suggested that for some overseas students the greatest threat to their successfully completing their educational programmes is loneliness, rather than lack of language or appropriate study habits. This is because isolation from colleagues is not only unfortunate in itself, but also blocks linguistic and educational advance.

So far in this Setting I have concentrated on that aspect of ESP activity which puts a premium on educational response and responsibility, because this has been a major concern in the Episodes in the second half of this volume. Nevertheless, the other and older tradition of linguistic responsibility had been continuing, even if at times its importance and relevance seemed to have been put at risk by other matters. It therefore seems right to choose for the final Episode a paper that describes research into the characteristics of certain Scientific English texts rather than discusses the place and use of such texts in an ESP programme. With the choice of the paper by Tarone and her co-workers, connection can also be made with the opening Episode by Barber because the first and last Episodes in this volume are the only two (except perhaps for Lackstrom, Selinker and Trimble) that are essentially descriptive of the language of Science. Both papers aim to provide information that will be of use to teachers of EST, but both refrain from indicating how that information might be best used. The two papers also share a concern to be explicit about their research procedures and to be cautious about the wider applicability of their results. Yet there are enormous differences between Barber and Tarone *et al.* and these differences reflect both our increase in knowledge and our increase in ambition over the twenty years that separate them. I list some of the differences below:—

(1) Barber took three texts that 'straddled' disciplines and also covered two of the major text-types (textbooks and journal articles) in an attempt to say something about general scientific style. Tarone *et al.* are extremely restrictive; they have studied two papers from one Journal; moreover, the two papers deal with the same subject. Therefore, when Barber observes that his is 'only a small-scale study, confined to a limited body of material, and this must be borne in mind when the results are considered', this is all the more true of Tarone.

(2) Barber is concerned with the frequency of occurrence of a range of syntactic features (such as voice) and certain syntactic structures (such as types of subordinate clauses). Tarone *et al.* are only interested in *voice*, and even here with the choice of active and passive in certain contexts.

(3) Barber is content to offer statistical information. Tarone *et al.* are much more ambitious; they are concerned to find an explanation of the use of the passive as opposed to *we* plus an active verb. They also make use of statistical data but in this case to provide *evidence* for their findings and to ensure that the reader has sufficient facts to challenge the conclusions if he or she should so wish.

(4) For Barber a text is a text; in other words, he makes no attempt to correlate findings with different sections of texts. For Tarone the organizational and discoursal structure of her material is crucial.

(5) Barber worked on his own; for Tarone a key aspect of the research design is to involve a specialist from the content field—in her case an astrophysicist acted as 'specialist informant'.

(6) Barber is descriptive whereas Tarone *et al.* are experimental; they develop a set of hypotheses and test them out against their data.

(7) Barber's work implies no challenge to the adequacy of traditional grammatical explanations such as 'the passive is used when the agent is unimportant'. Tarone *et al.*, on the basis of their data, offer such a challenge by purporting to show that in their contexts explanations may lie in rhetorical function and rhetorical structure, rather than in single-sentence semantics.

Episode Fifteen is a direct descendant of Episode Six. It reflects the strong American tradition of rhetorical research and its senior author, Elaine Tarone, has become an increasingly influential member of the now-scattered 'North-Western' US School of ESP. Indeed, one can even detect some stylistic similarity between the two papers, especially in the way they make claims about originality and discuss findings. *On the Use of the Passive in Two Astrophysics Journal Papers* is not an easy paper because it does not set itself an easy task. It raises questions of the true nature of explanation of linguistic phenomena—not from the standpoint of the nature of deep linguistic structure, but from the position of the writer of a journal article and the implications he or she should be aware of when making choices in the process of writing that article. In so doing it raises a number of other issues that need to be discussed; one is the matter of the most useful type of categorization of 'Scientific English' as a whole; another is whether linguists concerned with syntax are providing the kinds of explanation that the consumers (the ESP practitioners) need; and a third is whether certain contexts preferentially require their own explanations of the use of English or whether a unitary explanation is adequate. In all these matters, Tarone *et al.* offer us responsible statements about a minute fragment of the enormous volume of scientific writing. As the ESP practitioner must select from that volume and is often placed in the position of having to make observations and offer advice, this final Episode is also only a beginning. Just as I have been stressing the need for a cautious and situationally-moderated acceptance of the ideas of Phillips and Shettlesworth or Johns and Dudley-Evans or Hutchinson and Waters, so the same need for caution applies to the pedagogical use of Tarone *et al.* In all cases, and in both traditions, the work is full of interest, but it also usually requires some form of verification.

The final Episode is also something of a small celebration in that it signals the appearance of *The ESP Journal*, the first (and so far, the only) professionally produced and distributed journal in the field.

II

TEXT AND COMMENTARY

On the Use of the Passive in Two Astrophysics Journal Papers*

by Elaine Tarone, Sharon Dwyer, Susan Gillette *and* Vincent Icke
University of Minnesota

While extensive use of the passive is shown by frequency counts of verb tense and aspect which are performed on corpora combining texts from a variety of scientific and technical fields, significantly different results may be obtained when one compares the frequency of the passive and active voices within a single scientific or technical field. In this paper we examine the frequency of the active and passive verb forms in two astrophysics journal articles, finding that *we* plus an active verb occurs at least as frequently as the passive in both articles. On the basis of consultation with an informant in astrophysics, we propose four rhetorical functions of the passive as opposed to *we* plus an active verb: (1) *we* indicates the author's unique procedural choice, while the passive indicates an established or standard procedure; (2) *we* is used to describe the author's own work and the passive to describe the work of others, unless that work is not mentioned in contrast to the author's, in which case the active is used; (3) the passive is used to describe the author's proposed studies; and (4) the use of the active or the passive is determined by focus due to the length of an element or the need for emphasis.

Introduction

It has long been accepted that one of the most salient grammatical features of the register of English for Science and Technology (EST), as compared to registers of 'general English', is its relatively frequent use of the passive form of the verb. Frequency counts of verb tense and aspect performed on corpora of data which combine texts from a variety of scientific and technical fields do seem to show that, overall, the passive voice is used extensively in EST (cf. Cooray 1965, Duskova and Urbanova 1967, Fernalld 1977, George 1963, and Swales 1976). For example, Robinett (1980) performed such an analysis on a combination of texts from scientific, as opposed to *belles lettres* fields, and found that when all verb phrases containing *be* in each group of fields were analysed, 46% of those occurring in scientific texts were passive constructions, while only 29% of those in the *belles lettres* corpus were passive. The only study of which we are aware which examines the frequency of usage of the passive voice within one particular field is Wingard's (1981) study of verb forms and functions in six medical texts;
(a) interestingly, Wingard finds that verbs in the active voice outnumber verbs in the passive.

We are unaware of any other studies which (a) examine the frequency of usage of passive
(b) voice within a single field, and within a single genre within that field (e.g. textbooks, journal papers, etc.); or which (b) perform a rhetorical analysis to determine the systematic functions of passive voice, as opposed to active, within the text as a whole. Lackstrom, Selinker and

* Paper presented at the 1981 TESOL Convention, Detroit. We are grateful for substantive comments on the content of this paper to Kathryn Hanges, Tom Huckin, Eric Nelson, our anonymous reviewer, and many others.

Trimble (1970) and Widdowson (1981) have argued for such an analysis in terms of rhetorical function.

(c) In this study we examine the occurrence of passive and active verb forms in journal papers in one field, astrophysics, in order to determine whether writers in this field do prefer the passive over the active, and we investigate in depth the rhetorical functions of these forms.

Procedure

An initial survey of journal papers in astrophysics suggested to us that the passive verb form was not used to such a great extent as we might have expected. For example, we found the following abstract of this type of journal paper:

> (1) We *study* further the flow of accreting material into black holes from Keplerian disks surrounding them. Solving the system of radial structure equations in Schwarzschild geometry for the case where the kinematic viscosity v = constant, we *discover* a boundary layer at the disk's inner edge, where the flow *becomes* non-Keplerian. We also *show* that, despite the operation of viscous stresses across this inner edge and the presence of the boundary layer there, very little extra energy or angular momentum is *radiated* or *transported* outward from inside that radius—a result many *have* often *assumed* but no one *has* carefully *demonstrated.* These results *constitute* a solution to the problem of adequately describing the flow across the inner edge and properly setting the boundary conditions there and at the event horizon. (Stoeger 1980: 216, italics ours)

The use of active verb forms here, particularly the first person plural verb form, seemed quite
(d) unusual in light of the usual assumption that the passive voice predominates in scientific and technical English.[1]

We therefore undertook to examine in more detail the frequency of occurrence of the active and passive forms of the verb in two journal papers in the field of astrophysics, and to investigate in particular the rhetorical function of the passive in these texts. The two papers chosen for our investigation were both published in *The Astrophysical Journal*, and focus on research into the nature of black hole accretion disks:

[1] *The Manual of Style for the Astrophysical Journal* (University of Chicago Press, 1971) makes no recommendations at all regarding the use of the active and passive voice. Rather, authors are asked to 'at least attempt to conform to the elementary rules of grammar, syntax and punctuation'. Authors are warned to beware of only three common types of error: unattached participles, subject and complement of different numbers, and 'a sequence of nouns piled one on top of the other in Germanic tradition'. Aside from this, it is simply suggested that authors examine current issues of the *Journal* to familiarize themselves with the conventions.

(a) Five of Wingard's six texts were medical journal papers. It is indeed true that in these texts active verbs outnumber passive verbs but the preponderance of the active is less marked than in the two journals analysed in this Episode. The overall percentage of passives would seem to be in the 35–40% range. If existential uses of BE are excluded (see Episode One note *(k)*) then the frequency of actives and passives is broadly similar.

(b) It is worth noting the use of 'genre' here. There is a growing contemporary interest in 'audience analysis' and how this can be related to the achievement of communicative purpose. As a result, understanding the intended relationship between writer and reader has so increased in importance that conflating findings from, say, textbooks and journal articles (as we have seen in Barber and Huddlestone) is no longer a generally acceptable procedure. Work in 'genre-analysis' is taken up again in the Prospect.

(c) We can see that Tarone *et al.* have two aims and one is to check out the facts about the use of active and passive, and here I think we have to say that two short articles are an inadequate sample. The other aim is to 'investigate in depth the rhetorical functions of the forms', and this is the aspect of the article that justifies its inclusion in this volume.

(d) The footnote to the style-manual is another instance of a current concern to discover and evaluate the opinions of professionals involved in the *genre.* Until recently, it was generally argued that the only admissible data were the texts themselves; today at least some researchers are interested in discovering what the users of certain communicative conventions believe to be the rationale for those conventions.

Alan P. Lightman. Time-dependent accretion disks around compact objects. I. Theory and equations. *The Astrophysical Journal* 194: 419–427 (December 1, 1974).
William R. Stoeger, S. J. Boundary-layer behavior of the flow at the inner edge of black hole accretion disks. *The Astrophysical Journal* 235: 216–223 (January 1, 1980).

In our count and analysis, we counted finite verb phrases. We did not include bare *-en* participles such as 'the figures *given*'. (See Swales (1981) for an excellent discussion of bare *-en* participles.) Neither did we count verbs in footnotes or captions to charts. We did not count
(e) the symbol = as a verb, though at times it seemed to function as a verb, as in 'namely that po = po(r)'. We counted as passive all verbs which appeared in the subject + *be* + verb + *-en* form, regardless of whether they were true passive or stative (see Lackstrom, Selinker and Trimble 1970 for a discussion of passive and stative in EST). We decided to disregard the difference between passive and stative in our count because there were some cases in which it was difficult to clearly distinguish passive and stative based solely on context. We determined the number of active and passive verb forms used in these papers, section by section, and in the
(f) papers as a whole. We formulated hypotheses as to the apparent rhetorical function of choices between active verbs and passive verbs. One of us (V.I.) provided the astronomical interpretation of the text, and outlined the overall rhetorical structure of these papers.[2]

Results

A. Frequency of Active and Passive Verb Forms

(g) We were particularly interested in those uses of the active form of the verb which represented a clear decision to use either first person plural active *we* or the passive in referring to one's own research, as, in the Stoeger paper:

(2a) Previously (Stoeger, 1976b) we *pointed out* that the usual way of placing boundary conditions at r_{ms} was inadequate and misleading. (p. 216)

where the passive was clearly possible, as in our own paraphrase of (2a):

(2b) Previously (Stoeger, 1976b) it *was pointed out* that . . . (our paraphrase)

So, in addition to counting all active verb forms, we counted a sub-category of these: first person plural active verb forms. Then, because we were interested in examining those cases

---

[2] See Selinker (1979) on the importance in EST research of working with subject-area specialists as well as with linguists. We cannot stress enough the importance of Icke's contribution to our analysis. His knowledge of the subject matter was absolutely essential to our analysis of the rhetorical structure of these papers. Icke, while not a native speaker of English, has native speaker fluency and no perceptible accent. Further, he acts as a reviewer of papers in astrophysics for professional journals, and has very strong intuitions regarding the rhetorical and grammatical structure typically used in good writing in this field. Finally, we should point out that he checked and verified his interpretation of these two papers with several members of the Department of Astronomy at the University of Minnesota.

(e) See Peter Roe (Episode One, 'Related Readings') for an interesting analysis of equations and formulae embedded in technical texts.

(f) As note *(d)* above and Footnote 2 suggest, the contributions of specialist informants have proved valuable. There remain a number of unanswered—and perhaps unanswerable—questions, however. Is a specialist informant necessary? Or can a wider coverage of data compensate? Who *is* the real specialist informant? In this case, is it Icke? Or is it Stoeger and Lightman for their respective papers? In fact, there is some very recent work which has used the original author as specialist informant, but as we know from literary criticism, there may be problems attached to taking the author's own views at face value.

(g) There exists a large but rarely illuminating literature on the reasons for the use of the passive both in studies of General and Scientific English and in both scholarly and pedagogical grammars. The decision by Tarone and her co-workers to concentrate their attention on contexts in which a *real* choice of voice has been made will lead to very interesting results, and is probably the key research design feature of their paper.

where a clear decision had been made to use active or passive verb forms, we counted again, this time omitting the existential verbs *to be*, *to have*, *to exist*, *to become* and *to get* (when used in the sense of *become*), none of which has a passive form. The results of our frequency count of the active and passive verbs used in these papers appear in Table 1. (A breakdown of the frequency of usage of active and passive in each section of the papers appears in Appendices A and B).

TABLE 1

Overall Frequency of Active and Passive Verbs[a] in the Stoeger and Lightman Papers

	Stoeger		Lightman	
Total Number of Verbs[b]	244		370	
Active Verbs	217	(88.5%)	301	(81.4%)
Active *we* Verbs	58	(23%)	40	(10.8%)
Passive Verbs	27	(11.5%)	69	(18.6%)
Total Verbs, Existentials Omitted[c]	137		248	
Active Verbs	110	(80%)	179	(72.2%)
Active *we* Verbs	52	(37%)	40	(16.1%)
Passive Verbs	27	(20%)	69	(27.8%)

[a] There was only one *we* passive in our entire corpus (including both papers: 'We are faced . . .' (Stoeger p. 218). There were no occurrences of the verb *to be* in the first person plural *we* form.

[b] The percentages here are determined by dividing the total number of verbs into the total number of active verbs, active *we* verbs (subset of the former), and passive verbs. Existential verbs are included in the corpus here.

[c] Here the percentages are determined by dividing the total number of verbs excluding the existential verbs *to be*, *to have*, *to exist*, *to become*, and *to get* (in the sense of *become*) into the total number of active verbs (excluding existentials), and so on. We felt it was important to look at the percentages in this way as well, in order to eliminate any possible bias in the data which might make it seem that the active was used more frequently than the passive when in fact it wasn't. While the difference between active and passive usage
(h) is somewhat reduced when we look only at nonexistential verbs, we can still see a clear preference for the active over the passive.

In both papers, active verb forms greatly outnumber passive verb forms, regardless of whether existential verbs are counted. If we look only at the incidence of active *we* verb forms as opposed to passive, we find that Stoeger uses about twice as many first person plural active *we* forms as passive; in the Lightman paper there are more passives than active *we* forms.[3]

We feel we can say that, while there does seem to be some individual variation in the frequency of active *we* verb forms and passive verb forms, the overall tendency for both writers is to prefer the active to the passive. Icke maintains that, while he feels that the Lightman paper is better written than the Stoeger paper, he does not feel that either author is unusual in his use of the active verb form as compared with others in the field of astrophysics. Thus, if
(i) these two papers are representative of the writing style in this field, it would seem that in professional journal papers in the field of astrophysics, the passive verb form occurs much less frequently than the active, and that the first person plural *we* verb form occurs just about as often as the passive.

[3] It is interesting to note here that, while Lightman used fewer *we* subjects than Stoeger did, Lightman also used the impersonal subject *one* (as in, 'One may think of the system . . .') 12 times. Stoeger, on the other hand, never used *one* as the subject. Lightman's combined tokens of *we* and *one* as subjects amount to 52, or 21% of the subjects of his nonexistential verb phrases.

(h) But we need to remember that on the available evidence, this preference is less clear in other data.
(i) Further research may well show that this is a rather big 'if'.

B. Rhetorical Function of the Passive and Active Verb Forms

What is the rhetorical function of the active and passive verb forms in these two professional journal papers? When do the authors prefer the active over the passive? We outline below four generalizations which we claim account for the use of active and passive verb forms in these papers. The first three generalizations are, we believe, specific to writing in this genre, i.e., journal papers in astrophysics. It may be that future research will show these three
(j) generalizations to be true for related fields, such as physics or chemistry, in the same genre. To our knowledge, this is the first time these generalizations have been made and documented in the literature. The fourth generalization is commonly accepted for 'general English' usage of the passive and active voices.

It should be pointed out that the first three generalizations may be taken as having both a strong and a weak interpretation. The weak interpretation is that the generalizations will apply only when a verb which can be passivized is used. That is, the selection of verb is made first, and then, if that verb can be passivized, the generalizations apply. The strong interpretation is that the author will use vocabulary and locutionary devices to ensure that if the generalization calls for a passive, the passive will be used. So, if the generalization calls for a passive, the author will use the verb which can be passivized over the verb which cannot. That is, rhetorical
(k) and syntactic choices are made first, and then the lexical verb is used which fits into that structure.[4] It is possible to conceive of either interpretation of the following generalizations, and the data may enable us to select one or the other. However, it may also be that neither interpretation is completely correct. The writer may at times be influenced in use of voice by the nature of the verb previously selected, or s/he may at other times reject one verb and use another in order to use the desired voice.

Generalization I: Writers of astrophysics journal papers tend to use the first person plural
(l) active WE form to indicate points in the logical development of the argument where they have made a unique procedural choice; the passive seems to be used when the authors are simply following established or standard procedure, as in using accepted equations or describing what logically follows from their earlier procedural choice.

---

[4] We thank *The ESP Journal's* reviewer for these observations regarding the strong and weak interpretations of our generalizations.

(j) In contrast to the previous commentary note, at this point Tarone *et al.* seem unnecessarily restrictive when they state that 'the first three generalizations are, we believe, specific to writing in this genre, i.e. journal papers in astrophysics'. As we shall see, the generalizations do not seem to relate to specific conceptual structures of Astrophysics, but rather to decisions whether 'to use either first person plural active *we* or the passive in referring on one's own research'. Thus, there must be some expectation that in the *genre* of journal articles and in the *context* of the decision just referred to the three generalizations would at least be relevant to our understanding of the rhetorical function of voice-alternation in *other* fields. It is not that Tarone's highly intriguing generalizations are 'specific' to Astrophysics, but that so far they have only been *attested* in that subject area.

(k) An interesting discussion, but one slightly distanced from most people's introspection into their composing process. In fact, it would seem that if there is an early and preliminary *rhetorical choice* it is that of *subject* rather than of the lexical or syntactic shape of the main verb-predicate.

(l) Generalization I opens up all sorts of possibilities. For one thing, it questions much of the received wisdom about adopting a consistent 'narrative style', i.e. either use *we* or the passive. For another, it can be related to thematic subject—in the sense that *we* as subject indicates that *we* have done something noteworthy. But most interesting of all is whether the choice of *we* or passive has predictive value for the regular reader of the genre. Modern discourse analysts, especially those working with Professor John Sinclair at the University of Birmingham, have considerable interest in predictive structures and predictive signals in texts. It would indeed be interesting to see whether (in this case) astrophysicists encountering a sentence beginning with *we* plus active verb have immediate expectations of a 'unique procedural choice' about to be made.

The overall rhetorical structure of a professional journal paper in astrophysics takes the shape of a logical argument in which the author attempts to solve a problem by choosing from among various accepted procedures and equations that combination which will best solve the problem. The use of the active and passive forms of the verb in such a way as to mark those points at which the authors are making such choices is very common. Since the entire structure of these papers is made up of such a logical argument, there are a great many cases where choices are being made, or accepted procedure implemented (equations 'plugged in' at the appropriate time, and so on). Usually, the typical structure of theoretical papers such as those analysed here shows a marked 'inverted pyramid' design, as illustrated in Table 2. Thus, there is a gradual narrowing down of the scope of the paper, as the writer makes a series of choices; these choices are guided by a mixture of intuition, common-sense, technical ability, experience, luck, and so on. It is at these choice points that the writer will tend to use the first person plural active *we*. Where established or standard procedure follows from these choices, the passive is used. Table 2 makes clear the way in which both the Stoeger and Lightman papers follow this logical structure. In the Stoeger paper, for instance, Section I corresponds to 'general physics and all observations', Section II to 'general physics and special observations', and so on.

TABLE 2

Logical Structure of a Theoretical Paper in Astrophysics with Glosses[a] for Stoeger and Lightman Papers

Content	Choice Made by Writer	Stoeger section	Lightman section
general physics and all observations		I	I
	choice as to what phenomena to explain		
general physics and special observations		II	II
	choice what physics are likely to be relevant		
specific physics and observations		III	III, VI, IX
	choice what specializations and approximations to make to simplify the equations		
specific equations		IV, V	IV
	choice of boundary conditions, picking out a few solutions among many		
specific solution		VI, VII, VIII	V, VII, VIII

[a] Glosses provided by Icke.

Below we provide several passages from the two papers, together with glosses[5] in the margins to indicate where the author has made a unique procedural choice or followed established procedure.

[5] Glosses provided by Icke.

choice choice	(3)	In this paper we *develop* the theory of time-dependent disks. The underlying physics is essentially the same as that of the stationary models above, except that we *allow* variables to evolve in time on the 'drift' (radial flow) time scale . . . (Lightman p. 419)
choice estab.	(4)	The fundamental variables we *will use* are: . . . The laws governing these variables *are delineated* below: . . . (Lightman p. 420)
choice estab.	(5)	At this point we do not *need* any details of the shear stress . . . The fluid shear *is* simply *derived* from the assumed Kepler (orbital) velocity of the gas . . . (Lightman p. 420)
  estab.	(6)	From our assumption of radiative transport (assumption x of II) as the energy transport mechanism and assumptions vi and vii, the radiative transport *is described* by the radiative diffusion equation . . . (Lightman p. 421)
choice	(7)	For $r > r_{ms}$, there is a definite sense in which we *can neglect* viscosity—in that the flow follows, to good approximation, the circular geodesics. (Stoeger p. 218)
choice choice	(8)	Because we *want* to focus our attention on the flow across r_{ms}, a problem of radial structure, we *assume* for our purposes that $h \simeq$ constant . . . (Stoeger p. 217)
estab., ch. choice	(9)	Iteration *can be continued.* It *turns out*, however, that the first two iterations *give* satisfactory results . . . (Stoeger p. 219)
estab.	(10)	Energy *is generated* locally by viscous heating through action of the shear stress $t \phi r$. (Lightman p. 422)
choice	(11)	But they do not readily *lend* themselves to detailed modelling . . . (Stoeger p. 216)

There are a great many more examples of this sort—more than we can include in a paper of this length.

There are also a few exceptions to Generalization I in the Stoeger paper, though not in the Lightman paper. These possible exceptions appear below, together with some discussion.

(12) The important relationship for determining k is equation 16 which *was obtained* by inserting the expression 13 . . . (Stoeger p. 220)

Here, the insertion of expression 13 to obtain equation 16 was not standard procedure, but an earlier procedural choice of the writer. As a procedural choice, Generalization I suggests use of the active voice here.[m] However, the writer may be using both the past tense and the passive voice here in order to highlight the fact that this was an earlier procedural choice; Generalization I does call for use of the passive in describing what follows from an earlier procedural choice. (It is interesting to note that all our earlier examples of established procedure showed the passive being used in the present tense.)

(13) Then, if x *is taken* to be of order unity within the layer in the region $r > r_{ms}$ . . . (Stoeger p. 219)

Here again, making $x = 1$ is not standard procedure, but a choice of the writer. It is less easy to see here why the passive is used. It is worth noting with regard to both these exceptions that, as we have pointed out above, Icke is rather critical of Stoeger's writing style in general. He is particularly critical of (13) above, feeling that such examples do not provide 'clear signals' to the reader of the writer's line of argumentation.

In that only two exceptions were found in these two papers, and that a great many examples were found in support of Generalization I, we believe that there is ample evidence to conclude that this first generalization is indeed characteristic of writers of astrophysics journal papers.

(m) By this time the reader may well have become convinced that Tarone *et al.* are on to something, and that the exceptions are both marginal and to be expected.

Generalization IIA: When these authors contrast their own research with other contemporary research they use the first person plural active for their own work, and the passive for the work being contrasted.

Generalization IIB: When these authors cite other contemporary work which is not in contrast to their own, they generally use the active form of the verb.

(n) This second generalization holds for those portions of the astrophysics paper which deal with the review of the relevant literature. At first glance, it would seem that Generalization I, and IIA and B, are too similar to be included as separate generalizations. There are, however, two differences between I and II. First, contemporary literature on a given physical phenomenon and established procedure in the field of physics are not the same. In this case established procedure refers to systems of physics such as Keplerian physics or Schwarzschildian geometry, composed of long accepted paradigms. Contemporary works, however, usually attempt to describe specific physical phenomena in terms of the established systems, just as the two authors we have chosen to study have done, these interpretations may be subject to discussion by other physicists.

Secondly, Generalizations I and II apply at different levels of generality. Generalization II operates at a lower level of generality, stating that within this section of the paper, the writer highlights the contrast between his/her own work and other contemporary work in contrast by the use of voice. Generalization IIA may at first seem similar to Generalization I, in that the active is used for one's own unique contribution to the field (IIA) as well as for unique procedural choices (I). However, Generalization IIB also calls for the use of the active for other work not in contrast to one's own; it seems to us that such 'other work' may or may not be viewed as unique contributions to the field. It seems to us to be an entirely different criterion used here in Generalization II—a criterion operating at a lower level of generality, and one which focuses on whether other work is in contrast to one's own work or not, rather than on the issue of 'choice vs. established procedure'.

We will provide several examples which seem to support Generalization IIA, together with seeming exceptions to IIA, and then we will provide the examples supporting Generalization IIB (to which there are no exceptions in these papers).

(14) In this paper we *discuss* an aspect of accretion disk structure which *has* never *been* adequately *dealt with* . . . (Stoeger p. 216)

(15) All of the accretion disk models of the above authors are time-independent. A constant mass flux for the normal star into the disk *is assumed.* In this paper we *develop* the theory of time-dependent disks. (Lightman p. 419)

(16) In the actual literature on stationary disks, the function H(T) and consequently the multiple- and no-root phenomena *are* not *encountered* because the equations *are solved* under the imposed restriction of equation (34) and *done* so not exactly, but only approximately . . . (Lightman p. 427)

(17) In all previous calculations involving stationary disks (e.g. SS & NT) the dimensionless viscosity parameter *has been assumed* to be constant. The assumption probably becomes increasingly tenuous as an increasing degree of time dependence *is* allowed in the problem and as one *looks* at shorter and shorter time scales. We *shall make* the assumption that α is constant in radius and time on the drift time scale . . . (Lightman p. 433)

Clearly, in examples (14)–(16), it is the first person plural active form of the verb which is used to refer to one's own work in contrast to the work of others, which is described in the

(n) Note that the authors of this Episode are perfectly willing to accept that some observations are confined to sections of texts rather than texts as a whole; in this instance they are suggesting precisely how Stoeger and Lightman deal with the relevant literature.

(o) passive. In (17) also there seems to us to be a definite contrast between the first two, and the last, verb phrases in the passage: *has been assumed* and *is allowed* versus *shall make.*

The verb phrase *looks* seems to be less clear; this may be an exception to the strong version of IIA. The weak version of this generalization stands here, however, as *look* cannot be passivized. If we wish to argue for the strong version of Generalization IIA, we can point out that the subject of the verb is the abstract and impersonal *one*, and thus can perhaps be viewed as equivalent to the passive in some way. This is a weak argument however. A stronger argument is that Lightman is not just referring to other work here; he is criticizing it and building the case for his own choice of assumptions. As he moves from assumptions of others (passive voice) to a criticism of the limitations of these assumptions (passive and active) to his own work (active), voice shifts accordingly.

Another possible exception to IIA follows:

(18) Though our discussion *is confined* to geometrically thin, Keplerian accretion disks, the
(p) results are pertinent . . . Our discussion *is* also *specialized* to Schwarzschild geometry—but generalization to Kerr is straightforward. (Stoeger p. 216)

Here, it could be argued that in (18) Stoeger is not really contrasting his own work to that of others. Rather, the use of passive may follow from Generalization I, as Stoeger is describing the limits placed on his discussion by established procedure following from earlier choices.

Evidence for Generalization IIB (that the active form of the verb is used when other work is
(q) not being contrasted with one's own) is cited below:

(19) This will be true near r_{ms}. And it *generalizes* Lynden-Bell's (1976) results obtained from the Newtonian equation to the general relativistic case. (Stoeger p. 219)

(20) In fact, Pringle (1974) and Cunningham (1973) *have developed* models of vertical structure which *suggest* that the inner region of the disk is convectively unstable . . . (Lightman p. 426)

(21) Rees *has pointed out* (see Pringle *et al.* 1973) that failure of the above requirement *leads* to a thermal instability . . . (Lightman p. 420)

(22) In these models the elements of the accreting fluid *follow* circular geodesics to very good approximation . . . (Stoeger p. 216)

No exceptions to Generalization IIB were found.

Generalization III: When these authors refer to their own proposed future work, they use the passive.

(o) I believe it could be argued that (17) is more easily characterized as an instance of Generalization 1.

(p) However, we can note that a first person pronoun is still used though in the possessive; at the end of the day there seems little *rhetorical* difference between:

(18) Our discussion is confined to . . .
(18c) We confine/restrict the discussion to . . .

And we can also notice that the second verb (is *specialized*) does not allow a straightforward [*we* plus active verb] formulation. I think it is possible, therefore, that further work would show that [*our* +NP] might well need to be incorporated within a more complex analysis—an analysis that would include nominalized variants of 'reporting' verbs.

(q) Although Generalization IIB may work for these two texts, there is no doubt that it is the one most likely to fall down when applied to literature review sections in other papers. A number of other structures are well attested. Consider these alternatives to (20):

(20a) Models of vertical structure have been developed by Pringle (1974) and Cunningham (1973) which suggest . . .
(20b) Models of vertical structure have been developed which suggest . . . (Pringle 1974; Cunningham 1973).
(20c) In some models of vertical structure the inner region of the disk is convectively unstable (Pringle 1974).

This is not the place to discuss possible factors affecting a choice from (20) to (20c) (but see below, under 'Related Readings'). However, we can note that Tarone's two journal-authors appear to adopt a consistent *previous-researcher-as-subject* orientation. Such an orientation may be personal or preferred by the journal. Other orientations are widely used.

(T) There seems to be ample evidence that the authors tend to use the passive when referring to their own proposed future work. The main exceptions are Lightman's references to Paper II, which actually is not 'future work', but rather a paper written simultaneously with this paper, Paper I. (The submission dates of both papers are the same, and they appear contiguously in volume 194 of *The Astrophysical Journal.*) Several examples of the use of the passive to refer to future work are:

(23) This *will be dealt with* in a succeeding paper. (Stoeger p. 222)
(24) Whether such a situation is stable under perturbations *will be investigated* in Paper II. (Lightman p. 427)
(25) In this section we give exact, although implicit, solutions for those variables in terms of Σ, which are valid in all regions and which *will be used* in future numerical work (see Paper II). (Lightman p. 424)

A possible exception to Generalization III appears in example (26), where Stoeger uses one active and one passive verb form to refer to future work.

(26) It will be interesting to see what *happens* when these considerations *are extended* to Rosen's bimetric theory of gravity. (Stoeger p. 223)

The weak version of III is preserved here, as *happen* cannot be passivized. However, the verb *is obtained* could have been substituted for *happens* here, so this must be considered an exception to the strong version of Generalization III.

Another possible exception is:

(27) Hopefully further observationally oriented theoretical work along these lines *will yield* results . . . (Stoeger p. 223)

Again, the weak version of III is preserved here, as *yield* does not seem to have a workable passive in this context. We also are uncertain whether Stoeger is referring to his own future work here, or that of others; if he is referring to the work of others, the strong version of III is not violated here.

The only other exceptions to III are from Lightman's references to companion Paper II:

(28) In a companion paper (Lightman 1974, hereafter referred to as Paper II) we *solve* our evolution equation and auxiliary equations numerically . . . (Lightman p. 419)
(29) In our explicit models (see Paper II) equations (18), (19) & (20) *will turn out to be satisfied* . . . (Lightman p. 423)

Example (28) is clearly an active voice. Example (29) may be considered a passive, if the aspectual verb is not considered. If the aspectual verb is considered, it can be pointed out that *turn out* doesn't have a passive form, and thus is no problem for the weak form of Generalization III.

However, even if we want to argue for the strong interpretation of Generalization III, we believe that these two examples are not really problematic. This is because of the ambiguous nature of Paper II, mentioned earlier. Paper II has actually been written simultaneously with the present paper and is not 'future work' in one sense. The fact that the writer wavers between active and passive voice in referring to Paper II (see examples (24), (25), (28), (29)) probably reflects the fact that the paper itself can be viewed as either future work (not yet published) or as current other work (submitted simultaneously with Paper I). If Paper II is viewed as the latter, then Examples (28) and (29) are simply illustrative of Generalization IIB: they are examples of Paper II viewed as other work not in contrast to Paper I.

(T) A remarkable finding, and one which should be worth further investigation. Indeed the whole discussion of Generalization III is a model of careful and explicit linguistic and rhetorical analysis.

Generalizations I, II and III seem to us to be specific to the sort of English used in writing professional journal papers in astrophysics; at least, we are not aware that such generalizations have been made about other genres of English writing. Further investigation is needed to determine whether professional journal papers in other theoretical fields (such as other areas of physics, for example, where similar sorts of logical argumentation guide the development of the paper) use active and passive verbs in similar ways.

Generalization IV seems to be descriptive of general English patterns as well as patterns found in these papers. This generalization has been discussed in grammar books such as Quirk *et al. A Grammar of Contemporary English* (1972).

Generalization IV: The use of active as opposed to passive forms of the verb seems to be conditioned by discoursal functions of focus—as when the author chooses to postpose or to front certain sentence elements for emphasis—or by the excessive length of those elements.

(s) One of the most striking characteristics of the sentences used in these papers is the fact that lengthy equations are embedded within them, and must be arranged in such a way as not to interfere with the reader's processing of the basic grammar of the sentence. Because of end-weight such equations are often placed at the ends of clauses, and the use of active or passive verb forms is often conditioned by this requirement. We did not notice any overall influence towards either active or passive voice here.

(30) The radiative transport *is described* by the radiative diffusion equation ... (Lightman p. 421)

$$q = -\frac{1}{\kappa\rho}\frac{\partial}{\partial z}\left(\tfrac{1}{3}\, cb\, T^4\right)$$

(31) Equating the two temperatures, for example, yields: ... (Lightman p. 426)

$$\Sigma_{\text{crit}}\,(r) \approx 0.15\left(\frac{r^3}{M}\right)^{1/16}\alpha - 7/8$$

Conclusion

To summarize, then, we have found that a count of active and passive verb forms in two professional journal papers in astrophysics shows that the active voice is used much more frequently than the passive, and, more importantly, that the active first person plural *we* verb form seems to be regularly used at strategic points in these papers. An investigation into the functions performed by the active and the passive verbs in these two papers has allowed us to make the following generalizations:

Generalization I: Writers of astrophysics journal papers tend to use the first person plural active *we* form to indicate points in the logical development of the argument where they have made a unique procedural choice; the passive seems to be used when the authors are simply following established or standard procedure, as in using accepted equations or describing what logically follows from their earlier procedural choice.

Generalization IIA: When these authors contrast their own research with other contemporary research they use the first person plural active for their own work, and the passive for the work being contrasted.

Generalization IIB: When these authors cite other contemporary work which is not in contrast to their own, they generally use the active form of the verb.

Generalization III: When these authors refer to their own proposed future work, they use the passive.

Generalization IV: The use of active as opposed to passive forms of the verb seems to be conditioned by discoursal functions of focus or by the excessive length of certain sentence elements.

(s) A short but lucid discussion of a very complex topic.

We have pointed out that the first three generalizations seem so far to be specific to these papers, or perhaps (though future research will have to verify this) to other papers in professional astrophysics journals or in professional journals in physics or chemistry. The fourth generalization has been established for general English, and is merely noticeable here because of the need for the embedding of lengthy equations.

Huckin (personal communication) has asked whether our four generalizations ever conflict with one another, and if so, which one wins out. At this point, we do not know. However, we suspect that some of the apparent exceptions to our generalizations (notably [18] but also perhaps [28] and [29]) may be due to such a conflict. More research is needed to investigate this problem.

It should be noted that we only claim these generalizations to hold for professional journals. We would expect that the predominance of the active verb form relative to the passive would not be found in popular journal papers on astrophysics, as for example, survey papers in the *Scientific American.*[6] Such papers tend to be summaries of research in the field, with minimal reference to the authors' own work, whereas the major thrust in the professional journal papers we have just described is the reporting of one's own work within a fairly set logical framework, and the contrasting of that work to the work of others. Our first three generalizations would
(t) thus not seem to be applicable to the *Scientific American* papers, since different rhetorical functions are required in the two types of papers.

We believe that more research of this type is needed into the use of the active and passive forms of the verb. It should not simply be assumed that the passive is generally used more frequently in EST. The complexities of the picture should also be investigated: Is the passive used more frequently in all genres of EST? If not, why do we find variation in its usage? How do
(u) voice and tense interact? Do our four generalizations ever conflict with one another? If so, which one holds? It is extremely important to determine what rhetorical functions condition the choice of the passive in particular EST genres. Only when we have addressed these issues will we be able to provide accurate information to students of EST.

[6] We thank William Perry for drawing our attention to related *Scientific American* papers.

(t) Tarone *et al.* are at pains to distinguish between professional and popular journal papers and they surely are right to do this. However, such distinctions lead us to consider whether there are usefully identifiable sub-types within the two broad categories; and whether any established sub-types are restricted to particular fields or are more general. To my mind, these are questions for the eighties and in attempting to answer them we need to evaluate the virtues and vices of complicated sub-categorizations.

(u) Some of these questions, and the ones raised under note *(t)*, are considered in items listed in the related readings.

APPENDIX A

Frequency of Usage of Active and Passive Verb Forms in Stoeger (1980) Arranged by Section and as a Whole					
		Active Verbs			
Section of Paper	Total Verbs	With *we*	With Exis.	Total	Total Passive Verbs
Abstract	8	3	1	7	1
I. Introduction	31	6	11	26	5
II. Basic Equations	36	7	18	32	4
III. Boundary Layer Approach	58	11	32	56	2*
IV. Approximation Scheme and Solution	23	12	7	22**	1
V. Matching with the Keplerian Models	41	12	19	34	7
VI. Characterization of Flow	12	4	5	11	1
VII. Energy and Angular Momentum	23	3	12	20	3
VIII. Conclusion	12	0	2	9***	3
COLUMN TOTALS	244	58	107	217	27

* includes one use of passive with *we* ('we are faced with . . .')
** includes one use of first person singular ('I have included . . .')
*** includes one use of first person singular ('I am indebted to . . .')

Percent of Total Verbs $\frac{x}{244}$

% Active Verbs = 88.5%
% Passive Verbs = 11.5%
% Active *we* Verbs = 23%

Percent of Total Verbs with Existentials Omitted $\frac{x}{137}$

% Active Verbs = 80%
% Passive Verbs = 20%
% Active *we* Verbs = 37%

APPENDIX B

Frequency of Usage of Active and Passive Verb Forms in Lightman (1974)
Arranged by Section and as a Whole

Section of Paper	Total Verbs	Active Verbs			Total Passive Verbs
		With *we*	With Exis.	Total	
Abstract	8	1	2	5	3
I. Introduction	23	5	7	18	5
II. Assumptions and Approximations	57	3	25	48	9
III. Fundamental Equations	45	8	16	36	9
IV. Model for Viscosity and Resultant Equations	28	3	9	23	5
V. Approximate Regional Solutions	11	1	3	7	4
VI. Discussion of Consistency	48	7	22	44	4
VII. Reduction of Equations	32	6	4	21	11
VIII. Temperature Function and Solution Regimes	81	4	22	70	11
IX. Comparison with Stationary Models	37	2	12	29*	8
COLUMN TOTALS	370	40	122	301	69

* includes two uses of first person singular

Percent of Total Verbs $\frac{x}{370}$

% Active Verbs = 81.4%
% Passive Verbs = 18.6%
% Active *we* Verbs = 10.8%

Percent of Total Verbs with Existentials Omitted $\frac{x}{248}$

% Active Verbs = 72.2%
% Passive Verbs = 27.8%
% Active *we* Verbs = 16.1%

References

Cooray, Mahinda. (1965), 'The English Passive Voice.' *English Language Teaching* 21, 3: 203–210.

Duskova, Libuse and Vera Urbanova. (1967), 'A Frequency Count of English Tenses with Application to Teaching English as a Foreign Language.' *Prague Studies in Mathematical Linguistics* 2: 19–36.

Fernalld, Faith. (1977), 'A Study of the Comparative Frequency of Passive in Some College Freshman Texts.' *Indian Journal of Applied Linguistics* 3, 2: 53–70.

George, H. V. (1963), 'A Verb-Form Frequency Count.' *English Language Teaching* 18, 1: 31–37.

Lackstrom, John, Larry Selinker, and Louis Trimble. (1970), 'Grammar and Technical English.' *English as a Second Language: Current Issues*, 101–133. Robert C. Lugton (Ed.). Philadelphia, Pennsylvania: Center for Curriculum Development.

Lightman, Alan P. (1974), 'Time-Dependent Accretion Disks around Compact Objects. I. Theory and Basic Equations.' *The Astrophysical Journal* 194: 419–427.

Quirk, Randolph, Sidney Greenbaum, Geoffrey Leech, and Jan Svartvik. (1972), *A Grammar of Contemporary English.* London: Longman Group Limited.

Robinett, Betty. (1980), *Final Report: Delineation of Linguistic Features of Scientific and Technical English.* Unpublished manuscript submitted to Control Data Corporation.

Selinker, Larry. (1979), 'On the Uwe of Informants in Discourse Analysis and "Language for Specialized Purposes".' *International Review of Applied Linguistics in Language Teaching* 17, 3: 189–215.

———, Elaine Tarone, and Victor Hanzeli (Eds.). (1981), *English for Academic and Technical Purposes: Studies in Honor of Louis Trimble.* Rowley, Massachusetts: Newbury House Publishers.

Stoeger, William R. (1980), 'Boundary-Layer Behavior of the Flow at the Inner Edge of Black Hole Accretion Disks.' *The Astrophysical Journal* 235: 216–223.

Swales, John. (1976), 'Verb Frequencies in English'. *ESPMENA Bulletin* 4: 28–31.

———. (1981), 'The Function of One Type of Participle in a Chemistry Textbook,' in Selinker *et al.*, 40–52.

Widdowson, G. H. (1981), 'English for Specific Purposes: Criteria for Course Design,' in Selinker *et al.*, 1–10.

Wingard, Peter. (1981), 'Some Verb Forms and Functions in Six Medical Texts,' in Selinker *et al.*, 53–64.

III

ACTIVITIES

(1) Study Appendix A and Appendix B. Do you accept or reject the following conclusions? And why?

(i) Stoeger contains a higher proportion of existential verbs.
(ii) Overall, Stoeger and Lightman are at opposite extremes as far as the relative frequencies of [*we* + active] and the passive are concerned.
(iii) The percentage of passives in Stoeger is consistently low; in Lightman it is higher but still low except for Section VII.
(iv) The two appendices would have been more useful if the Passive Verb columns had been divided into passives where the underlying subjects were the authors and where they were not. In that way we could have seen whether there were significant differences between sections in the choice of [*we* + active] as opposed to the passive with underlying *we*.
(v) Eight and nine sections respectively is rather too many if we want to obtain a general picture of changes between one part of an article and another.

(2) It is easy to see that the first and second generalizations proposed in this *Episode* depend crucially on authors of articles alternating on occasion between *we* and impersonal statements. Not all authors, of course, do this; for instance, in this collection Barber and Higgins are consistently personal whereas Ewer and Hughes-Davies and Herbolich are impersonal. However, some of the other authors do alternate.

How far do Generalizations I and II explain the choice of voice in at least *one* of the following:—

Episode Six: from *Rhetorical Considerations* to *Choice of Tenses*
Episode Seven: from *The Use of Language in Discourse* to *Matter and Volume*
Episode Nine: from *Authentic Materials* to *Two Methodologies for ARMS*

(Incidentally, Chris Kennedy in *The ESP Journal*, 2, 1, 1983, made an appeal for the analysis of applied linguistics texts themselves, particularly for teacher-education purposes. Perhaps now a start is being made.)

(3) Suppose that one of your responsibilities in your institution is to offer help to your colleagues on the writing of Journal articles. Briefly outline a scheme of work that would incorporate the findings of Tarone *et al.*

IV

EVALUATION

(1) Tarone *et al.* summarize Generalization III as 'when these authors refer to their own proposed future work, they use the passive'.

This is more of an observation than an explanation. What would be an explanation? How could it be arrived at? Would the search for an explanation necessarily involve a specialist informant or informants?

(2) This volume began by examining an analysis of Scientific English published in 1962 and closes with an analysis of similar data twenty years later. What sort of paper on EST do you think will be published in 2002?

V

RELATED READINGS

In the *References* the paper by Selinker on the use of informants is important and influential. Widdowson's paper makes a distinction between goal-oriented approaches to course design and process-oriented approaches, of which Hutchinson and Waters (Episode Fourteen) would be an example. Widdowson advocates the latter approach but stresses the employment in ESP course design of the 'cognitive styles that define the methodology of the subject of their specialization'. There has already been some discussion of this in the Setting to Episode Seven.

Other work that can be related to this Episode includes:

Sandra Oster, 'The Use of Tenses in "Reporting Past Literature" in EST' in the collection entitled *English for Academic and Technical Purposes* already mentioned in the References (and in Episode One). In fact, Oster's hypotheses have not been universally accepted, but it is interesting to compare a 'voice-driven' to a 'tense-driven' approach to similar data.

John Swales, *Aspects of Article Introductions* (LSU, the University of Aston in Birmingham, 1981). This is a monograph that attempts to explore the tense and voice aspects we have discussed, along with other matters, from an information-structure viewpoint.

A. S. Wood, 'An Examination of the Rhetorical Structures of Authentic Chemistry Texts', *Applied Linguistics* III, 2, 1982. An elegant discussion of the rhetorical structure of certain types of article from Chemistry Journals set against a consideration of how such articles could be 'simplified'. Wood concludes: 'In pedagogic terms this paper has suggested to the teacher an intermediate procedure between the stark alternatives of producing his own text which bears no resemblance to any actual scientific article, or mutilating an existing article by cutting out the parts which his students find indigestible. The suggestion put forward here offers some hope to the EST teacher that there is another option.'

— RETROSPECT —

In the Introduction I made it clear that I would not attempt to write the history of ESP over the last twenty years or so; and at the conclusion of this volume I am more conscious than ever of how personal the selection of Episodes has been. In fact, the most I have tried to do is to establish links between the fifteen Episodes themselves, and between them and various linguistic and educational developments. I have tried to tell a story and to draw some lessons from it. Presumably if I had chosen a different fifteen Episodes—and there is no shortage of candidates for inclusion—it would have been in many respects a different story. I have also declined a historian's responsibility in another way. I have made no real attempt at chronological accuracy; in particular, I have only on a few occasions been bold enough to suggest who first came up with such-and-such a concept and when and where. The precise origins and causes of certain new directions have remained obscure, and may well continue to do so. One contributory factor to the uncertainty of the historical record lies in the variable gap between conception and publication. On this point all I can safely say is that the key features of the Episodes were usually being worked out some one to three years before they were published in the forms given here.

And what of the lessons that I would wish to draw? The first concerns the relationship between ESP and its parent occupation of English Language Teaching. Some established figures in the ELT world have maintained from time to time that 'there is nothing new about ESP', whereas, as we have seen, there have been those on the ESP side who have advocated that the many widely-supported attitudes and activities in the teaching of 'General English' would benefit from falling under the influence of ESP approaches. Taking partisan positions in this way is not very helpful. ESP is not a young cuckoo determined to eliminate all other birds from the nest that it has infiltrated; it is better seen as a recently-evolved species that best thrives in certain secluded and restricted kinds of habitat.

A second observation can be related to the conduct of argument in the language teaching field in general. Often disagreements that arise are not really about matters of principle because the disagreements are ultimately reducible to protagonists reflecting on experience drawn from very different educational environments. The debate about the place of formal grammar teaching is a clear instance of this type of dispute. Those who oppose 'formal grammar' typically have experience of younger or highly heterogeneous classes, of programmes with a heavy emphasis on 'functional survival', of programmes that are more concerned with speaking rather than writing, and of those of relatively short duration. On the other hand, those who support 'formal grammar' have often been teachers of classes in which there has been some emphasis on developing professional skills including writing, composed of well-educated and relatively mature students who will eventually be sitting for some official examination. And so it is with some of the disagreements in ESP. As I hope I have shown, several disagreements in ESP are essentially different sorts of response to different sorts of situation. Of course, this is not to imply that if several experienced ESP practitioners were all confronted with identical versions of the same situation they would all miraculously arrive at the same solution; only to suggest that we need to establish that there exist important factors in common before being sure that opposed points of views are really being upheld.

A third lesson I would like to draw is that it seems preferable to aim for a combination of both linguistic and educational responsibility. Most of the earlier Episodes in this volume stressed their concern for the former, most of the later ones for the latter, and some of the reasons for this pattern of development I have attempted to explain in various Settings. After all, ESP is one of the relatively few types of teaching within ELT (teaching 'advanced conversation' is another) in which there is some fairly obvious and direct responsibility to find out what linguists and other scholars have had to say about the kind of English you want to teach. ESP is not simply a matter of teaching a traditional description of the English language *well.* In ESP, methodology alone may not suffice, however much it may be the crucial factor in a beginners' General English class. It seems to me, therefore, that we need to be ready to compensate for an unbalanced attention to either linguistic or educational responsibility. And as part of this readiness we need to recognize the role of individual 'professional temperament'. There is clear evidence that, temperamentally, some ESP practitioners put a higher value on methodology (activities) than they do on information about the use of language (content), and others the converse; and this phenomenon may be related to whether particular holders of ESP positions are *at heart* language teachers or linguists. As a result, those ESP practitioners who are *methodologists* (who are busy setting up series of 'engaging' activities) need to remind themselves to verify that the language behaviour they are generating is as appropriate and as utilizable as possible. On the other hand, those who are by temperament and training *demonstrators* (busy working out explanations, examples and rules of thumb) need to remind themselves that there may always be better ways of communicating and exploiting the chosen content.

A fourth lesson that follows from a consideration of these fifteen Episodes in English for Science and Technology is that, despite considerable progress, there is still a long way to go. There is no need to look further than the final Episode to see how much remains to be done before we can with any confidence make pedagogically useful generalizations about scientific papers or articles published in English. And the scientific paper is no minor genre or obscure area. In many academic libraries around the world English-language scientific and engineering journals take up as much as 50% of the total book and periodical budget. An increasing percentage of scholarly papers written in English (over 80% in some areas) inevitably means that an increasing proportion of papers are being both written and read by members of the scientific and technological community who do not have English as their first language. In many senses, the scientific paper is one of the most important manifestations of the role of English as a language of wider international communication—and yet we still know insufficient about it to be able to provide a proper handbook for those NNS scientists who wish to further their results and their careers by publishing in English.

Finally, I hope it has become clear that the generally-accepted story of ESP as a series of repeated attacks on the inadequacy of previous approaches is a superficial one. As I see it, the real tale told by the last twenty years is quite different. It shows that we have steadily been expanding the number of aspects of the learner's situation that we need to take into account—from Barber's narrow perspective on the syntactic properties of target texts to the wide-ranging and multi-level facets described by Johns and Dudley-Evans, on to further and more subtle explorations of the articulation of discourse by Tarone and her co-workers and, finally, on to some of the research in progress described in the following section. Necessarily there have been great technical developments, in methods of language analysis, in understanding the classroom, in new methodological techniques, in analysing the students' needs and in characterizing their study and work habits, but behind all these there has been a fluctuating but growing determination to bring *English for Specific Purposes* to educational maturity. And that has been the most difficult lesson to learn; 'never to make an end of the means, never to be so immersed in the medium, the formulae, the techniques, as to forget the end to which they were but subsidiary'.

— PROSPECT —

In this final section I would like to comment on developments in the eighteen months since the first appearance of Episode Fifteen. In doing so, I also hope to reconnect EST to the wider field of ESP and thus take up one or two matters that were mentioned in the Introduction.

One striking development has been a new interest in the training of ESP teachers. The first clear sign of this was the theme of the 1981 SELMOUS Conference (see Episode Twelve) at Essex University—*The ESP Teacher: Role, Development and Prospects.* Until then Jack Ewer had been almost alone in insisting that the ESP teacher needed courses that would be somewhat different to those provided for general English teachers or those run by Departments of Linguistics and Applied Linguistics. But in the last year or so a small but significant number of one-year Master's-level courses in ESP have been started and much hard thought has been given to developing realistic objectives for shorter in-service training programmes. In the Postscript I put forward the view that the effective ESP practitioner of the nineteen-eighties needs a wide range of skills: capacities for discourse analysis and exercise construction, access to what is currently known about reading and writing processes, an eclectic methodology, insights into the educational and professional environments for which the students are learning English, some research capability, and skills of administration, negotiation and public relations. As a profession we are beginning to see how these skills might be transferred from more experienced to less experienced practitioners, and it is not surprising that a complete recent issue of the *ESP Journal* (2, 1, 1983) is given over to teacher-training.

In fact, the investigative skills of ESP specialists are beginning to take on at least two new dimensions. In the seventies, ESP course designers relied heavily on the standard social-science techniques of questionnaires, tests of various kinds, structural interviews and occasional and random direct observation of subject classes. One recently-developed line of enquiry has been the case-study. According to Schmidt (1981), 'the advantages of this method over the others are the possibility of an in-depth study over a period of time, the opportunity to appeal to the students' intuitions about his or her difficulties and needs in more detail than in the oral interview or questionnaire, and the occasion for the curriculum developer to do direct observation of the student in the classroom and study situation to gain insight into the students' own methods of learning'. A particularly interesting recent example of this case-study approach is James's longitudinal study of an overseas student's struggles with his doctoral dissertation (James, forthcoming). The parallels between this type of investigation and those in other areas such as discourse analysis are quite striking: the research is narrow and deep rather than broad and shallow; and secondly, there is a strong emphasis on *process* rather than *product*—on the processes of studying, reading, writing and so on.

The other main dimension involves reducing the importance attached to the study of the *product* (or spoken or written text) in another way. Standard approaches to language varieties and the nature of text or discourse are now being seen, *for ESP purposes*, as over-concerned with the text itself and within the texts over-concerned with factors that relate to their social appropriacy. As a consequence, there is greater contemporary interest in the educational and professional environment and in the *values* that environment places on certain types of communication. I can illustrate this contrast between older and newer approaches with a made-up example relating to English courses for students of economics.

Imagine that Country X has six institutions that offer a BSc in Economics and Social Science. Also imagine that lectures take place in the first language but the main textbook for the First Year Economics course is written in English. Let us further assume that three institutions use *Samuelson* as their textbook, whilst the other three use *Hanson*. We therefore arrive at the following picture:—

Institutions

1, 3, 5	Samuelson	2, 4, 6	Hanson

A text-based approach to the design of Service English courses for these institutions would conclude that the best thing to do would be to analyse *Samuelson* and *Hanson* respectively and develop support reading courses based in some way on those analyses. The courses might actually contain extracts from the textbooks, they might (following Hutchinson and Waters) be a preparation rather than a 'rehearsal', or they might (following Moore *et al.*) offer more general materials which would nevertheless develop reading skills appropriate to *Samuelson* and *Hanson*; but whatever the relationship between subject-readings and English course, the fact that the textbook was *Samuelson* or *Hanson* would be the crucial variable.

Now let us suppose that the *role* of the set textbook differs in the six Economics Departments that we are concerned with. Imagine that in Departments 1 and 2 the textbook is the core of the year's course, the lectures are fully supportive of *Samuelson* or *Hanson*, the students are expected to learn the content of the textbook, and will be asked to reproduce in their examinations the basic principles of economics as laid down by the distinguished textbook authors. In Departments 5 and 6 quite a different set of attitudes prevail. Here we find the view that, because of the contemporary crisis in economics, there is no point in teaching standard theories. Rather, the students will be asked to develop a capacity to think critically about all economic generalizations and apply that critical thinking to the world's contemporary economic difficulties. Lectures lead the way in this attack on conventional wisdom; *Samuelson* and *Hanson* are to be read as examples of the inadequacies of traditional views. Finally, let us assume that Institutions 3 and 4 adopt an intermediate position between these two extremes. Therefore, the picture must now be redrawn as follows:—

Institutions

1—reading to retain information—2
3—mixed reading purposes—4
5—reading to develop critical—6
faculties

Thus, a text-driven approach to course design would be likely to produce (for instance) a fair degree of similarity between materials for Institutions 1 and 5, whereas a text-use approach would produce very different course material for those two same institutions. (Of course, the situation I have just set up is much simplified; there are certainly more approaches to text than I have allowed for, as recently demonstrated by Johns and Davies, 1983.)

As a result of such considerations, there is now a tendency to look beyond the content and its linguistic expression to institutional attitudes and expectations regarding that content; and to look for shared and conflicting expectations of the various groups that make up the members of the institution. Widdowson (1981), among others, has tried to integrate different types of learning and different attitudes to learning into ESP course design, and this is one way in which ESP is becoming concerned with educational as well as linguistic research. Another is the current interest in the role and influence of various kinds of academic, professional and occupational 'sub-cultures'. The work of educationalists such as Becher (1981) and Entwistle (1979) is becoming of increasing relevance to ESP because of their investigations into 'disciplinary cultures', and the answers to many of the questions I raised in the Introduction will eventually lie here, perhaps with some co-operation from the ESP practitioners. What are the belief-systems, initiation ceremonies, rites of passage, rituals, taboos, value judgments of excellence or otherwise, codes of practice, etc. of doctors, lawyers, navigators, geologists, and so on? The ESP practitioner as 'insider' rather than 'outsider' clearly needs to have some appreciation not only of the conceptual structure of the discipline (as Johns and Dudley-Evans have pointed out) but also of the conventions of conduct imposed upon its members. In this respect, it is perhaps worth noting that I choose to illustrate the difference between text and textual-environment approaches to reading course design from the field of economics rather than from one of the sciences. I have a feeling that such marked differences in educational orientation are more plausible in the social sciences than in the physical sciences, thus suggesting that the potential influence of a 'departmental culture' may be stronger in some branches of knowledge than in others.

The foregoing discussion of the conventions of professional behaviour leads us to another promising line of development—that of genre-analysis. Unfortunately, the terminology in this new area is very confusing, as labels have been liberally borrowed from other fields: *genre* itself from literary criticism, *speech-event* from linguistics, *activity-type* from anthropology, *topic-type* from reading research, *communicative event* from ethnography and *text-type* from discourse analysis. I use *genre* here partly because this was the term preferred by Tarone *et al.* in Episode Fifteen. By *genre* is meant a more or less standardized communicative event with a goal or set of goals mutually understood by the participants in that event and occurring within a functional rather than a social or personal setting. Well-established genres are reports of laboratory experiments, scientific papers, testimonials and job references, sermons, cross-examinations, medical case reports and so on. In these terms, a classic attempt at genre-analysis in the applied linguistics literature is the study of the structuring of doctor–patient interactions in Casualty (Candlin *et al.*, 1976). Two very recent examples are the study of dictated post-operative surgical reports (Pettinari, 1983) and Bhatia's investigation into the rationale underlying the complex expression of legislative provisions (Bhatia, 1983). Such studies differ from traditional register or text analysis in the importance they attach to communicative purposes within a communicative setting, and in that context it is interesting to note that both Pettinari and Bhatia stress the valuable contributions that specialist informants have made to their understanding of those underlying purposes.

Work on genres would appear to have a number of implications for the future development of ESP. Genre-analysis has reiterated the importance of information structuring and ordering. Consider, for example, one type of administrative or commercial letter—that which communicates an administrative decision. The letter may communicate 'good news' ('you have been awarded a scholarship') or it may communicate 'bad news' ('you have been refused one'). Both letters will probably be written in the same bureaucratic style but they will probably be organized very differently. The 'good news' letter will announce the award early, whereas the 'bad news' letter will prepare the ground by what is known as a 'buffer statement' and the 'bad news' will come late. Equally important is the difference between the purposes of the two letters beyond the shared superficial intent of providing information about the success or failure of the application. The 'good news' letter will be constructed in such a way that the continuation of the correspondence is encouraged, whereas the other one will be designed to terminate the correspondence by giving the unlucky recipient the least possible opportunity for objection or complaint. One obvious implication of such attempts at genre-analysis is that they could be equally useful for teachers and materials writers of English as a first language as for those of English as a second or foreign language; and indeed there have been recent and welcome signs that ESP and Communication Studies are beginning to recognize certain mutual interests and concerns (see the reference for James's paper). Conversely, interesting questions now arise about the cultural specificity of genres; for instance, are 'bad news' letters based on the same underlying (and possibly unconscious) considerations around the world—or do such letters differ from one culture to another? The answers to such questions have, in turn, clear pedagogical implications, as we saw in the discussion of Episode Seven.

Further, it may turn out that it is only within genres that viable correlations between cognitive, rhetorical and linguistic features can be established—for it is only within genres that language is sufficiently conventionalized, and the range of communicative purpose sufficiently narrow, for us to hope to establish pedagogically-employable generalizations that will capture useful relationships between function and form. But, despite its undoubted promise, it looks as though genre-analysis has a price to pay. If it manages to reveal something of the internal logic and external language of a conventionally-constrained communicative event, it follows by reason of its orientation that it may have little to say about other, apparently quite similar, communicative events. Tarone stressed the narrow scope of her generalizations and in my own work I have found that there is no such thing as *an* Introduction in academic writing. Of course, opening sections are often called 'introductions' but they would appear to be quite differently organized in different genres such as scholarly papers, theses, projects and essays.

Some of the most interesting developments in methodology have been brought about by the new technologies of the microcomputer and the video-recorder, and here again ESP practice has been no respecter of received ideas or traditions. With regard to computer-aided language learning, one small but influential school of thought is leading further and further away from carefully-graded discrete-item materials derived from programmed learning principles and requiring fairly sophisticated equipment. Instead, enthusiasts such as John Higgins and Tim Johns (Higgins and Johns, forthcoming), look to arcade games like 'Space Invaders' for their inspiration; they see the computer as tirelessly offering to play a challenging language game made more exciting by competitive scoring systems. For instance, in *Storyboard* the computer offers nothing but blank spaces representing letters of a short text. The learner must reconstruct the text from this next-to-nothing by either using informed guessing strategies or using his or her limited stock of 'capital' to buy information. In other developments deliberately simple rules are given which the learner is asked to check out and improve. Thus the computer has no God-like omniscience but is a relatively feeble adversary who can be taken on and defeated—and this 'low profile' image is reinforced by the efforts of the program-writers to design their products in such a way that they will go into the smallest and cheapest microcomputers.

In a parallel way, the emerging video methodology has turned its face against any perceived similarity between the video language lesson and educational television. For instance, the size of the video-chunks shown is steadily being reduced, and today it is not uncommon to hear people maintain that ninety seconds of video material is quite sufficient for a sixty-minute EAP class. Further, there is currently much interest in allowing only part of the class to see the video extract or to deprive sections of the class of either sound or vision because of the increased communicative pressures such 'information gaps' impose on the participants. In both areas, it remains to be seen whether these interactive methodologies will turn out to be a *reductio ad absurdum* or a brilliant educational application of technical facilities.

And finally we come to the matter of vocabulary teaching in ESP, which we have recognized as having suffered serious neglect throughout the years covered by this volume—and this despite the promising early work by Herbert. In my view, the situation still remains very unsatisfactory. It is true that a number of people have been applying techniques of collocational and componential analysis to ESP material, but with rather uncertain results. Perhaps the best-known work in this area is the *Longman Dictionary of Scientific Usage* by Godman and Payne (1979). Although Godman and Payne's dictionary demonstrates impressive intellectual endeavour, few students seem able to cope with the complexity, and the ESP profession might have paid greater attention to Lehrer's observation (Lehrer, 1974) on her own roughly-comparable work that 'perhaps the analysis is only understandable if the reader knows the meanings of all the words already', which is hardly likely to be the position of our students—or, if it is, we should be teaching them something else. Another and more recent publication of some relevance is *The Words You Need* by Rudska, Channel, Putseys and Ostyn (1981), although it is not directed to an ESP market. This textbook follows the displays of collocational and componential features with some interesting practice and exercise material, and this is obviously valuable. However, many teachers do not accept the usage restrictions (or lack of them) in the displays themselves and this difficulty perhaps follows from the authors' decision to offer a lexical analysis that aims to encompass a wide variety of registers and styles in the English language.

If there has been a thread that connects the themes that I have briefly discussed in this closing section it is that of *process* and *interaction*; in training new entrants into the ESP profession, in understanding student behaviour, in designing courses, in understanding why communicative events take the forms they do, and in ESP uses of computers and video-recorders. Unfortunately, it is precisely that interest in *process* and *interaction* which is missing in vocabulary work; interactions between specialized vocabulary support materials (technical dictionaries, glossaries, lexical fields, etc.) and the language learner and user are under-researched, and the processes of technical and subtechnical vocabulary acquisition imagined rather than investigated. Twenty-one years have passed since the publication in Stockholm of 'Some Measurable Characteristics of Modern Scientific Prose' and in many ways English for Specific Purposes has grown to a considerable degree of maturity in that time, but until we can find ways of ensuring the collaboration of learners, practitioners and specialized lexicographers and lexicologists in the experiment and trialling of new and more efficient ways of coping with the vocabulary problem, I do not think ESP can really be said to have come of age.

References

Tony Becher (1981), 'Towards a Definition of Disciplinary Cultures', *Studies in Higher Education* 6, 2.

V. K. Bhatia (1983), *An Applied Discourse Analysis of English Legislative Writing*, LSU ESP Monograph, the University of Aston.

C. N. Candlin, C. J. Bruton and J. M. Leather (1976), 'Doctors in Casualty: Specialist Course Design from a data base', *IRAL* 14/3.

Noel Entwistle, Maureen Manley and Dai Hounsell (1979), 'Identifying Distinctive Approaches to Studying', *Higher Education* 8.

A. Godman and E. M. F. Payne (1979), *Longman Dictionary of Scientific Usage*, Longman.

Higgins and Johns (forthcoming), *Computers and Language Teaching*, Collins.

Ken James (1984), 'The Writing of Theses by Speakers of English as a Foreign Language: the results of a case-study' in *Common Ground: Shared Interests in ESP and Communication Studies* edited by Williams, Kirkman and Swales, Pergamon, Oxford.

Tim Johns and Florence Davies (1983), 'Text as a vehicle for information: the classroom use of written texts in teaching reading in a foreign language', *Reading in a Foreign Language*, 1, 1, University of Aston.

Adrienne Lehrer (1974), *Semantic Fields and Lexical Structure*, North Holland.

C. Pettinari (1983), 'The function of a grammatical alternation in fourteen surgical reports', *Applied Linguistics* 4, 1.

B. Rudska, J. Channell, Y. Putseys and P. Ostyn (1981), *The Words You Need*, North Holland.

Maxime F. Schmidt (1981), 'Needs Assessment in English for Specific Purposes: The Case Study' in *English for Academic and Technical Purposes* edited by Selinker, Tarone and Hanzeli, Newbury House, Massachusetts, 1981.

H. G. Widdowson (1981), 'English for Specific Purposes: Criteria for Course Design' in *English for Academic and Technical Purposes* (op. cit.).